D1260770

HALAKHAH IN A THEOLOGICAL DIMENSION

Program in Judaic Studies
Brown University
BROWN JUDAIC STUDIES
Edited by
Jacob Neusner,
Wendell S. Dietrich, Ernest S. Frerichs,
Calvin Goldscheider, Alan Zuckerman

Project Editors (Project)

David Blumenthal, Emory University (Approaches to Medieval Judaism)
William Brinner (Studies in Judaism and Islam)
Ernest S. Frerichs, Brown University (Dissertations and Monographs)
Lenn Evan Goodman, University of Hawaii (Studies in Medieval Judaism) (Studies in Judaism and Islam)
William Scott Green, University of Rochester (Approaches to Ancient Judaism)
Ivan Marcus, Jewish Theological Seminary of America
(Texts and Studies in Medieval Judaism)
Marc L. Raphael, Ohio State University (Approaches to Judaism in Modern Times)
Norbert Samuelson, Temple University (Jewish Philosophy)
Jonathan Z. Smith, University of Chicago (Studia Philonica)

Number 68
HALAKHAH IN A THEOLOGICAL DIMENSION

by
David Novak

HALAKHAH IN A THEOLOGICAL DIMENSION

by
David Novak

Scholars Press
Chico, California

HALAKHAH IN A THEOLOGICAL DIMENSION

by
David Novak

© 1985
Brown University

Library of Congress Cataloging in Publication Data

Novak, David, 1941–
  Halakhah in a theological dimension.

  (Brown Judaic studies ; no. 68)
  1. Jewish law—Philosophy—Addresses, essays,
lectures. 2. Ethics, Jewish—Addresses, essays, lectures.
I Title. II. Series.
BM520.6.N68 1984   296.1'8   84–10661
ISBN 0–89130–757–5

Printed in the United States of America
on acid-free paper

CONTENTS

PREFACE

When Professor Jacob Neusner invited me to put together this collection of some of my more recent essays on Halakhah, I was both honored and pleased. Professor Neusner, more than any other scholar today, has been responsible for the wide dissemination of Judaic learning in North America, not only by the publication of his own prolific work, but also by his encouragement and promotion of the work of fellow Judaic scholars. I am grateful to him for including me among the distinguished authors in the Brown Judaic Studies Series.

The title of this work, *Halakhah in a Theological Dimension*, indicates that it is to a large extent a continuation of the project of my earlier two part work, *Law and Theology in Judaism* (New York: KTAV, 1974-76). This new title perhaps better demonstrates my basic assumption of the *interpenentration* of Halakhah qua law and Aggadah qua theology throughout the history of Judaism. One rather unsympathetic reviewer of the second part of my earlier work, however, contended that it lacked methodological focus and the "Law *and* Theology" could cover just about anything "in Judaism." Perhaps in this work, both by its title and in its content, I will be more successful in convincing more of my readers that the "and" in "Law *and* Theology" designates a real internal relation and is not just a literary juxtaposition.

Aside from the usual egotism which motivates any author to accept opportunities for the publication of his work, there is a more publicly valid reason for my acceptance of Professor Neusner's kind invitation at this time. The interest in halakhic discourse present in the mid-1970's and to which my earlier work was addressed, is far more pronounced now in the mid-1980's. This is due, it seems to me, to the even more pronounced general interest in normative ethics among educated people and, also, to the growing intellectual maturity of the American Jewish community, which is requiring more of the authenticity and intellectual rigor of Halakhah in finding cogent Jewish approaches to the problems of the day. However, inasmuch as the community per se is not halakhically constituted in toto, one cannot assume that the sociological consensus for Halakhah, which could be assumed in pre-modern, non-secular, Jewish societies, is present today. Therefore, in order to cogently present Halakhah at this time, one must show it in a theological dimension, that is, in a dimension which deals with the covenantal character of Judaism, a dimension prior to the constitution of any particular

Jewish society in history. The very fact that Halakhah is not the status quo forces us to examine its precepts and concepts in a more comprehensive way. This is what I try to do here.

The origins of the chapters in this book are as follows:

Chapter 1, "Can Halakhah Be Both Authoritative and Changing?" was first published in a different version in the *Proceedings of the Rabbinical Assembly* 40 (1980). This revised version has been augmented with selections from the articles, "Review of J. David Bleich's *Contemporary Halakhic Problems*," *Judaism* 27/4 (Fall 1978); "Status Quo and Change," *ibid.* (Summer 1980); and "Transcending Denominational Labels," *SH'MA* 13/258 (September 30, 1983). I am grateful to Rabbi Jules Harlow, Dr. Robert Gordis, and Dr. Eugene B. Borowitz, the editors of these respective publications, for permission to use these articles in this collection.

Chapter 2, "The Conflict between Halakhah and Ethics: The Case of *Mamzerut*," was originally a paper at the annual meeting of the American Academy of Religion in New York City in December 1982.

Chapter 3, "Annulment in Lieu of Divorce in Jewish Law," was first published in the *Jewish Law Annual* 4 (1981). I thank the editor, Dr. Bernard S. Jackson, for permission to republish this article here.

Chapter 4, "Divorce and Conversion: Is A Traditional-Liberal Modus Vivendi Possible?" was originally a paper read at a conference sponsored by the National Jewish Resource Center at the University of Denver in June 1981. I am grateful to Dr. Irving Greenberg, the Director of the Center, for permission to publish the paper in this collection.

Chapter 5, "Women in the Rabbinate?" was originally published in *Judaism* 33/1 (Winter 1984); and chapter 6, "Alcohol and Drug Abuse in the Perspective of Jewish Tradition," was originally published there (33/2, Spring 1984) too. Again, I am grateful to Dr. Gordis for permission to republish these articles here.

Chapter 7, "Judaism and Contemporary Bioethics," originally appeared in the *Journal of Medicine and Philosophy* 4/4 (December 1979). I thank the associate editor, Dr. H. Tristram Engelhardt, Jr., for permission to republish the article in this collection.

Chapter 8, "The Threat of Nuclear War: Jewish Perspectives," was originally a paper read at a symposium sponsored by the Synagogue Council of America and the

United States Catholic Conference at the University of Notre Dame in October 1982.

Chapter 9, "The Logic of the Covenant: An Essay in Systematic Jewish Theology," is being published here for the first time.

My gratitude is due to my synagogue, Congregation Darchay Noam of Far Rockaway, New York, for encouraging me in my dual career of being their rabbi as well as being an active scholar. I feel that being their rabbi has enabled me to be a better scholar; I only hope that they feel that my being an active scholar has enabled me to be a better rabbi to them. Finally, I thank my wife, Melva, for her general encouragement as well as the donation of her specific literary skills to my attempt to make this book more readable, and my daughter, Marianne, who with her usual intelligence and industry, made the index.

Far Rockaway, New York
Adar II, 5744
March, 1984

CAN HALAKHAH BE BOTH AUTHORITATIVE AND CHANGING?

An approach to Halakhah which is traditional as well as historically conscious is based on two principles:

1. Halakhah is fully authoritative for Jews.

2. Halakhah is subject to change.

The first principle is a value statement whose immediate translation is normative, namely, Halakhah is to be followed. The second principle is a general description, namely, how Halakhah manifests itself in history.

One or the other of these principles has been rejected by fundamentalists and liberals respectively.

Fundamentalists accept the proposition that Halakhah is fully authoritative for Jews, but deduce it from the negation of halakhic change. For them Halakhah is authoritative precisely because it was, is, and will be unchanging.[1] In other words, for them history has no influence on Halakhah. All of Halakhah is *sub specie aeternitatis*.

Liberals, on the other hand, accept the changeability of Halakhah and some of them deduce from it that Halakhah is, therefore, non-authoritative.[2] In other words, for them the acceptance of the dynamics of history in Judaism has made Halakhah in the traditional sense inoperative.

Since one can easily show that the *phenomenon* of Halakhah has not been the same in every age, one cannot very well deny manifest change by any reference to experience. Hence, the real question is not whether Halakhah changes or not, but rather what that change is judged to be. It seems to me that both fundamentalists and liberals misjudge the meaning of halakhic change.

Fundamentalists assert that change is secondary in a deductive sense, namely, the general principles of Halakhah remain constant and only their particular applications change in the course of ruling for new situations arising in the history of the Jewish people. Thus all change qua subsequent application is potentially within the system already.[3] Halakhah judges and history is judged; the former is wholly active and the latter is wholly passive. Only the lack of our full political power prevents the sway of Halakhah over history from being complete.

Is this judgment of the deductive character of all halakhic change correct?

Deduction is the method of syllogistic reasoning. Let us choose an example of such reasoning from classical sources subject to much contemporary discussion because of the whole current debate over the role of women in Jewish ritual. The major premise proposes a universal category: "For *all* positive commandments, designated for a certain time only, women are exempt."[4] The minor premise is: "On the first day of the seventh month . . . is to be a day of blowing of the shofar for you" (Numbers 29:1). By deduction we conclude: "Women are (therefore) exempt from hearing the sound of the shofar on Rosh Hashanah."[5] Now if this were all there is to the halakhic process, I would agree with those who characterize it as "deduction." However, the matter is by no means so simple.

Neither the Written nor the Oral Torah is presented as a series of logically connected propositions, that is, a set of universals from which certain corollaries necessarily follow.[6] Rather, in the Written Torah we find a series of specific prescriptions, often interspersed among narrative descriptions of events, usually randomly presented, and if ordered, ordered only on the basis of topical similarity. Indeed, according to the prevalent rabbinic opinion, the very normative character of the Written Torah lies in its specificity rather than in its generality.[7] The prescriptions found in the Oral Torah, even in its most ordered presentation, the *Mishnah*, are also arranged topically rather than deductively.[8] In both Torahs data are presented in such a way as to make subsequent generalizations possible; the data are not deduced from the generalizations a priori. To miss this basic distinction is to confuse historical sequence with logical sequence *(post hoc ergo propter hoc)*, namely, to assume that temporal series are necessarily consequential, that what comes earlier solely determines what comes later.[9]

Returning to our example of women's participation in Jewish ritual, we see how the *Mishnah* characterizes their obligations and exemptions. The *Gemara* then shows how this is a generalization based on a number of specific prescriptions. And the *Gemara* also shows that there are a number of important exceptions to this general characterization.[10] "All" in truth means "many" or "most."[11] Simple deduction of the prescriptions from the general principle is not satisfactory because the principle itself is not an a priori ground of deduction. The principle is clearly a posteriori, that is, empirical. Here is where an unpredictable, historically conditioned, factor in the halakhic process must be acknowledged, for the data which form the basis of the generalization must be *selected* for comparison. Thus, in the principle I have presented as an illustration, the data are connected by *heqesh*-analogy (for example, mitzvah A exempts women; mitzvah B is similar to mitzvah A in other aspects; therefore, women are exempt from mitzvah B as well).[12] According to the Tosafists this type of analogical reasoning is selective *(dan me'atzmo)*.[13] The Palestinian Talmud much earlier showed how any such analogy is refutable on the basis of strict logic alone.[14] Therefore, in most cases of halakhic reasoning a process of selective prioritization precedes the actual deduction of a particular ruling and is presupposed by it. This process of selective prioritization applies any time a difficult new case calls for the employment of more than one rule.

Furthermore, even after the completion of the Talmud, when halakhic principles were supposed to have been permanently set,[15] new selective factors were introduced into Halakhah which changed the meaning of these principles. The most notable example of this, in the context of the classical texts chosen for illustration, is the permission introduced (or perhaps explicated) by Rashi and his grandson, Rabbenu Tam, in the twelfth century for women to recite the blessing before performing a positive commandment designated for a certain time only.[16] Theretofore women had been exempt from these commandments, thus making the recitation of the blessing before them seem to be contrary to the prohibition of uttering an unrequired blessing.[17] Surely this permission, accepted by Ashkenazic Jewry, illustrates how something as innovative as the awakened religious desires of women to take on themselves additional personal responsibilities played a crucial role in the halakhic process.[18] Finally, the rules set down in the Talmud and in post-Talmudic sources for choosing one normative opinion over another are essentially selective. Thus it was admitted that the halakhic views of the School of Shammai and R. Meir are more logically compelling, even though the actual law *(halakhah le-ma'aseh)* follows the School of Hillel and R. Meir's regular disputant, R. Judah.[19]

The denial of any change other than deductive application is assumed to be a dogma of Normative Judaism. The usual source for this dogma is supposed to be Maimonides. In his introduction to his comprehensive code, the *Mishneh Torah*, Maimonides opens as follows,

> All of the commandments were given to Moses at Sinai along with their
> interpretations, as Scripture states, "And I will give to you tablets of
> stone and the Torah and the commandments" (Exodus 24:12). "Torah"
> means the Written Torah; "the commandments" (ha-mitzvah) means what
> is called the Oral Torah. . . . Even though the Oral Torah was not written
> down. Moses our master taught all of it (kulah) in his court to the
> seventy elders.

The question is: Just what, for Maimonides, comprizes the Oral Torah as an unchanging
revealed datum?

The important thing to note in looking at this oft quoted text is that Maimonides is
paraphrasing a Talmudic text and his paraphrase of it is selective. The well-known text
reads,

> R. Levi bar Hama said in the name of R. Simon ben Laqish . . . "Torah"
> means Scripture (Miqra); "and the commandments" means Mishnah . . .
> "to teach them (le-horotam)" means exegesis (gemara). This teaches us
> that all of them were given to Moses at Sinai.[20]

Maimonides' most important omission from this text is gemara—"exegesis."[21] This, I
think, is not simply an economy of words. For, Maimonides in another passage in the
Mishneh Torah defines gemara as "understanding and discerning the end of a matter from
its beginning, and deriving one thing from another, and comparing one thing with
another . . . and how one learns the forbidden and the permitted and similar things from
revealed tradition (mi-pi ha-shemu'ah)."[22] Thus he makes a clear distinction between the
actual data of revelation and the various methods for theoretically understanding it and
practically applying it, methods ultimately philosophical.[23] Indeed, in a little known
responsum he actually criticizes the recitation of a Talmudically ordained blessing
thanking God for being "the teacher (he-melamed) of Torah to His people Israel."[24] He
explains there that "God does not teach it to us, but commanded us to study it and teach
it." Thus it would seem that for Maimonides the actual data of revelation are the words
of the Written Torah and those prescriptions of the Oral Torah referred back to Moses
because no other historical source can be found for them.[25] The whole process of
interpretation, however, and this surely includes judgment and subsequent
generalizations, is not revealed but is the ongoing work of reasoned human input. It is
thus the fundamental data not the general principles of Jewish law which must be taken

to be unchanging and unchangeable.[26] Thus Maimonides writes in a less often quoted passage in the *Mishneh Torah*.

> The Great Court in Jerusalem is the root *(iqqar)* of the Oral Torah. They are the foundation of legal authority *(ha-hora'ah)* and from them statutes and judgments go out to all Israel ... On equal footing are the things they learned from revealed tradition *(mi-pi ha-shemu'ah)* which is the Oral Torah, and the things they learned from their own knowledge ... which seemed to them to be so, and the things they devised as 'a fence for the Torah' and what the hour required ... Matters of tradition *(qabbalah)* were never disputed.[27]

We now see that Maimonides uses the term "Oral Torah" in both a general and a specific way. Specifically it means the undisputed and undated data of tradition. Generally it means the whole process of authoritative halakhic interpretation and innovation. It is clear that only the former, along with the 613 perpetual prescriptions of the Written Torah, are considered unchanging.[28] However, all of Normative Judaism cannot simply be deduced from them.

The fact that Normative Judaism cannot be viewed as a process totally predictable from the outset is stated in a well-known *aggadah* where Moses is miraculously transported across time into the classroom of R. Akibah.[29] He becomes depressed when he is unable to understand the subsequent halakhic discourse of R. Akibah, but his spirits are restored when R. Akibah indicates, in response to his students' query, that the source of his intricate ruling is "a law of Moses from Sinai."[30] The obvious intent of this *aggadah* is to show that Moses himself could not possibly foresee what would develop from the law he received at Sinai.[31] All he could do was to take comfort that what he received was still the foundation of all this development and is not contradicted by it but, rather, is fulfilled by it. Also, his authoritative leadership is being carried on in the person of his rabbinical successors.[32] Furthermore, along these lines one could say that the frequently cited rabbinic notion that "anything a senior student *(talmid vatiq)* will propose in the future was already given to Moses at Sinai" means that all authentic Jewish teaching is both rooted in Sinaitic revelation and fulfills its intent.[33] However, as we have seen, the empirical reality of the halakhic process itself precludes assuming that all subsequent teaching is merely further specification of earlier more general principles. Reference back to Sinai, in the specific rather than the essential sense, is retroactive, as it were.[34]

However, the authority of Halakhah as a normative principle cannot be consistently maintained if the principle of change is elevated from a description to a prescription, as some traditionally inclined liberals would like to do.[35] Although one cannot very well deny the factual observation of halakhic change, one can most certainly dispute the assertion that change is, therefore, an halakhic value. Because Halakah has changed does not mandate any further change unless there is an explicit intersystemic reason for such change, as indeed there had to be in the past.

I know of no classical halakhic source where change per se is mandated or even defended. Quite the contrary, one can cite numerous examples in the classical sources to show that the rabbis regarded change as a necessary, lamentable, evil rather than an exemplary good. The most oft cited example of change in the history of Halakhah is Hillel the Elder's enactment (taqqanah) of prosbul, which enabled the authorities to circumvent the scriptural law that cancelled all debts every seventh year.[36] However, no less an innovator than the Babylonian Amora, Samuel—the formulator of the radical principle "the law of the kingdom is the law"[37]—referred to Hillel's enactment as "the arrogance of the judges (ulbana de-dayyanay)" and said that if he had the power he would have it repealed and thus return normative Jewish practice to the original law of Scripture.[38] Furthermore, the Talmud stated that Hillel enacted prosbul "because he saw the people were prevented from lending one to another and transgressed what was written in the Torah, 'beware lest there be a despicable thing (dabar beli'al) in your heart, etc.' (Deuteronomy 15:9)."[39] The point in citing this verse, which concludes by denoting this "despicable thing" as the refusal to lend money to those who need it most, is that Hillel was forced to choose between two evils, namely, sacrificing the welfare of the poor or sacrificing the obvious meaning of the Scriptural law of the Sabbatical Year. His choice of the former was considered to be the best that he could do under these bad circumstances. He reacted, in effect, to a situation of moral regression among the Jewish people. Neither the text nor its treatment by the great medieval halakhists allows it to be a precedent for the theory which affirms change as an halakhic value. The point is that the burden of proof was never on those who advocated the status quo ante in Halakhah, but on those who advocated change.[40] It was they who had to show convincingly that the changes which they were advocating were required lest more radical changes come about willy-nilly.[41] It is clear that any change was considered a regrettable fact of living in an as-yet-unredeemed world.

The affirmation of change as itself normative is not only questionable historically, it is also objectionable philosophically. Being a description of a normative process rather than an identification or even interpretation of any specific operative principles therein, it can be considered an example of confusing general description and specific prescription. This is a serious logical problem as we have just seen. Moreover, to affirm a changeable source of authority is to affirm the ontological absurdity of an infinite regress. Even change requires at least one unchanging point of reference.[42] Authority cannot function (that is, change) unless it has a recognizable *terminus a quo* and *terminus ad quem*. Worse, to affirm a changeable source of authority is to commit the moral outrage of making those *who* change the law the final authorities. To do this is to affirm the principle of tyranny, namely, the most powerful will now make the law based on their own interests and opinions.[43] Thus, if Halakhah is to remain law, the unchanging element must be primary and the changing element must be secondary to it. If, on the other hand, one is unwilling to make changeability subordinate to that which is unchanging in Halakhah, then two dubious possibilities follow. Either there will be no objective source of authority in Jewish religious life, which means an affirmation of anarchy (inevitably followed by tyranny to fill the political vacuum), or the authority of Halakhah will be preempted by something else.

The "something else" usually presented as that which is to be prior to Halakhah in Judaism is "ethics."[44]

If ethics is to be prior to Halakhah, but one cannot find any convincing example of where it actually did function as such in the classical Jewish sources, then such ethics must come from outside Judaism itself. As such, Judaism becomes epiphenomenal, reducible to something external.[45] This is indeed the case when the egalitarian, universalistic, autonomous ethics espoused by liberals in our culture are used to judge Judaism. Since Judaism is so elitist, particularistic and heteronomous, such ethical grounding of it clearly leads to the dismantling of almost everything in it which makes Judaism unique. Much of Judaism cannot be justified on such ethical grounds, certainly not the halakhic system, as the example of Reform Judaism indicates.

If ethics is taken to be prior to Halakhah and is also taken to have been so in the past, then this ethics would seem to come from the non-legal aspect of Jewish tradition, Aggadah.   Certain contemporary liberal Jewish theologians, sensitive to the assimilationist consequences of judging Judaism by universally conceived ethical standards, attempt to use Aggadah (actually, certain *aggadot* only) to ground and even radically change Halakhah.[46]   However, since Aggadah is surely less systematic than Halakhah, how can Aggadah possibly ground it in any systematic way?[47]   Any attempt to do so would reduce Halakhah to Aggadah and thereby obliterate their essential difference.   Moreover, the aggadists themselves affirmed the normative priority of Halakhah.[48]   Clearly, then, if ethics is to truly ground Halakhah, it cannot be Aggadah, but must be something more precisely intelligible than either of them.   It must be nothing less than a philosophically cogent system of ethical principles of which Judaism is the chief example.   In such a system ethical principles are not naively presented as self-evident intuitions, but they must be constituted in an apodictic way.[49]   However, with the exception of Hermann Cohen, I know of no modern Jewish theologian philosophically gifted enough to be able to ground Judaism in such a philosophically cogent ethical system.[50]   And even Cohen's system can surely be disputed for valid philosophical, theological, and historical reasons.

Finally, too much philosophically naive discussion of the role of ethics in Normative Judaism ignores or is ignorant of the whole history of philosophical disputation over the supposedly self-evident principles it so facily invokes. These disputes are every bit as complex and prolonged as the halakhic disputes some liberals believe they can transcend by their simple invocations.   All too often what liberals mean by "ethics" are nothing more than the currently popular opinions held in their own community.[51]   Ethics is now confused with sociology (ethos).

Although there is a vast difference between the fundamentalist Jewish community and the liberal Jewish community, one point shared by both (without hardly ever being noticed by either of them), is a confusion of the unchangeable core of Halakhah with the most immediately manifest behavior of the community in customary usage *(minhag)*. These communities differ in that the liberal Jewish community seems to always look for standards more lenient than classical Halakhah, whereas the fundamentalist Jewish community seems to always look for standards far stricter than classical Halakhah.[52]   In both communities, nevertheless, sociological ideology seems all too often to be the norm. For if the law is *always* according to the latest *authorities (halakhah ke-batra'ay)*, then the Halakhah is always what is manifest here and now. The "absolutization" of this principle, which was by no means the view of all halakhists,[53] explains the vast power of certain "great men" *(gedolim)*. They basically reflect and enforce the current state of opinion in the community.[54] A more historically oriented approach to Halakhah sees customary usage as part of a changing and changeable process of general understanding and particular application of the primary prescriptions of the Written and Oral Torahs as commandments *(mitzvot)*. For this reason the very commitment to the primary authority of the Halakhah should actually stimulate us in our enterprises of textual and historical criticism, enterprises which see beneath customary usage by discovering its historical contingency. This is especially important today when customary usage can be seen at times as impeding the operation and intent of the primary prescriptions of both Torahs. This is particularly acute in a number of areas of Jewish family practice, where the radically changed social situation has placed the Jewish family in a very much altered position.[55]

This approach, which I have just outlined above, is more relevant to the basic theological ideas which have informed the halakhic process. The halakhic process stands between the revelation of Sinai and the full redemption of the days of the Messiah. The affirmation of revelation (an adequate theory of which is almost always absent from both fundamentalist and liberal rhetoric), as mediated by Jewish history, means that the Halakhah is in substance the commandments of God as men and women attempt to fulfill them. Change, then, is called for when the status quo prevents us from doing a mitzvah as fully and devotedly as we might. This often calls not only for new practical applications, but for new theories as well. The substance is everlasting; the form changes. To equate the status quo, which is customary usage, with the commandments themselves is to deify *minhag.* This is theologically unjustifiable. The affirmation of redemption follows from this. For our incomplete doing of the commandments of God is not only because we are lazy or obstinate. It is also because the world in which we live is not the kingdom of God and mere social survival often requires compromises which are necessary but not desired. Often Halakhah has to be changed lest far more drastic changes take place outside its "four cubits." Thus our recognition of this is not a cause for triumphalist rejoicing but a sober recognition of the as yet unredeemed character of this world.   Halakhah, then, is a self-contained system but is not self-sufficient existentially.   Without the affirmation of mediated revelation we reduce Halakhah to *minhag* and ill prepare our people for the radical social changes they must confront in modern western culture.   The dynamics of recent history require more than an acceptance of the past per se as automatically authoritative.   Faith must be more than antiquarianism.   Revelation presents a source of authority which transcends the customary usage of any generation.[56]   Without the affirmation of messianic redemption, in addition, we become utopians, convinced that our own ingenuity, even our own halakhic ingenuity, can solve our human problems with human solutions.[57]

   Halakhah requires our commitment and our understanding.   Commitment involves our personal faith that we are truly responding to the law of God and that our response is necessarily incomplete.   Understanding involves that we recognize that the Torah was given to human beings and not to angels.[58]   In modern language this means that it was given to historically contingent rational persons and not to programmed automatons or autonomous creators of simply man-made law.

THE CONFLICT BETWEEN HALAKHAH AND ETHICS: THE CASE OF *MAMZERUT*

1. *Introduction*

The case of *mamzerut* (bastardy) provides a classic example of the conflict which can arise between Halakhah and ethics. Halakhah prescribes a clearly inferior social status for persons born of certain forbidden unions: they may not marry most other Jews. In essence, then, the tradition prescribes a penalty for one person because of the sin of others. Ethics, understood as rationally evident norms, prescribes a penalty only for one's own sins.[1] As early as the book of *Jeremiah* the ethical objection is raised, "the fathers have eaten sour grapes and the teeth of the children are set on edge!" (31:28)[2] Clearly such a conflict is intersystemic in Judaism itself and cannot be dismissed as a conflict between the tradition and ideas borrowed from the outside.

In this chapter I shall examine some aspects of the historical development of the legal institution of *mamzerut* and how ethical considerations led to the restriction of its scope, if not altogether, then at least to a great extent. I shall also show a tendency in Halakhah which regarded *mamzerut* as an institution to be expanded and this was also based on ethical considerations, namely, the integrity of the Jewish family.

In the Midrash *Vayiqra Rabbah* the following poignant ethical indictment of *mamzerut* is made,

> "And I returned and saw all the persecuted." (Ecclesiastes 4:1) Hanina the tailor interpreted this Scripture; " ... all the persecuted *(kol ha'ashukim)*": these are the *mamzerim* ... their mothers committed a sin and these humiliated ones *(alybya)* are removed?! This one's father had illicit sexual relations; what did he do; why should it make a difference for him?! They have no comforter but "from the hand of their persecutors there is strength": this is the Great Sanhedrin of Israel which comes against them with the power *(koah)* of the Torah and removes them based on *(al shem)* "no *mamzer* shall enter the congregation of the Lord" (Deuteronomy 23:3). "They have no comforter." Thus God says, 'I have to comfort them,' because in this world they are refuse *(pesolet)*, but in the Messianic Age *(l'atid labo)* ... they are pure gold.[3]

The comparative lateness of this text, in relation to the halakhic rabbinic texts wherein the legal institution of *mamzerut* is developed, makes it especially important, for it is a subsequent reflection on this whole institution.[4] By carefully examining its nuances, we

can see how the rabbis dealt with the ethical problem raised by *mamzerut*.

This text can be seen as dealing with two general questions over and above the

specific question of the ethical value of *mamzerut*.

The first question concerns Divine versus human judgment. This comes out in the

following aggadic text.

> One verse (Exodus 20:5) states, "He punishes children for the sins of
> parents;" but another verse states, "Children shall not be put to death for
> the sins of their parents." (Deuteronomy 24:16) The two verses contra-
> dict each other. However, we learn there is no conflict *(la qashya)*: the
> first verse refers to when the children voluntarily follow *(ke-she'ohzin
> ... be-yadayhen)* the deeds of their parents; the second verse refers to
> when they do not voluntarily follow the deeds of their parents.[5]

The first verse cited refers to the judgment of God; the second refers to the judgment of

man. The conflict between them can only be resolved by reinterpreting one of them to

agree with the ostensive meaning of the other one.[6] In this homily the judgment of God

is reinterpreted to agree with the rationally evident ethical norm underlying the

judgment of man, namely, one is only to be punished for his or her own sin. In this

homily, dealing with the general question of sin and punishment, human judgment

manifests the ethical principle with which Divine judgment must now agree. In the

homily of Hanina the tailor, on the other hand, Divine judgment manifests the ethical

principle with which human judgment must now agree. However, the essential point in

common between both homilies is that an ethical principle calls for a reinterpretation of

a legal mode of judgment.

The second question concerns the abrogation of the Torah, or at least some of the

norms of the Torah, in the Messianic Age. Hanina the tailor seems to hold that "the

mitzvot are to be abrogated in the Messianic Age *(betelot l'atid labo)*."[7] In our case the

Divine kingdom will eliminate *mamzerut*. Now, undoubtedly because Christianity based

so much of its antinomian theology on this doctrine,[8] the Palestinian amorayyim, who

were most anxious to counter Christian claims, were quick to reinterpret it. For them it

no longer applied to the Messianic Age but, rather, to the world-to-come, conceived of as

the realm of life-after-death. Thus R. Johanan bar Nappaha interpreted this principle to

mean that "the dead are free" (Psalms 88:6), that is, the laws of clothing restrictions (kla'yim) do not apply to corpses.[9]   This reinterpretation of this doctrine, of course, presupposed that a clear distinction had been made between the Messianic Age and the world-to-come.   This distinction was clearly made by R. Johanan elsewhere, but in the Tannaitic period it seems not yet to have been made with any rigorous consistency.[10] Hanina the tailor, however, seems to revert to the earlier, literal, meaning of this principle.   Indeed the most important example of this doctrine is also found in *Vayiqra Rabbah*, namely, it is stated there that God Himself will issue a new Torah (*hidush Torah*) in this future time and the dietary laws, especially, will be abrogated.[11]   What emerges from this line of aggadic thinking is that the present laws of the Torah are already open for radical reinterpretation, something Hanina demands from the halakhic authorities of his day.

2. *Who is a Mamzer?*

The word *mamzer* itself is of unclear etymology.   Abraham Geiger gave, however, a highly plausible explanation of its original meaning.[12]   According to Geiger *mamzer* should be read as *me'am-zar*, namely, a child born of a gentile father and a Jewish mother, a prohibited union ("Kinder aus unehelichem Umgange").   He cites Zechariah 9:6 ("And a *mamzer* shall dwell in Ashdod . . . ") in the Septuagint where *mamzer* is rendered *allogeneis*, that is, "outsider" as in the Septuagint to Isaiah 61:5 ("And outsiders shall stand and shepherd your flock, and foreigners shall be your farmers and vintners").   Here "outsiders" (*zarim*) is rendered *allogeneis* and "foreigners" (*benay nekhar*) is rendered *allophyloi* (literally, "other tribes").[13]   Geiger refers to "an old Talmudic tradition" which states that "when either a gentile or a slave has had sexual relations with a Jewish woman, the child issuing from this union is a *mamzer*."[14]

Geiger's great insight brings into bold relief what are in fact two different halakhic understandings of who is a *mamzer*.   The first, as we have just seen, designates as *mamzer* the issue of an illicit union between a gentile man and a Jewish woman.   The second definition of a *mamzer* is the issue of an illicit union between two Jews.   As the *Mishnah* states,

> Whoever could not be married to this particular Jew, but could be
> married to another Jew (*yesh lah al aherim qiddushin*), the child issuing
> from this union is a *mamzer*.   Who is such a person?   Such a person is one

of the members of illicit unions mentioned in the Torah (Leviticus 18:6 and following).[15]

Elsewhere the *Mishnah* states, in a seemingly earlier version of the law,

> Who is a *mamzer*? Any relation with whom one is not to have sexual relations *(she-hu be-lo yabo)* is the opinion of R. Akibah. Simon the Temani says whomever one would be liable for *karet* at the hands of God if he had had sexual relations with her.[16]

This text appears, with the insertion of appropriate proof-texts from Scripture, in the *Sifre* on Deuteronomy 23:3.[17] In fact, this understanding of the meaning of *mamzer* also led to its own etymology of the word. The Talmud, no doubt reflecting on this whole tradition, sees *mamzer* as coming from *mum zar*, that is, a full Jew having a "strange blemish" in either his or her pedigree.[18]

The difference between these two understandings of the meaning of *mamzer*, although by no means mutually exclusive, can be seen, in the question of whether in matters of pedigree the emphasis is on patrilineal or matrilineal descent.

The Talmudic text cited by Geiger, namely, that the child issuing from a gentile father and a Jewish mother is a *mamzer*, reflects the older Scriptural notion that descent is determined solely by the father. In other words, children of a Jewish father (even if the mother is a gentile) are Jews; children of a gentile father and a Jewish mother are excluded from the Jewish people; they may not "enter the congregation of the Lord." This seems to be the plain meaning of the text because in the very next verse it states, "Neither an Ammonite nor a Moabite may enter the congregation of the Lord" (Deuteronomy 23:4), which the rabbis saw as not only prohibiting an authentic Ammonite or an authentic Moabite from marrying a Jewess, but, also, prohibiting their entry into Judaism altogether by conversion.[19]

Identity of children is determined by the father. Indeed there is no mention in Scripture of any specific *rite de passage* whereby the gentile wife of a Jewish man became part of the Jewish people. Even Ruth the *Moabitess* (!), who later became the paradigm for the true proselyte *(ger tzedeq)* simply verbally affirms her desire to be part of the people of Israel and accept their God (Ruth 1:16).[20] This desire is enough for no less an Israelite leader than Boaz to marry her (4:10) and for no less an Israelite king than David to be her direct descendant (4:22).

The new emphasis on matrilineal descent clearly had the effect of limiting the definition of *mamzer* to the second understanding, namely, the issue of an illicit inter-Jewish union. Like all such effects in a traditional legal system, it did not come about immediately.

We can see the change from matrilineal to patrilineal emphasis in the following text from the Palestinian Talmud.[21]

> Jacob the man of Neburaya went to Tyre. They came and asked him whether or not one may circumcize the son of a non-Jewess (*Aramayta*—and a Jew) on the Sabbath. His opinion was to permit them to do so based on (Numbers 1:18) "They were registered by the clans of their ancestral houses (*le-bayt abotam*)." When R. Haggai heard about this he said that he should be brought to be lashed. He said to him, 'on what basis would you lash me?' He said to him that it was from the following Scripture (Ezra 10:3), "And now let us make a covenant . . . to remove all the foreign women and those born from them. . . ." He said to him, 'from the authority of the Hagiographa (*u-min ha-qabbalah*) you would lash me?' He said to him that it could be done from the authority of the Torah. He said to him, 'from which part of the Torah (*min hadayn Oraita*)?' He said to him from the following. 'R. Johanan said in the name of R. Simon bar Johai that you shall not marry them, etc.'

The citation of the first proof-text from the book of *Ezra* is important because we see that the beginnings of matrilineal concern are post-exilic. The full statement of R. Johanan in the name of R. Simon bar Johai, which is the development of this emphasis of Ezra and the *sofrim*, is brought in the Babylonian Talmud.

> That "he will turn your son away from Me" (Deuteronomy 7:4)—your son from a Jewess is called "your son," but your son from a non-Jewess is not called "your son" but "*her* son."[22]

Now the text in Deuteronomy specifically refers to the seven Canaanite nations alone. It is only by a rather tenuous inference that the Talmud generalizes "he will turn your son away from Me" to include all gentiles, who will turn the Jewish partner away from Judaism (*lerabbot kol ha-mesirim*). Furthermore, the "son" mentioned in the passage does not refer to a child issuing from this Jewish-Canaanite (or any Jewish-gentile) union, but, rather, as Rabbenu Tam pointed out, to the male Jewish partner in this mixed union, who will be turned away from Judaism by his gentile father-in-law (*ha-hoten*).[23]

The establishment of matrilineal identity required a clear departure from the plain meaning of the text of Scripture. In fact, Maimonides, who usually avoids any but the most evident Scriptural exegesis as a basis for Halakhah, here too avoided all of this and simply stated the law.[24] Thus the designation as a *mamzer* of the child born of a gentile father and a Jewish mother is actually a developmental stage in the movement from patrilineal to matrilineal descent, that is, one is a Jew because of his Jewish mother, but he is still a flawed Jew because of his gentile father. This is why R. Johanan bar Nappaha, the authority who holds that Jewish identity per se is determined by the mother, is also the same authority who holds that a gentile father makes his albeit Jewish child a *mamzer*.[25] It was only after centuries of debate among the Amorayyim that, probably sometime in the late fourth century C.E., the rule became "that when a gentile or a slave had sexual relations with a Jewess, the child is *kasher*, whether the woman was unmarried or married."[26] This edict undoubtedly had the effect of greatly limiting the number of *mamzerim* inasmuch as cases of intermarriage are far more publically ascertainable than cases of adultery and incest, the two causes of *mamzerut* when both parents are Jews.

This long process of development of the Halakhah must be understood in order to appreciate the ethical indictment of *mamzerut* in this particular text in *Vayiqra Rabbah*. For the whole *midrash* is based on the Scriptural account of the son of an Egyptian father and an Israelite mother who has blasphemed (Leviticus 24:10-12). According to the much earlier Tannaitic *midrash*, the *Sifra*, this blasphemer had the stigma of a *mamzer*.[27]

> He came to pitch his tent in the midst of the camp of Dan. They said to him, 'by what right (*mah tibekha*) do you pitch your tent in the midst of the camp of Dan? He said to them, 'I am descended from one of the daughters of Dan.' They said to him, 'Scripture (Numbers 2:2) states, "All the men of the Israelites, each shall camp with his standard under the banners of their ancestral house (*le-bayt abotam*)." . . . "He is the son of an Egyptian man" (Leviticus 24:10): even though there were no *mamzerim* at that time, it was as if he were a *mamzer*. . . ."Among the Israelites": This teaches that he converted (*she-nitgayyer*).

R. Abraham ben David of Posquières (*Rabad*) noted in his commentary on the *Sifra* that the author of this *midrash* is of the opinion that the son of a non-Jewish father and a Jewish mother is a *mamzer*. In other words, even though *mamzerut* was not officially decreed until the Deuteronomic code, it was in effect earlier. Nahmanides in his

commentary on the Torah[28] cites certain anonymous French scholars who stated that the
reason this man had to convert is because this was before the giving of the Torah (that is,
Deuteronomy), and before this time, as among the gentiles, a child followed the pedigree
of his or her father.[29] Thus, according to this interpretation, a *mamzer* was considered
at this time to be a non-Jew altogether.

Therefore, the complaint of this *mamzer* is that he has been denied any status at all
in Israelite society because of his gentile patrilineal descent. This would prevent him
from permanently owning land in Israel. Even his conversion would only give him the
status of a temporary resident-alien, a *toshab*. Indeed, the *Sifre* sees this as the reason
why Jethro refused the invitation of his son-in-law, Moses, to join the Israelites in the
Promised Land.[30] This complaint in the mouth of the blasphemer makes perfect sense in
the historical context of the *Sifra*, before the rabbis had eliminated the children of
gentile fathers and Jewish mothers from the stigma of *mamzerut*. Furthermore, at the
beginning of the section of *Vayiqra Rabbah* where *mamzerut* is discussed, the blasphemer
is considered to be either "like a *mamzer*" or "definitely a *mamzer (barur)*."[31]

Nevertheless, the complaint about *mamzerut* in *Vayiqra Rabbah*, unlike that in the
Sifra, is *not* made by the blasphemer but is now made by a contemporary, Hanina the
tailor. By this time the complaint is against *mamzerut* as an unjust stigma on the child
of an illicit inter-Jewish union.[32] And this is precisely why the complaint is directed
against the Great Sanhedrin, which should not be understood literally in that this
institution had long ceased to function,[33] but rather as a symbol of halakhic authority in
general. By the time of Hanina the tailor the rabbis, by legal fiat, had determined that
the children of intermarriages, when the mother was a Jewess, were not only full Jews,
but they were also removed from the stigma of *mamzerut*. In fact their only remaining
stigma was that, like others of less than pure pedigree, a woman born from such a union
could not marry a *kohen*.[34] Therefore, the meaning of Hanina's complaint is that if the
rabbis had the power, by fiat, to remove the stigma of *mamzerut* from the issue of mixed
marriages, a stigma which seems to be the original meaning of the very term *mamzer*, as
we have seen before, then why do the rabbis not remove the stigma of *mamzerut* from
the issue of adulterous and incestuous unions? In other words, why do the rabbis not
change the whole institution of *mamzerut* when they clearly have the legal power to do
so?

3. *The Aggadic Debate Over Inherited Guilt*

Despite various attempts to circumscribe *mamzerut*, there was rabbinic debate about the ethical value of *mamzerut*. Some rabbis were convinced that it was ethically unjustifiable and had to be radically circumscribed. However, there were other rabbis who were convinced that *mamzerut* was a necessary institution in order to promote the higher standard of sexual morality expected of the Jewish people. This ethical debate, carried on in aggadic discourses, had halakhic results. Those disapproving of *mamzerut* had the tendency to limit its range and devise means for helping *mamzerim* escape the stigma of their birth. On the other hand, those approving of *mamzerut* had the tendency to expand its range and devise means for increasing the number of *mamzerim*. These two differing halakhic tendencies, the one centripetal and the other centrifugal, can only be understood when seen in the context of the ethical debate over the essence of *mamzerut*, a debate conducted aggadically.

The *locus classicus* of this debate is in the following *Tosefta* text.[35]

> *Mamzerim* will be purified *(tehorin)* in the Messianic Age *(l'atid labo)* in the words of R. Jose. R. Meir said that they will not be purified. R. Jose said to him, 'is it not said (Ezekiel 36:25): "I will sprinkle pure water upon you and you will be pure."?' R. Meir said to him that the end of this verse states "from all your impurities and from all your idolatries" (only). R. Jose said to him that it says there "I will purify you": even . . . from *mamzerut*.

In the Babylonian Talmud this debate is discussed as follows,

> R. Judah said in the name of Samuel that the law is the opinion of R. Jose. R. Joseph said that if R. Judah in the name of Samuel had not said that the law is the opinion of R. Jose, Elijah would take from us many many groups.[36]

Although the printed text of the Palestinian Talmud,[37] as well as the critical edition of *Vayiqra Rabbah*,[38] state that the law is *not* the opinion of R. Jose, Professor Saul Lieberman brings a manuscript of the Palestinian Talmud from the Cairo Genizah which states, "if the law is not the opinion of R. Jose that *mamzerim* will be pure in the Messianic Age, then the generations will be humiliated *(alubin)* in the Messianic Age."[39]

Along the lines of this eschatological speculation about the status of *mamzerim* and what Elijah will do with them in the Messianic Age, the *Mishnah* states,

> R. Joshua said . . . that Elijah is not only coming to declare what is

impure and what is pure ... but to remove with force (bizro'a) those who have (wrongly) come close and to draw close those who have been (wrongly) removed. Thus the family of Bet Tzerifah was on the other side of the Jordan and Ben Zion removed them with force. And there was another family whom Ben Zion drew near with force. Like this will Elijah be when he comes to declare what is impure and what is pure, to draw near and to remove. .... But the sages say that he is not coming to remove or draw near but to make peace in the world as it says (Malachi 3:23-24), "Behold I send Elijah the prophet to you ... and he will turn the heart of the fathers to the sons and the heart of the sons to their fathers."[40]

Now according to Maimonides, commenting on this *Mishnah*, Ben Zion drew near a family that actually should have been put in the category of *mamzerim*, whereas the Bet Tzifirah family did not deserve to be put in this category. Elijah will act with the same force, but he will draw near the families who are truly *kasher* and will remove the families who are truly *mamzerim*. For the sages, on the other hand, Elijah will bring about peace and unity among the people and between the generations. Since *mamzerut* is a barrier to this type of total reconciliation, the opinion of the sages, in contradistinction to that of R. Joshua, is brought to show that they thought *mamzerut* will be ultimately abolished by supernatural means.

The amorayyim too were divided over whether *mamzerut* is beneficial or not.

R. Hama son of R. Hanina said that when God makes His presence manifest (mashreh Shekhinato) in Israel, He does so only on the pedigreed families (mishpahot meyuhasot) in Israel as it says (Jeremiah 30:25), "In that time, says the Lord, I will be God for all the families of Israel, and they will be a people for Me." It did not say 'to all Israel' but "to all the families." ... R. Joshua ben Levi said that money (kesef) purifies *mamzerim* as it is said (Malachi 3:3) "He shall sit like a smelter purging silver (kesef) ..." What does "they shall present offerings in righteousness (bi-tzedaqah)" mean? R. Isaac said that God did charity (tzedaqah) with Israel in that a family that has become intermingled (she-nitma'ah) is left intermingled.[41]

The reasoning behind the pro-*mamzerut* attitude is expressed in *Vayiqra Rabbah*.

"A closed garden" (Canticles 4:12): R. Phineas said in the name of R. Hiyyah bar Abba that because Israel protected (she-gadru) themselves in Egypt from sexual immorality (min ha'ervah) they were redeemed from Egypt ... because there was none among them who was promiscuous (parutz ervah) except, you should know, one woman, and Scripture publicized her, that is, "Shlomit bat Dibry of the tribe of Dan" (Leviticus 24:10) . . . "bat *Dibry*": R. Isaac said that she brought pestilence *(deber)* on her son.[42]

In other words, according to this view, what prevents promiscuity among the Jewish people is the awareness of the consequences it is likely to bring, namely, that one's children will suffer the stigma of *mamzerut*. That children do suffer because of their parents' mistakes is, to be sure, a sad fact of both heredity and environment.

4. Some Halakhic Remedies

In the Babylonian Talmud the following Tannaitic fragment is brought.

They asked R. Eliezer (ben Hyrkanus) about the status of a female *mamzeret* after ten generations. He said to them, 'were it only after three generations that I could purify her!'[43]

Almost the exact fragment appears in the parallel text in the Palestinian Talmud.[44] Nevertheless, in both Talmuds what the halakhic reasoning of R. Eliezer would be is not presented. Rather, as we shall see shortly, it is connected with aggadic speculation about how long *mamzerim* actually survive. It would seem, then, that R. Eliezer's statement is the statement of a wish that he could not himself fulfill within the limits of the law.[45]

Nevertheless, the *Mishnah* brings a statement of a generation later which makes a similar claim about a male *mamzer*[46] and, also, demonstrates the claim halakhically.

R. Tarfon says that male *mamzerim* can be purified. How? A *mamzer* marries a gentile slave woman *(shifha)* and the child born of this union will thus have the status of a slave. Let him then free him *(shihrero)* and his son will have the status of a free Jew *(ben horin)*. R. Eliezer says that he will have the status of a slave who is a *mamzer*[47]

R. Eliezer, as we have just seen, is clearly sympathetic with the motivation of R. Tarfon's later ruling, but he still cannot accept its halakhic validity. Nevertheless, both Talmuds record the conclusion of R. Judah in the name of Samuel that the law is according to the opinion of R. Tarfon.[48]

The Babylonian Talmud questions whether R. Tarfon's opinion is to be advocated *ab initio*, or only accepted *ex post facto*. If the former, then it implies, according to Rashi, that the prohibition of marrying a gentile slave woman does not apply to a *mamzer*.[49] If the latter, on the other hand, it implies that even a *mamzer* may not marry a gentile slave woman, but if he did the children of this union do benefit from her *changeable* status and do not suffer from his *unchangeable* status. In other words, the *mamzer* is advised to become as incognito as possible, marry a slave woman, and correct the status of his children before it is too late.[50] As Maimonides notes, however,

> Because of this matter they permitted a *mamzer* to marry a gentile slave woman in order to purify his children. . . . They did not rule against a *mamzer* marrying a gentile slave woman because of the rectification of the status of the children *(mipnay taqqanat ha-banim).*[51]

It is obvious from this that Maimonides regarded the prohibition of marriage with a gentile slave woman as rabbinic and, therefore, the rabbis have the power to restrict it as they see fit. This interpretation is clearly in line with the Talmud.

Despite the fact that the Babylonian Talmud concludes that R. Tarfon's solution may be followed openly *ab initio*,[52] the other halakhic method of solving the problem is a sort of benign neglect. Thus the aggadic statement of R. Isaac, which we examined shortly before, namely, that "a family that has become intermingled is left intermingled *(nitma'ah)*"[53] is interpreted halakhically. In other words, in matters pertaining to *mamzerut*, we assume that all Jews are *kasher*, that is, not *mamzerim*, and that the burden of proof as in all such matters in on the accuser.[54] Moreover, this rule of benign neglect is seen as being based on the aggadic view of R. Jose, which we examined earlier, namely, that *mamzerim* will not be singled out in the Messianic Age. Since they will not be singled out in the future, we are under no obligation to single them out in the present. Thus R. Joel Sirkes *(Bah)*, a sixteenth century Polish halakhist, writes,

> It is written in the notes of Mordecai on *Yebamot* that R. Isaac bar Samuel was questioned about this as being nothing but eschatological speculation *(hilkhata de-meshiha)*, and he answered that we derive from this that according to R. Jose one need not remove himself (that is, marry) from unknown families.[55]

5. *Some Halakhic Impediments*

The strictest view of *mamzerut* was that of R. Akibah.

> R. Akibah held that there is no valid marriage *(ayn qiddushin tofsin)* when the union is in violation of any negative commandment *(l'avin)* . . . it is taught in a *baraita* that R. Simai said that R. Akibah declared the issue of any such union to be a *mamzer*, except a widow who married the High Priest, because there the Torah stated (Leviticus 21:15) "he shall not sire disqualified children." Disqualification *(hillulim)* he makes but not

> *mamzerut.* But R. Yeshbab said, 'come let us protest about Akibah ben
> Joseph who is saying that any Jewishly invalid intercourse *(kol she'ayn lo*
> *bi'ah be-yisra'el)* makes the issue a *mamzer.*'[56]

Now the *Gemara* earlier indicated that no one would say that relations with one's wife

when she was a menstruant *(niddah)* make the issue a *mamzer.*[57] Undoubtedly this was

the ruling because such a transgression is too widespread and would be next to impossible

to detect. This would, however, be a logical conclusion from R. Akibah's position, and

this is undoubtedly why both Talmuds take special efforts to eliminate this easy

conclusion.[58]

Despite the fact that the law is not the opinion of R. Akibah, the tendency of the

Halakhah was to expand the category of *mamzerut* in doubtful areas. Thus the *Mishnah,*

in listing the ten categories of Jews (and quasi-Jews) who returned from Babylonian exile

with Ezra, mentions the categories of *shetuqay* and *asufay.*

> Who are the *shetuqay*? Anyone who knows who is his mother but not who
> is his father. Who are the *asufay*? Anyone who was taken in from the
> marketplace and who does not know his father or his mother. . . . . All
> who are prohibited from marrying other Jews are permitted to marry
> each other. R. Judah prohibits it. R. Eliezer says that those who are
> prohibited because of the certainty of their status *(vada'an)* may marry
> others in similar status, but those who are prohibited because of doubtful
> status *(bisfeqan)* may neither marry those who are prohibited because of
> the certainty of their status nor others prohibited because of their
> doubtful status.[59]

Although there were various attempts to limit if not eliminate these two categories of

doubtful *mamzerim,* the general principle underlying all of this legislation was expressed

as "they made a higher standard *(ma'aleh)* concerning pedigree *(be-yuhasin).*"[60]

With the repeal of the old rule that the issue of a union between a Jewish mother

and a gentile father is a *mamzer,* the main source of *mamzerim* was the issue of

adulterous unions between two Jews. However, adulterous unions of the ordinary

clandestine variety are rarely detected. Hence, adulterous unions of the "technical"

variety, that is, women who hastily remarried not having been properly divorced from

their first husbands, became the main source of *mamzerim.* The children of the improper

second marriages suffer the stigma of *mamzerut* because of the carelessness of their

parents. Indeed this consequence was seen as good motivation for women to take special care in obtaining proper divorces from their husbands before remarrying. Thus the *Mishnah* states,

> A woman whose husband went abroad, and people came to her and said, 'your husband is dead,' and who remarried afterwards, and then her first husband returned: she must leave both men and obtain a *get* from both of them. She receives no *ketubah* payment . . . and any child from either marriage is a *mamzer.* [61]

This whole *Mishnah* is correctly explained by Rashi, who states that although the rabbis permitted remarriage even if only one witness reported the death of the first husband, the woman herself is, nevertheless, expected to make her own thorough investigation *(de-hi gufa dayqa)* before hastily remarrying.[62] It seems as though this much is required by the covenantal faithfulness *(qushta)* of Jewish marriage. Rashi also explained that the child of the first husband is only a *mamzer* if the first husband took his wife back, and the child of their remarriage is a *mamzer* according to rabbinic law *(me-dibrayhem).*[63] This is because of the child's doubtful status, a status resulting from his or her mother's questionable conduct in hastily remarrying.

However, the rabbis were aware of the havoc that would be wrecked in Jewish family life if husbands were permitted, what was conceived as their Scriptural right, to cancel bills of divorcement after they were sent by agent. Thus the *Mishnah* states,

> In earlier times *(ba-r'ishonah)* one would convene a *Bet Din* in another place and nullify *(u-mebatlo)* it (the *get* he sent by agent). Rabban Gamliel the Elder decreed *(hitqin),* for the good of society *(mipnay tiqqun ha'olam)* that this not be done.[64]

Now the Babylonian Talmud explains the legal force of Rabban Gamliel's decree as being the rabbinic power to annul marriages, that is, even if the *get* was subsequently invalidated, the woman's marriage is terminated anyway.[65] The Palestinian Talmud explains this decree as being based on the even broader principle that the rabbis have the power to abrogate part of the Scriptural institution *(oqrin dibray Torah).*[66] Nevertheless, one of the reasons why the principle of rabbinic annulment must be restricted to the case mentioned in the *Mishnah* is stated by the Tosafists as follows,

> R. Samuel raised the objection that if this principle is more broadly applied *(im ken),* then an uncle married to his niece might cover up *(yehappeh)* her adultery so that when a witness comes that she has commited adultery, he will send her a *get* and then nullify it not in the

> presence of the agent and the marriage would thus be annulled
> retroactively. Her status would then be that of an unmarried woman
> (penuyah) retroactively. . . . In answer to this objection . . . that
> mamzerim will thus be purified . . . if we know that this was his intention
> in so doing (she-le-kakh mitkavven), then we do not annul the marriage,
> because the sages made a constructive decree (de-le-taqqanah) and not a
> destructive decree (ve-lo le-taqqalah). For if this happens, Jewish
> women would become promiscuous.[67]

Here again we see the consequence of mamzerut presented as a strong deterrent to
Jewish promiscuity.

6. The Existence of Mamzerim

The most radical solution to the problem of mamzerut is to deny that mamzerim
really exist. Thus the statement of R. Eliezer ben Hyrkanus, which we examined earlier,
where R. Eliezer expresses his wish that he could purify female mamzerot, is connected
in the Babylonian and Palestinian Talmuds with the following Amoraic opinion (which I
quote in the Babylonian version),

> One might therefore say (alma) that he (R. Eliezer) thought that a
> mamzer does not survive (la hayay). And so did R. Huna say that a
> mamzer does not survive. But does not our Mishnah say 'Mamzerim are
> prohibited (from marrying other Jews) and this prohibition is everlasting
> (isur olam)?' R. Zera said that this was explained to me by R. Judah that
> when he is known to be a mamzer, he survives; when unknown, he does
> not; when known and unknown, he survives three generations and more
> than that he does not survive.[68]

Rashi explains "known and unknown" to be the normal case when people check pedigree
for three generations, but not more than that.[69]

Now this statement can be interpreted to be in the tradition of treating mamzerut
with benign neglect, that is, assuming mamzerim do not survive and there is no point,
therefore, in looking for them. This comes out in the Palestinian Talmud.[70] If this is so,
then we have one more example of where a Scriptural legal category is treated as a null
class. As such, its import becomes solely theoretical and is not treated practically. In
other words, its import becomes aggadic rather than halakhic. This would then be the
same line of interpretation employed elsewhere in the Talmud.

> A *baraita* taught that the 'rebellious son' *(ben sorer u-moreh)* never existed and never will *(ve-lo l'atid lehiyot)*. So why was it written in Scripture (Deuteronomy 21:18-21)?   Profitably expound it *(darosh ve-qabbel sekhar)*. . . . the 'idolatrous city' *(ir ha-nidahat*—Deuteronomy 13:15-18) never existed and never will ... the 'stricken house' *(bet ha-menuga*—Leviticus 14:33-53) never existed and never will . . .[71]

Now these three opinions are definitely disputed as the Talmud duly notes. However, this passage does represent a tradition which interpreted some ethically troubling Scriptural institutions as purely theoretical. One could interpret the above treatment of *mamzerut*, which the Palestinian Talmud traces back to Rab,[72] to the very beginning of the Amoraic period, along the same lines.

Nevertheless, in the development of this notion in both Talmuds the exact opposite line of interpretation is developed. Thus both Talmuds report accounts of rabbis actually exposing *mamzerim* in order to save their lives, that is, in keeping with the earlier view that only known *mamzerim* survive.[73] Now, it seems to me, that the original statement meant that *mamzerim* do not survive infancy.[74]   Nevertheless, the later Talmudic tradition sees *mamzerim* surviving into adulthood and that only their exposure assures their continued survival. In other words, it is better to be a live *mamzer* than a dead one! Thus exposing the *mamzer* saves his or her life, just as an earlier Tannaitic source advocated that *mamzerim* be exposed so that *kasher* Jews will not be fooled and erroneously intermarry with them.

> A *baraita* taught: R. Judah said that there was a case of a man who came before R. Tarfon who had six fingers and six toes, twenty-four digits in all. He said to him, 'may there be many like you in Israel!' R. Jose said to him (R. Judah), 'what kind of proof is that?!' This is what he (R. Tarfon) said to him, 'may there be few *mamzerim* ... like you in Israel!'[75]

Now this text is placed by the editors of the Babylonian Talmud in the *Gemara* which deals with the *Mishnah's* listing of physical disfigurements which disqualify a *kohen* having them from officiating at the altar in the Temple.[76] Therefore, R. Tarfon, with his well known sympathy with the plight of *mamzerim*, hoped that *mamzerim* would not have such noticeable disfigurements so as to be so readily detected. A related Amoraic text seems to indicate that we can actually tell who are *mamzerim* because they look so much like their adulterous fathers.[77] Although this text is brought in the context of establishing halakhic criteria for positive identification of corpses, this particular text is clearly aggadic.[78]

7. Conclusion

In examining the development of the institution of *mamzerut* we have noticed two tendencies in approaching it and dealing with it. The first tendency is centripetal, attempting to restrict its range as much as possible. The second tendency is centrifugal, attempting to extend its range. Indeed in virtually all such major questions in the history of Judaism one can show similarly dual tendencies.

Discussion of the interrelation between law and ethics, despite the antiquity of the data examined, can never be totally descriptive. For even if our project is only to examine the laws of some long dead society, once we attempt to uncover the ethical questions dealt with in the development of these laws in their society, we are already making analogies with the laws of our own society. This is so because the underlying foundation of our project is concern with ethical questions which are presupposed in the development of the laws of *any* and *every* society.[79] Indeed, on logical grounds, how can the examination of the prescriptive data have no prescriptive meaning? Therefore, what normative conclusions can our brief examination of the legal institution of *mamzerut* lead to? Furthermore, *mamzerut* is not a legal institution of a dead society; Halakhah still governs the lives of a definite (and growing) segment of the Jewish people. Hence, neither the ethical continuum nor the legal continuum here has been broken. The ethical continuum has not been broken because of the immutability of essentially human sociality, which always has to deal with the question of family status. The legal continuum has not been broken because of the continuity of Jewish history. The question now becomes: where do Jews go from here?

At this stage we must establish the parameters of possible solutions. Here we must reject two extremes. The first and most obvious extreme is to simply eliminate *mamzerut* in principle. This extreme must be rejected because it entails the abrogation of the authority of the law. The *Mishnah* established the operative principle in Halakhah that once it is posited that a Toraitic institution does not exist (*l'aqor et kol ha-guf*), one cannot talk about a normative halakhic process at all anymore.[80] The authority of any legal system cannot tolerate picking and choosing which institutions are to be upheld and which are to be dropped.[81] On the other hand, we must also reject the extreme which extends *mamzerut* to areas the tradition already barred it from entering, as we have surely seen before.

We have seen before that the basic thrust of the centripetal approach to *mamzerut* has been the ethical objection that children not be made to suffer for the sins of their parents, that everyone receive what he or she deserves.   The basic thrust of the centrifugal approach, conversely, has been based on the ethical consideration of the integrity of the family as the basic unit of human society in general, and the basic unit of Jewish people especially.

Now, it seems to me, that this second consideration is no longer served, but is actually dis-served, by an emphasis on *mamzerut*. This is so because the overwhelming number of *mamzerim* today are the issue of improperly conducted second marriages where the ignorance of the parents has led to a consequence that rarely was known, much less appreciated, by them when they violated Jewish law in their remarriage.

The only ennunciated solution we have is that of R. Tarfon, namely, that the *mamzer* marry a gentile slave woman and thus produce gentile children who are not *mamzerim* and can, then, be converted to Judaism on the basis of their matrilineal descent which does not have the strain of *mamzerut* in it. This solution, even in its own day, was only partial because it did not help female *mamzerot*. In our own day, when slavery is an institution which has been long and happily abolished, this solution is no longer available. (Where would one find such "slave women" today anyhow?)

Thus today the only real solution for the *mamzer*, male or female, is intermarriage, for only outside of the Jewish people will these persons be able to live a normal family life.   Intermarriage and assimilation are two sides of the same coin.   The Talmud recognized this grave possibility.   Commenting on the verse, "Cursed is the man who makes a graven image and idol" (Deuteronomy 27:15) the following point is made,

> This refers to one who had sexual relations with someone forbidden to
> him *(al ha'ervah)* and fathered a child.   This child went among the
> gentiles and became an idolator. His parents caused him to do this.[82]

Rashi points out that the *mamzer's* shame in his *mamzerut* caused him to leave the Jewish people altogether.[83]

Here, as so often in the history of the interrelation of law and ethics, a choice has to be made between two evils, inclining to the lesser of the two. Since the preservation of the Jewish people has always been a paramount concern in both Jewish law and Jewish ethics, and is certainly a point of universal Jewish consensus after the Holocaust, we must ask ourselves here and now: what is a greater threat to that preservation, intermarriage or *mamzerut*? If our answer is the former, then there are two things that can be done within the Halakhah as it has developed heretofore. The first thing that can be done is to assume that all Jews are *not mamzerim* and conduct no investigations of pedigree *(ayn bodqin)*, when we know we are dealing with persons born Jews.[84]   The second thing that can be done, when *mamzerut* is too evident to ignore, is to annul the first marriage *(afqa'at qiddushin)* of the offending mother thus making her children the issue of *de jure* "fornication" *(be'ilat zenut)* but not adultery *(ni'uf)*.[85] This would only give such children an informal social stigma *(pegam)* and prevent some others from marrying them.[86]   It would not, however disable them socially with the stigma of *mamzerut*. This solution was proposed some years ago by the late Israeli Supreme Court Justice Moshe Silberg in an open letter to the Ashkenazic Chief Rabbi of Israel, Shlomoh Goren.[87]

The main argument against this solution, as we saw before, was that the Tosafists feared it would lead to sexual immorality since any violated marriage could be annulled retroactively. However, the answer to this objection today is threefold: (1) in today's atmosphere of unprecedented ignorance and apathy among the majority of the Jewish people, fear of the consequence of *mamzerut* is no longer operative in their sexual decision making; (2) improperly initiated second marriages, which can easily be performed under either secular or non-halakhic Jewish auspices, are not considered "fornication" by the majority of the Jewish people; (3) any situation which could lead a segment of the Jewish people to believe that intermarriage is the only solution to their personal and familial dilemma must be rectified since intermarriage and its attendant assimilation pose today's greatest threat to the survival of both the Jewish people and Judaism. As the *Mishnah* noted in a famous passage, changes in the law are called for when worse results will emerge from staying with the *status quo,*

> "It is time to act for the Lord; they have violated your Torah." (Psalms 119:126). R. Nathan said, 'violate the Torah because *(mishum)* it is time to act for the Lord!'[88]

ANNULMENT IN LIEU OF DIVORCE IN JEWISH LAW

1. *The Modern Crisis in Jewish Divorce*

The problem of a woman still legally married to an absent husband is one which has been of perennial concern to halakhists from early rabbinic times until the present. Such a woman is termed an *agunah,* namely, "one who has been deserted."[1] Her situation has always been considered unfortunate and halakhists have tried to alleviate it as much as was possible within limits of the Law, and in a way which did not demean the sanctity of the marital bond which Judaism has always regarded as being of the greatest importance.

A woman can become an *agunah* under two very different circumstances. On the one hand, her husband can be lost through an accident such as war and it is unknown whether he is dead or alive. On the other hand, the husband's whereabouts can be well-known and the woman is an *agunah* because he is exercising his Scriptural privilege to either give or not give her a proper *get.* Interestingly enough, in modern times the first type of *agunah* problem has become easier to solve in most cases whereas the second type has become more difficult.

In cases of the husband being accidentally lost the rabbis of the Talmud already made two major concessions. One, to ascertain the death of such a lost husband they were willing to accept the testimony of only one witness rather than the two or more required by Scriptural law. Two, they allowed this one witness to be just about anybody, rather than insist upon the precise qualifications for a qualified witness set down in the *Mishnah.*[2] If we look at how much easier long-range communication is in modern times, how much easier it is to search remote places, we can see how the *de jure* leniency of the Talmud is extended by this *de facto* ease. Air travel and world-wide telecommunication, for example, have helped ascertain the deaths of many lost husbands whose deaths would have been impossible to ascertain in previous periods.[3]

However, in those cases where a husband refuses to give a *get,* even when ordered to do so by a rabbinical court, the *agunah* problem becomes more acute in modern times. This is so for two reasons. First, whereas in former, pre-modern, times Jews lived under the semi-autonomous authority of a society governed by Jewish law, today virtually all the Jews of the diaspora—the majority of world Jewry—live as *individuals* in societies

29

governed by secular law. Jewish communities only have the status of corporations voluntarily entered into by individuals who can secede from them at any time. Therefore, whereas in former times Jewish authorities could exert political, social, economic, and even physical pressure on a husband whom they considered obligated to give his wife a *get*,[4] today such ecclesiastical pressure is illegal in a secularly constituted society. Even the informal social pressure that could be exerted in the self-contained, pre-modern, Jewish societies is now of little effect in an open secular society, where privacy and individuality are considered rights the society is to fully protect. Furthermore, whereas in former times the larger non-Jewish host society very frequently helped enforce Jewish autonomous rule (probably as a general check of a suzerain against internal anarchy *within* any subject community),[5] today democratic authorities are usually loathe to interfere in religious questions which are considered to be essentially private.[6] Hence husbands can wrongly refuse to grant their wives Jewish divorces with impunity. It is this type of *agunah* problem that is our own peculiarly modern vexation. No rational and sensitive halakhist could possibly regard this situation as a tolerable state of affairs. It clearly calls for a practical solution, or even a partial practical solution, within the four cubits of the Halakhah. To allow a situation like this to go unchecked is to jeopardize the moral authority of the Law both in general and, specifically, in its matrimonial aspects. To allow a situation like this to go unchecked is tacitly to encourage anarchy, which is the very antithesis of all law.

2. *Rights Subsequent to Obligations*

In a brilliant essay devoted to the Talmudic basis of annulment in Jewish law, an essay I will return to frequently in this paper, the eminent Talmudist and Jewish philosopher, my late revered friend, Professor Samuel Atlas, emphasized the essentially social character of the institution of marriage. "For the institution of marriage in and of itself is a social institution *(mosad tzibburi)* affecting the whole community in that the legal consequences flowing from it extend to all Israel."[7] Professor Atlas illustrated his point by citing the Talmudic text which states that the necessity for witnesses in a marriage ceremony at all times is because the relationship between the man and the woman affects "others."[8] According to several important medieval commentators, these "others" so affected are the whole society who are now, by virtue of the *witnessed* marriage ceremony, prohibited from marrying this woman.[9] The witnesses function as surrogates for the whole community.

From this follows a fundamental point in the philosophy of Jewish law, namely, that any individual freedom (in this case the freedom to divorce one's wife or not) is not a right prior to the Law but, rather, a personal prerogative which is allowed by the Law when it is consistent with the purposes of the Law. When, however, it contradicts the purposes of the Law, any individual freedom may be curtailed or even removed by those persons endowed as authorities by the community committed to the authority of the Law. The history of the Halakhah is filled with examples of this process of curtailment and abrogation. This background is important to describe in order to place any solution to the second type of *agunah* problem in proper historical context.

In Judaism the Law is fundamentally the revealed will of God and the purpose of the Law is to make the kingship of God the most important political factor in the life of the covenanted community. "I am the Lord your God . . . you shall have no other gods in My presence" (Exodus 20:2-3).[10] From this fundamental principle it follows that all human authority is limited. Practically, this means that no one covenant member could exercise unlimited authority in the life of another covenant member. Where this practical meaning was not spelled out in Scriptural law, it was interpreted to be so by rabbinic legal exegesis. Thus, in the case of a full covenant member, slavery became a form of finite indentured servitude because "the children of Israel are servants unto Me and not the servants of servants."[11] Later, even in the case of non-Jewish slaves their covenantal status entitled them to more and more privileges in relation to their Jewish masters.[12] I cite examples from the law of slavery because here is where the full authority of one human person over another is most explicitly seen.

Coming closer to the area of matrimony, we see that whereas Scriptural law seemed to enable any jealous husband to subject his wife to the ordeal of the bitter waters (Numbers 5:11-31), rabbinic interpretation qualified that right by making the woman's voluntary defiance of objectively verifiable criteria a necessary pre-condition for her being subjected to this ordeal.[13] In addition, she had to submit to it voluntarily.[14] Finally, the first C.E. authority, Rabban Johanan ben Zakkai, abrogated this male privilege on the grounds that male abuse required its forfeiture.[15] A similar situation pertained in the severe curtailment of the seeming Scriptural right of parents to have an incorrigible son *(ben sorer u-moreh)* executed.[16]

Rabbinic interpretation also limited the seeming Scriptural right of the husband to divorce or not divorce his wife at will (Deuteronomy 24:1). First, a woman had to be divorced on objectively verifiable grounds.[17] Second, a woman could petition the court to force her husband to divorce her on the grounds of specific neglect or general incompatibility.[18] Third, the institution of the *ketubah* (marriage contract) protected her economic security and made divorce financially difficult for most husbands.[19] Finally, in the case of levirate marriage (Deuteronomy 25:5-10), whereas Scripture seems to assume that it is always in the best interest of the childless widow to remain part of her deceased husband's family by being automatically considered the wife of his brother, rabbinic interpretation recognized that this was not always the case. They made the ceremony of release *(halitzah)* easier and without subsequent stigma to either party.[20]

All of this, it seems to me, reflects the rabbinic recognition that marriage is a mutual covenant between husband and wife, one which is analogous to the covenant between God and Israel.[21] As such, everything possible was to be done to encourage it and strengthen it as a state of human completion and fulfillment both for the man and for the woman.[22] Such completion and fulfillment are only possible in a situation of real mutuality. When this is irrevocably absent, then continuing the legal status of the marriage prevents the partners from finding that mutual completion and fulfillment with someone else. Thus divorce becomes an obligation under these specific conditions rather than a nonspecific right of the husband to exercise at will or whim.[23]

Here and now we have a situation where the law as it stands enables a lawless person, the husband, to use a specific law to reject the authority of the Law in general and to fulfill his avaricious or sadistic designs against his wife. She, on the other hand, will be penalized precisely because her very lawfulness prevents her from remarrying without a *get*. In the Talmud we find a refusal to accept any legal situation where "the sinner is rewarded" *(hot'e niskar)*.[24] To allow such a situation is to affirm the priority of the individual right over the social authority of the Law. This surely runs counter to the whole tendency of Jewish law. Thus in the very discussion of annulment in one Talmudic text we find that the adherence of the fourth century C.E. Babylonian amora, Rava, to the rule that a man may not abrogate a *get* if accidentally prevented from doing so *(ayn ones be-gittin)*, is interpreted as follows:

Rava himself was of the opinion that it was on account of both virtuous (tzenu'ot) and non-virtuous (perutzot) women. It was on account of virtuous women because if one ruled that this get were not valid, there will be times that there will be no accidental prevention but they will assume that there was, and they will thus remain in a state of agunah. And it was on account of the non-virtuous woman because if this get were not valid, there will be times when he will be accidentally prevented from giving the get and they will say he was not so prevented. And such a woman will remarry anyhow (ve'azla uminasva) and the get will be invalid (batel) and her children will be illegitimate mamzerim.[25]

The husband's refusal to give a get, therefore, when the law requires he do so, involves an interference with the Covenant, which essentially constitutes the community of Israel and is interpreted by them. It follows that the husband's right to withhold that divorce involves a direct conflict with the covenanted community of Israel, who have ruled that his duty is now to divorce his wife. Hence that right should be curtailed if not altogether abrogated in such cases. The question is: How can this be done within the system of Halakhah? For although theological reflection can inform the process of halakhic decision making, a halakhic decision itself must be directly based on legal criteria alone.[26]

The solution to this problem in one way or another is going to have to limit the usual range of cases where a normal get pertains. There was a general reluctance in the Talmud to do this and, as we shall shortly see, this general reluctance influenced many medieval halakhists who refused to draw the full legal consequences from Talmudic precedents for annulment in lieu of divorce. Thus in several cases where a marriage could quite easily be annulled because of irregularities in its initiation, the Talmud nevertheless stated, "the sages did not have the power to release her (lehotzi'ah) without a get."[27] The general Talmudic assumption seems to have been that one does not leave the state of matrimony (when, of course, the husband is still alive) without a get.[28] Such an approach made annulment in lieu of divorce harder, to be sure, but not legally impossible, as we shall see.

3. *Annulment of Improperly Initiated Marriages*

The power of rabbinic authorities to annul a marriage retroactively is seen in two separate cases presented in the Talmud. (These cases should be clearly distinguished from those marriages which were regarded as never having existed at all, for example, incestuous or adulterous unions, or unions with non-Jews.)[29]   In the first case we find that a man kidnapped an orphan girl and betrothed her just before her wedding to another man. In the second case a man kidnapped a woman and forced her to consent to marriage with him.[30]   In both cases the late fourth century Babylonian authority, R. Ashi, indicated that the marriage had been annulled because the man "acted improperly *(she-lo ke-hogan)*, so the rabbis acted 'improperly' with him and they removed *(ve'afqa'inhu)* the marital status *(leqidushay)* from him." The attribution of improper action to the rabbis is an obvious hyperbole simply designating that the rabbis treated the man "measure for measure" *(midah keneged midah)*, namely, he got what he deserved.[31]   The Talmud then reports that R. Ashi's disciple and colleague, Rabina, could well understand how the rabbis had the legal power to declare the money of the marital acquisition null and void, if indeed the marriage had been so initiated. But he questioned how they could annul a marriage initiated by intercourse.   R. Ashi's answer was that such intercourse is considered to be nothing more than fornication *(be'ilat zenut)*, having no binding status whatsoever.

Rabina's argument that it is simple to annul a marriage initiated with money was interpreted as being based on the principle "what the court declares null and void *(hefqer bet din)* is null and void."[32]   Undoubtedly this was the reality in the overwhelming majority of cases in his time because several generations earlier the Babylonian Amora, Rab, prohibited initiating marriage by an act of intercourse as a measure to prevent public lewdness *(mishum peritzuta)*.[33]   Now this equation of the money used to initiate marriage with the money used in an ordinary commercial transaction is significant. For much earlier the tannayim, R. Akibah and R. Tarfon, disputed whether witnesses in cases involving matrimonial law were to be examined by the strict standards required in capital cases *(dinay nefashot)*, or by the more lenient standards required in civil cases *(dinay mamonot)*.[34]   Although the law follows R. Akibah's view that the analogy is with civil cases, nevertheless, one could show how subsequent Talmudic and medieval interpretation did not regard matrimony and commerce as essentially the same.[35]   Despite this tendency, Rabina's analysis indicates that there was no hesitancy to extend this analogy when needed.

From these two cases it would seem that there is precedent for retroactively annulling marriages improperly initiated, *ex post facto*. Whether or not this precedent was practically applicable or not, however, was debated by the great medieval halakhists.

On the one hand, the important Spanish halakhist, R. Solomon ibn Adret *(Rashba)*, wrote in a responsum that,

> If the communities *(ha-qehillot)* want to prevent these abuses let them make a decree *(taqqanah)* by unanimous consent to remove *(veyafqiʿu)* ... any money given to any woman is totally removed, totally ownerless *(hefqer gamur)*.[36]

In another responsum he states that such a procedure is indeed proper provided it has the consent of the leading scholar in the community. He reports that such a case arose in his city (Barcelona) and that he argued his point in the presence of his teacher, Nahmanides, who agreed with him.[37] Nevertheless, he hedges from giving full practical endorsement to such a procedure, indicating that the matter needs further reflection. Furthermore, in what seems to be a later responsum, he indicates that the power to annul marriages is limited to the cases explicitly *(be-ferush)* mentioned in the Talmud and that we may not generalize that every marriage improperly initiated may be annulled.[38] Despite these reservations, the fourteenth century Spanish halakhist, R. Isaac ben Sheshet Parfat, cited Ibn Adret as the prime authority who permits such innovative procedures based on Talmudic precedent. Nevertheless, he too expresses reservations, indicating that he would not practically rule in such cases until he obtained the consent of all the other Spanish rabbis.[39] Obviously if such consent were obtainable then or at some other time, the whole legal justification for the procedure is ready-made.

On the other hand, theoretical difficulties, aside from the question of practical implementation, were raised by other medieval halakhists. Thus the fifteenth century Italian halakhist, R. Joseph Kolon *(Mahariq)*, objected that if the annulment of marriages improperly initiated were indeed a current rabbinic option, then why did the rabbis not annul polygamous marriages which have clearly violated the ban *(herem)* of the eleventh century Franco-German halakhist, Rabbenu Gershom?[40] This is based on the opinion of the thirteenth century halakhist, R. Mordecai ben Hillel Ashkenazi, who argued that the rabbis refrained from annulling certain marriages: not only those in violation of the ban of Rabbenu Gershom but also those in violation of rabbinic law (sheniyot) and even some in violation of Scriptural law (aberot de'orayta).[41] These counter-examples seem to indicate that one may not generalize from the two cases discussed in the Talmud, that the rulings there were *ad hoc* in character. This argument is repeated by R. Joseph Karo, R. Moses Isserles and R. Elijah of Vilna—a most formidable halakhic trio.[42]

Although many other rabbis disputed this point, some inclining towards the generalizing view of Ibn Adret, others inclining to the restrictive view of R. Mordecai, there was an attempt by the sixteenth century halakhist, R. Joseph Boaz, to reconcile the two views. His point was that it all depended on how the decree of a particular community was exactly worded (nusah ha-taqqanah). If the community merely placed a ban (herem) on those who improperly initiated a marriage (as did Rabbenu Gershom), then the marriage is valid even though its participants are transgressors and may be punished. If, on the other hand, they ruled *ab initio* that any such marriage is to be regarded as null and void, then it is so indeed and is considered as if (ke'ilu) it never was.[43] This type of reasoning did have results later on and was the basis of such decrees in a number of Sephardic and Oriental communities in the late nineteenth and early twentieth centuries.[44]

4. *Annulment in Lieu of Divorce*

Looking at the two Talmudic precedents alone it would seem to be very difficult to infer from them a general rabbinic power to annul marriages. The precedents obviously involve cases where a marriage was improperly initiated. Even in cases closely similar we saw an overall reluctance practically to implement rabbinic annulment even by those authorities who argued that it was theoretically possible. How much more reluctant must we then be to attempt to institute rabbinic annulment for marriages which were indeed properly initiated? Our problem is clearly compounded.

Nevertheless, the Talmudic treatment of annulment is not limited to cases where a marriage was improperly initiated. The power to annul marriages is also invoked in a situation where a get was already written and then cancelled by the husband, which is considered his privilege according to Scriptural law.

> Rabban Simon ben Gamliel says that the husband may not cancel the *get* (*le-batlo*) ... because if he could wherein would lie the power of the court *(koah bet din)*?—Can it be? The cancellation of a *get* is a Scriptural right *(miydiy de'orayta)*. For the sake of the 'power of the court' do we permit a married woman to remarry?—Yes, because anyone who betrothes does so with the implicit understanding that the act is in consonance with rabbinic standards *(ada'ata de-rabbanan)*, and the rabbis removed the marital status from him ... [45]

The point that immediately catches our attention here is that although the rabbinic power to annul marriages seems to be transposed from the two earlier cases, a new principle is introduced, namely, that the act of betrothal carries with it the built-in condition that *the rabbis can annul a marriage irrespective of how it was initiated* (or even how long ago it was initiated). The Talmud then explains the specifics of this type of annulment in the exact same way that it explained the specifics of the simpler type of annulment, that is, either the marriage money is declared null and void, or the act of initiatory intercourse is declared to be fornication. Even though the law does not follow Rabban Simon ben Gamliel, minority opinions rejected in one generation can be used in another.[46]

The Tosafists indicate that this implicit acceptance of *continuous* rabbinic approval is made explicit by the addition of the words "according to the law *(ke-dat)* of Moses and Israel" to the betrothal formula.[47] Professor Atlas astutely points out that the betrothal formula would be legally binding even if this phrase were omitted.[48] Nevertheless, although conditions stipulated by the rabbinic authorities *(tenai bet din)* need not be explicated, such explication makes their force that much more obvious.[49]

The specific difference between the two earlier cases of annulment, and this case of annulment in lieu of divorce, is that in the former cases the marriage was not initiated properly. In this case, however, the marriage was initiated properly. This point was not lost on the medieval halakhists. The Tosafists noted that in the former two cases the key phrase "in consonance with rabbinic standards" is absent.[50] They infer from this absence that the aforementioned principle only applies where the marriage was properly initiated, that is, in consonance with rabbinic standards. In the two earlier cases this is obviously not so. In other words, the initiation of marriage in consonance with rabbinic standards carries with it the implication that if the marriage is to be terminated, it is to be terminated by those same rabbinic standards, that is, what they *now* require.

R. Mordecai goes further and indicates that this legal fact is a condition *(al tenai)* of every properly initiated marriage, namely, that if the husband should *in the future* transgress *(ya'avor le'ahar zeman)* rabbinic standards, then his marriage is thereby annulled *(shelo yihyu qiddushin halin)*.[51] From this two highly significant points emerge. First, whereas in the Talmud conditional marriage is treated as the exception rather than the norm,[52] now *all* properly initiated marriages are considered to be conditional as the norm, and only improperly initiated marriages are considered to be unconditional as the exception. Second, whereas the view of R. Mordecai was used by R. Joseph Kolon as the main precedent for limiting the power of communities to annul marriages improperly initiated, the same view of R. Mordecai, when analyzed in its entirety, serves as an excellent precedent for granting communities the power to annul marriages where there are irregularities in the delivery of the *get* or no *get* is possible.

If one takes the introduction of the principle of annulment in this case literally, then it would seem that the rabbis were declaring that there had *never been* a marriage between the two parties. In other words, annulment by literal definition is *retroactive*. Professor Atlas points out that such literalism leads to further problems. First, whereas a transaction can be declared to be null and void *(hefqer)* at the time it was transacted, it is difficult to assume that it can be similarly declared null and void years, even decades, after it was transacted and accepted as valid. Second, whereas an act of intercourse can be declared to be fornication at the time it happened, it is difficult to assume that it—and every subsequent act of marital intercourse between the couple—are nothing but fornication.[53] In both cases the gap between legal fiat and empirical reality is just too wide.

To resolve these problems Professor Atlas engages in some very insightful Talmudic text criticism. He argues that the transposition of the principle of the rabbinic power to annul marriages is an example of legal fiction, that is, extending an old legal principle out of its original context and applying it in a new context.[54] Such extension involves an inner contradiction on the literal level, namely that annulment is by definition retroactive, yet we may not assume that rabbinic annulment to uphold a *get* was meant in this case to be retroactive. For whereas retroactivity in cases of annulment of improperly initiated marriages entails no absurd results, retroactivity in the case of an improperly handled divorce does involve the absurd results that a long–standing and long–accepted transaction is now deemed non–existent, and that a long–standing and long–accepted marital relationship is now deemed fornication. Because the principle of rabbinic annulment was the only precedent which could help resolve the problem of the cancelled *get*, it was invoked in this context even though the amorayym did not mean to draw all of the logical conclusions it entails.

Professor Atlas' use of the theory of legal fiction here is heavily indebted (and duly acknowledged) to the analysis of this theory by the American legal scholar, Professor Lon L. Fuller.[55] The fruitful use of Fuller's analysis indicates the value of comparative jurisprudence in the study of the development of Jewish law.

Nevertheless, despite the seeming restrictions on the use of this principle by the amorayyim, the medieval halakhists were concerned with some possibly unwanted consequences. The two most unwanted consequences of the use of this principle in cases of properly initiated but improperly terminated marriages are the possible avoidance of penalty for adultery (if there was no marriage, then there was no adultery), and the possible removal of the stigma of offspring from adulterous marriages (if there was no marriage, then there are no subsequent *mamzerim*). The Tosafists indicate that it is precisely because of such undesired results that the principle should only be applied by competent rabbinic authorities, exercising the greatest care. Here the purpose of the law "to morally improve and not to morally corrupt" (*le-taqqanah* . . . *ve-lo le-taqqalah*) must be kept in mind in rendering decisions involving this principle.[56] Thus the famous attempt to invoke it by the nineteenth century Galician halakhist, R. Shalom Schwadron, to alleviate a certain unfortunate case of illegitimacy, has been the subject of much rabbinic debate until the present time.[57]

The problem, however, with attempting to use this application of the principle of rabbinic annulment of marriages is that the necessary conclusion (at least since the middle ages) that such annulment is retroactive involves the general absurdity of assuming that an often long–standing marriage had never existed, and the specific difficulties of justifying adultery and illegitimacy. Finally, rabbinic annulment in lieu of divorce, as presented here, involves a case where there was indeed a *get*, however we might judge its subsequent validity. In the case we are trying to solve today, on the other hand, there is no *get* nor was there ever one.

5. *The Rabbinic Power of Abrogation*

In analyzing the specific distinction between the two earlier cases of annulment and that involving an improper divorce, the Tosafists remark that whereas in the latter case rabbinic annulment is a consequence of the implicit condition in all properly initiated marriages, namely, that the marriage's duration is contingent on compliance with rabbinic standards, in the former cases, where this condition is absent, rabbinic annulment is the result of the rabbinic power to abrogate a Scriptural right in certain cases (*le'aqor dabar min ha-Torah*). In one place R. Isaac the Younger *(Ri)* is uncertain whether this principle is actually the basis of this earlier type of rabbinic annulment, but in another place an anonymous Tosafist expresses no doubt that this indeed is the basis for this procedure.[58] It is somewhat puzzling that the Tosafists did not quote or even refer to the Palestinian Talmud's discussion of the decree of Rabban Simon ben Gamliel to annul marriages where the husband rescinded the *get*. For this principle is broad enough to cover any case where annulment might be required.

The Palestinian Talmud in analyzing the rationale for the decree of Rabban Simon ben Gamliel indicates that this is not the only instance where the rabbis abrogated a Scriptural right.[59] To counter charges that the rabbis have no such power an example was brought from the laws of the heave offering *(terumah)* given to the priest. According to Scriptural law one could give the priest olives in lieu of oil and grapes in lieu of wine. The rabbis removed this privilege from individuals and ruled that if olives or wine were so given such a heave offering was invalid *(ayn terumato terumah)*. The reason given for this is that such a Scriptural right too easily lent itself to fraud *(mipnay gezel)*.[60]

Coming closer to abrogation of a specific application of a Scriptural law in the context of marriage, we find the following relative precedent.

The *Mishnah* rules that if a woman were told that her husband died across the sea and she remarried, and afterwards her first husband returned, she then is required to be divorced by both men, and she forfeits her normal right to the payment of her *ketubah* (and the children from both men are now *mamzerim*).[61] The Tosafists point out that although the *ketubah* is the Scriptural right of a virgin bride she is, nevertheless, penalized by the rabbis in order to facilitate her divorce. (Under normal circumstances the payment of the *ketubah* was seen as a means to impede divorce.)[62] *Rashi* explains that although the rabbis permitted remarriage even if only one witness reported the death of the first husband, the woman herself is, nevertheless, expected to make a thorough investigation *(dehi gufa dayqa)* before hastily remarrying.[63] It seems as though this is required by the covenantal faithfulness *(qushta)* of the Jewish marital relationship.

The *Gemara* later on questions whether a rabbinic court can "stipulate *(matnin)* to uproot something from the Torah." The answer is that this is indeed the case inasmuch as according to Scriptural law the children of the first husband are certainly not illegitimate.[64] Clearly, then, a rabbinic court may stipulate what an individual may not stipulate in terms of abrogating an aspect of Scriptural law.[65] An individual's motives are assumed to be selfish whereas the rabbinic authorities are assumed to be acting on behalf of the common good and in the interest of the Torah system as a whole.

Taken at face value the principle that the rabbis have the power to abrogate a Scriptural law seems to do away with the Divine law altogether. Obviously this was not the meaning of this principle, in that the primacy of the Divine law is one of the dogmas of Rabbinic Judaism.[66] Clearly one has to induce from the contexts in which this principle is enunciated just what its meaning is. First, it is never invoked to justify the total and permanent abrogation of any Scripturally ordained institution but, rather, it is used to limit certain uses of that institution which were considered abuses. Most of these abuses were monetary, that is, where an individual could take advantage of a loophole in the law for purposes of private greed, as we have seen already. Second, it was used to remove certain personal privileges whose abuse was considered detrimental to the common good or to some higher good within the Torah system as a whole. The best known example of this is the institution of *prosbul,* where the need to lend money, especially to the poor, was considered to be of *greater Toraitic priority* than the right not to repay a debt during the Sabbatical year.[67] Third, it was negative in character *(sheb ve'al ta'aseh),* that is, it ruled that an act positively ordained not be done under certain circumstances, but it did not rule that a prohibited act be done, this latter option being considered too radical.[68] Thus the rabbinic prohibition to sound the *shofar* when *Rosh Hashanah* falls on the Sabbath only involves the non-performance of the Scriptural commandment to sound the shofar on the first day of the seventh month.[69]

Not only does the invocation of the principle of rabbinic abrogation of some specific aspect of a Scriptural law give the most cogent foundation for the institution of rabbinic annulment of certain marriages, it also avoids the problems raised by retroactive annulment. In other words, the invocation of this principle enables a marriage to be annulled by rabbinic authorities *from that time on.* The use of this principle, then, avoids the legal fiction of the analogy between a marriage improperly initiated and one properly initiated but only improperly terminated. Thus the nineteenth century halakhist, R. Akibah Eiger of Posen, wrote in his comments to the *Mishnah* wherein Rabban Simon ben Gamliel's view is presented, that "for an important reason *(di-be-ta'am)* the sages have the power to abrogate something from the Torah."[70] Elaborating on R. Eiger's comment the contemporary Israeli scholar, R. Shlomoh Zalman Auerbach, writes, "it is better to uproot *(la'aqor)* the marriage henceforth on *(mik'an ulehab'a)* than to annul *(melafiqi'a)* it completely. It is possible that this is so because annulment would retroactively make all their previous marital intercourse fornication."[71] Rabbi Auerbach makes this point in the context of arguing against the suggestion of R. Shalom Schwadron that the principle of the retroactive annulment of marriage could be invoked to alleviate an unfortunate case of illegitimacy.[72]

The most direct precedent I could find for permitting rabbinic annulment of marriages where a husband refuses to give his wife a *get* to which she is clearly entitled is presented by the sixteenth century halakhist, R. Moses Isserles of Cracow. In order to appreciate the force of the text from R. Isserles the Talmudic background of it must first be presented.

The *Mishnah* states that if a Jewish woman were captured by gentiles in a situation where they might very well execute her, then she is forbidden to return to her husband.[73] Some later authorities limited this to the case of where the husband is a *kohen;* others said that it applied even if her husband were an ordinary Israelite.[74] However, R. Isserles in his note to the *Shulhan Arukh* reports a view that states that in a time of mass killing and turmoil this restriction does not apply.[75] The eighteenth century commentator, R. Judah Ashkenazi of Tiktin, explained that since under such circumstances a woman could not save herself by offering herself sexually to her captors, there is, therefore, no reason to assume she would do so.[76] In his own commentary on the *Tur,* R. Isserles identifies this ruling and elaborates upon it.

> In the decree of Austria these women were permitted to their husbands, even if they were *kohanim,* by the authority of great men *(al pi*

gedolim). And it seems to me that it is possible that these great men permitted this not through strict legal deduction *(midina),* but because of the need of the time *(tzorekh sha'ah).* For they saw that we must be concerned that, God forbid, in the future if women know that they could not return to their husbands of their youth, they would not compromise themselves *(she-lo yeqalqalu)* and thus these great men were lenient. . . . It seems to me they relied on the principle . . . that the court has the power to annul marriages and, thus, these women were as if they had not been married *(ke-penuyot)* . . .[77]

The concern of those great men who formulated the decree of Austria was that Jewish women might actually die rather than be raped if they thought that rape would destroy their marriages. This is, no doubt, based on the principle that a woman is not to die as a martyr in the event of rape since she is only a *passive victim.*[78] Furthermore, we see that in a pressing situation, where the integrity of the Jewish family is threatened, great men did not hesitate to invoke Talmudic principles radical enough to rectify a morally unacceptable situation, that is, a situation unacceptable on *internal Jewish criteria of morality.*

6. Conclusion

It would seem that the principle that the rabbinic authorities have the power to abrogate a Scriptural privilege in a specific situation is the most satisfactory basis for the rabbinic power to annul marriages deemed unacceptable where it is beyond our power to have the husband authorize the writing of a proper *get.* I believe that the line of reasoning which runs from the tanna, Rabban Simon ben Gamliel, to the amorayyim, R. Ashi and Rabina, to the medieval authorities, R. Solomon ibn Adret and R. Isaac ben Sheshet Parfat, to the later authorities, R. Moses Isserles and R. Akibah Eiger, to the modern Sephardic communities which did indeed implement the rabbinic power to annul marriages—this whole line of reasoning, which is willing to employ radical options within the Law when the common good is threatened by evil individuals, gives us ample legal means to annul the marriage of a woman whose husband refuses to give her a *get,* either for reasons of blackmail or vengeful spite.

It is obvious that such annulments should only be granted by rabbinic courts, comprised of outstanding scholars, having the support of a large number of rabbis.[79] Needless to say, every effort should be made to attempt to persuade the husband to give his wife a *get*. It is clear that this is an emergency measure and will in no wise supplant the normal procedure of *gittin* which will still suffice in the great majority of cases.

In an earlier work I wrote about marriage annulment sympathetically, but stopped short of endorsing it, hoping that it would first gain universal Jewish consent.[80] Subsequent experience and further research into the classical halakhic sources has convinced me that such universal consent is neither forthcoming nor is it necessary. I am now convinced that without the practical power to annul such marriages the law is in effect encouraging immoral blackmail and vengeance. If the greatest threat to the halakhic system is the fact that many Jews are no longer respectful of it, then correction of the moral evil of the specific type of *agunah* we have been discussing will go a long way in making that system more inspiring on its own grounds to both the committed and the alienated. After all, in our secularly constituted societies the Law only has moral persuasive power, not political coercion any more. In the present state of affairs, concerning this specific problem in Jewish divorce law, the law neither benefits the virtuous nor the non-virtuous. A non-virtuous woman will not wait for the *get* she knows is not forthcoming and will thus remarry in a non-halakhic way (an option not open to pre-modern Jews short of apostasy) and so become an adulteress whose children are illegitimate. The virtuous woman will wait in lonely suffering. Both states of affairs are totally contrary to the Law and its purposes.[81]

DIVORCE AND CONVERSION: IS A TRADITIONAL-LIBERAL MODUS VIVENDI POSSIBLE?

1. *Introduction*

When the journal, JUDAISM, was launched over thirty years ago, as an effort to enhance inter-Jewish dialogue, my teacher, Professor Robert Gordis, wrote,

> We are committed to the proposition that Judaism has positive value for Jews and for the world . . . At the same time, we disassociate ourselves from the dangerous tendency toward the hardening of party lines on the contemporary Jewish scene . . . Undoubtedly, our differences will find expression in these pages . . . for we share the conviction of the Talmud that 'Both these and the others are the words of the living God.'[1]

The model he chose was the dialogical relationship between the School of Shammai and the School of Hillel in tanaitic times. The principle that the words of both are considered to be "the words of the living God"[2] had practical consequences as the *Mishnah* notes, "Even though they prohibit and the others permit, they invalidate and the others validate, the Shammaites were not inhibited *(lo nimne'u)* from marrying Hillelite women and vice-versa."[3] The *Tosefta* interpreted the overall atmosphere of comraderie as being due to the fact that "they practiced fidelity *(emet)* and peace among themselves."[4] Indeed, the Talmud indicates that the prevalence of the Hillelite position in Halakhah was precisely because of their greater respect for the views of their opponents.[5]

As attractive as this precedent is, however, it does not seem to be sufficient for our purposes. First of all, both schools were clearly Pharisaic and, therefore, their differences were within a much narrower range than the earlier differences between the Pharisees and the Sadducees. Indeed their differences do not seem to be any wider than those which divide factions within each of the three major groupings in American Judaism today. Furthermore, their differences seem to have been more halakhic than theological. Even such disputes as to whether heaven or earth was created first[6] seem to be more issues of exegesis than of theological principle and far less profound than the issues of revelation and religious authority, which certainly divide Jews today. As such, the situation described in this precedent presupposes a far greater theological unanimity than we can realistically assume for ourselves. Thus the practical community that existed between the Hillelites and the Shammaites can only be seen as subsequent to the more fundamental unanimity we have yet to establish.

The relationship between the Pharisees and the Sadducees, embracing as it did much wider differences of theology and law, might provide a more sufficient model for us. Now the real relationship between the two groups (as the historians would say, *wie es eigentlich gewesen*) is difficult to ascertain because as "heirs of the Pharisees" (the felicitous term introduced by my friend, Professor Jakob J. Petuchowski), our rabbinic sources are pro-Pharisee and the Sadducees receive a consistently "bad press" in them. Nevertheless, we do know that despite these profound differences between the two groups, they both interrelated in the Sanhedrin[7] and that the Pharisees regarded that whatever consensus they shared with the Sadducees was a minimal public standard in practical matters. In the Talmud we read,

> R. Judah said in the name of Samuel that a court is not liable for misleading the people until it rules on a matter on which the Sadducees would not agree. However, in a matter on which even the Sadducees would agree, the court is exempt. What is the reason for this?—Because such a matter would even be known in elementary schools *(zeel qeray bay rab).*[8]

In other words, because the Sadducees only accepted explicit Scriptural legislation, such legislation could be assumed to be known as a matter of common Jewish consensus. Thus we see a practical consensus even though there were major theological and halakhic differences between the Pharisees and the Sadducess, most notably their difference concerning whether or not Oral Tradition *(Torah she-b'al peh)* was revealed and authoritative.

This analogy is not meant to designate who are our contemporary "Pharisees" and our contemporary "Sadducees." Such designations inevitably use "Saducee" as a pejorative term, but I do not think we have enough non-Pharisaic information about them to be able to compare any other group in a later period to them.[9] My point in making this analogy is simply to show that the clear theological and halakhic differences between the two groups did not prevent the Pharisees at least from attempting to constitute some sort of practical standard that could be used as the basis of a minimal common consensus among the Jewish people. When we examine the question of evidence *(edut)* in both divorce and conversion proceedings, we shall see further specifications of this common, albeit *de facto,* consensus which lend themselves to the kind of contemporary version of it we seem to be trying to achieve here and now.

2. *The Halakhah and Personal Status*

Traditional and liberal Jews seem to be most evidently and seriously divided on the question of divorce and conversion. Because many liberal Jews have opted not to adhere to the *objective halakhic criteria* (I will later return to the importance of this categorization) in these two areas, traditional Jews have been unable to accept the validity of civil divorces recognized by the liberals as well as conversions conducted by them. At this level there can be no modus vivendi, nor do I think there ought to be one. Nevertheless, several important liberal Jewish thinkers have realized that a religious community, any religious community, must be defined by *objective normative criteria* if it is to be able in good faith to call for unambiguous commitment on the part of its members. Therefore, commitment to "Catholic Israel" *(kelal Yisrael)* as the very foundation for keeping inter-Jewish differences clearly Jewish prompted Professor Jakob J. Petuchowski over ten years ago to write,

> It is thus the Halakhah dealing with 'personal status' which guarantees the underlying unity of the 'holy community' ... They ... must be prepared to conform to the law at least in this respect. For, only if the 'holy community' remains undivided on the basic level of its existence, ... there can be an unqualified acceptance of one another as fellow Jews ...[10]

Professor Petuchowski's call for objective public criteria in the area of personal status of Jews lays the necessary foundation for a common consensus between traditional and liberal Jews.

I would contrast Professor Petuchowski's cogent approach with the much less cogent approach of the Committee on Jewish Law and Standards of the Rabbinical Assembly (Conservative). In 1966 the committee, undoubtedly acting in good faith on behalf of Catholic Israel, issued the following statement authored by Rabbi Eli Bohnen,

> We recognize the fact that in some instances it may not be possible, or even advisable, to insist that *tevillah* must be accomplished. It is conceivable that a great traumatic hurt could be inflicted on converts who have been loyal to the Jewish faith for years ... Indeed, we have been informed of cases where in extraordinary circumstances outstanding

> Jewish authorities accepted evidence of having bathed at sea as
> fulfillment of the requirment of *tevillah*.[11]

Since these "outstanding Jewish authorities" are not cited, I assume the source
concerning bathing in the sea that Rabbi Bohnen had in mind is from the *Shulhan Arukh*.

> A woman whose menstrual flow had concluded, who immersed herself
> without specific intention *(be-lo khavvanah)*, for example, she fell into
> the water or went in to cool off, she is permitted to resume sexual
> relations with her husband.[12]

However, this opinion only refers to a woman in this case *(niddah)*; it is rejected by a
number of important authorities; and the author of the *Shulhan Arukh* himself insists that
a proper immersion in a *mikveh* be initially required.   Moreover, Maimonides, the
immediate source for this opinion (the ultimate source is the Talmud), noted that such
accidental or incidental immersion is not acceptable, even *ex post facto*, as preparation
in certain priestly rituals *(terumah, qodashim)*, where full religious intention *(kavvanah)*
is required.[13]   This proviso is important to bear in mind because conversion would
certainly be inconceivable by anyone's criteria without the element of this very
intention. An unintentional conversion is an absurdity.[14]

It would seem that this *de facto* acceptance of accidental or incidental immersion in
the case of a post-menstruant is taken to be analogous with the following two rulings
brought together in the Talmud.

> The servant of R. Hiyya bar Ami had a certain gentile woman immerse
> herself for purposes of marriage. R. Joseph said that he was able to
> validate her Jewish status . . . according to the view of R. Assi who
> ironically queried, 'who has not immersed herself after menstruation *(mi
> lo tablah le-niddotah)*? As for a certain man called 'son of an Aramean,'
> R. Joshua ben Levi ironically queried, 'who has not immersed himself
> following seminal emission *(mi lo tabal le-qeryo)*?[15]

Now these rulings are of no help to those who wish to grant *de facto* recognition to
non-halakhic conversions, because *it is only immersion in a miqveh for another religious
purpose which is sufficient, ex post facto, for conversion.* As the Palestinian Talmud
notes,

> R. Assi bar Bun stated that because both of these immersions are for the
> sake of specifically Jewish sanctification *(le-shem qedushat Yisrael)*, one
> suffices for the other.[16]

Maimonides, on the other hand, only regards these and other immersions as evidence of a general commitment to Judaism and insists upon another immersion for the sake of conversion under all circumstances.[17] Nevertheless, even those authorities who are more lenient than Maimonides on this question, regard these cases as unusual and are certainly attempting to alleviate embarassment and hardship in some very particular instances.[18] They are not attempting to generalize from these cases to set up a new halakhic category of converts.

The approach of the Rabbinical Assembly Committee on Jewish Law and Standards actually creates more halakhic problems than it solves. For it would seem that this type of proof of conversion, retroactively as it were, requires that the convert be strictly observant of the details of Jewish ritual law most frequently violated by most Jews throughout history and certainly in this age.[19] (Indeed, immersion after a seminal emission was not even legally required in the amoraic period).[20] It is most unlikely today that a convert who had not been immersed for the sake of conversion would subsequently become observant of the most stringent area of Jewish law and pietistic practice. Finally, a conversion which omitted immersion *by design,* as is indeed the case in most liberal conversions, cannot be said to fulfill the requirement of acceptance *(qabbalah)* of the commandments of the Torah *in toto,* the undisputed essence of halakhically valid conversion.[21] Such omission by design is in direct violation of the rabbinic rule, "a gentile who came to accept *(le-qabbel)* the words of the Torah except for one thing — we are not to accept him. R. Jose bar R. Judah says this means even one detail of rabbinic law."[22] This does not mean that the convert is expected to observe every aspect of Jewish law—a clearly impossible demand intellectually, morally and religiously.[23] Rather, it means that conversion must involve an unconditional acceptance of the valid authority of Jewish law in general and the initial rejection of none of its specifics *ab initio.* As long as we are all open to the Torah and Tradition, absolutely rejecting none of it in principle, then our various levels of practical observance do not invalidate this general acceptance.[24] Here we see how an overly lenient approach might create more halakhic problems than it solves.[25]

3. *Two Major Stumbling Blocks*

Even when the objective halakhic criteria of personal status are accepted, divorce and conversion entail two further problems which have direct halakhic consequences:

divorce presents an ethical problem and conversion presents a sociological problem. Both of these problems are by no means extraneous halakhically. Let us first look at the sociological problem which conversion entails, especially in our own day.

In the Talmud the following is stated,

> Both a man who converted for the sake of marying a Jewish woman, and a woman who converted for the sake of marrying a Jewish man . . . they are not converts (aynan gerim) in the opinion of R. Nehemiah.[26]

Even though such converts are considered Jews ex post facto according to the subsequent Halakhah,[27] the question arises concerning whether or not Jewish authorities are permitted to accept such converts ab initio. Now I know Orthodox rabbis who will not accept such converts and dissuade what may be deception by making the preparation for conversion so long that even the most ardent suitor would be discouraged from going through such a process in order to marry a Jew. Nevertheless, we all know that most conversions today (although, happily, we are seeing more converts from a purely religious motivation) are motivated by at least the initial desire to marry a Jew. Moreover, rabbinical experience has taught me and other rabbis that there is often an underlying consistency in the dual desire to marry a Jew and become one. For in many cases the non-Jew seems to be essentially attracted to the Jewishness of the Jew he or she desires as a man or a woman.

Two important halakhists earlier in this century, R. David Zvi Hoffmann, the late rector of the Orthodox rabbinical seminary in Berlin, and R. Ben Zion Meir Uziel, the late Sephardic Chief Rabbi of Israel, dealt with this question, both recognizing that a lack of rabbinical leniency here would most likely lead to civil marriage and the inevitable loss to Judaism of both the Jewish partner and the children born of such a union.

On the one hand, R. Hoffmann approaches the question in the spirit of making the best of an inherently bad situation by bending the law somewhat lest a far worse transgression result. He furthermore suggests that the convert make a formal declaration or promise (Eidesstattliche Versicherung/auf Ehrenwort), something a little less grave than an actual Jewish oath (shebu'ah), to observe such basic Jewish laws as the Sabbath and the dietary restrictions.[28] Of course, one must be careful in requiring such a promise that it in no way imply that only these institutions of Judaism need be accepted, for this could also imply a conditional acceptance of Judaism, which, as we just saw, invalidates the conversion. Moreover, such a formal promise also entails the problem that more often than not the Jewish partner in this imminent marriage is a Jew of lax or haphazard observance. The requirement of this type of promise could only have meaning if it included the Jewish partner. This, if anything, compounds the sociological problem of conversion involving marriage.

R. Uziel also emphasizes that one must make the best of a bad situation, insightfully bringing the Talmudic justification for the Scriptural permission to convert and marry a gentile warbride (eshet yefat to'ar), namely, "Scripture takes into account human inclination (yetzer ha-ra)," as well as a responsum of Maimonides.[29] On the other hand, however, in his conclusion he makes a striking point which causes his treatment of this question to be far more meaningful for us here and now than that of R. Hoffmann. He writes to the Chief Rabbi of Istanbul, "It is because this Jewess or this Jew does not want to transgress but, rather (aderaba) wants to save him or herself from transgression (le-hatzil atzmam me'isur)." Here we see an extraordinary sociological insight in the very heart of a halakhic judgment. What Uziel recognized is that the sociology of intermarriage has changed in this century. Whereas in earlier times intermarriage was most often an expression of apostasy, in this century it has become a consequence of greater social interaction between Jews and non-Jews. Thus the contemporary Jew who is drawn into a love relationship with a non-Jew, and who also urges the non-Jew to seek conversion to Judaism, is attempting to reconcile his personal involvement with his or her own authentic commitment to Judaism. The motivation, then, is the exact opposite of that which seeks apostasy.[30] Hence this important precedent by such an outstanding halakhist enables an halakhic approach to be formulated which recognizes certain fundamental sociological changes in the modern world, a point most often emphasized by liberal Jewish scholars.

Jewish divorce today raises a grave ethical problem, one which more than any other, I believe, has led sensitive liberal Jews to turn away from Halakhah in this area. The ethical problem is the question of the agunah, unable to remarry because of the obstinate refusal of her husband to grant her a Jewish divorce (get).[31] Although Scriptural law vests the power to grant a divorce solely in the hands of the husband, as the Halakhah developed the wife gained the right to request that the rabbinical court force her husband to grant her a divorce, even against his own evident will, on the basis of the

woman's objective charges.[32] However, the effective exercise of this right presupposes
a Jewish community with at least internal political autonomy, and also few chances if
any for the husband to hide in anonymity. Usually these were sufficient safeguards to
protect the wife from an unscrupulous husband, although the problem of the apostate
husband vexed medieval halakhists, for here internal Jewish autonomy and public Jewish
identity were not effective safeguards for a wife from a husband who was now beyond
the pale of Jewry.[33] Various solutions have been attempted by modern halakhists, all of
which have at best been only partially helpful.[34] I argue elsewhere in detail that the
only solution to this problem, both halakhically and ethically, is the most radical one
possible within the "four cubits of Halakhah," that is, rabbinical annulment of marriages
where the husband has totally prevented the giving of a *get* called for by the law *(afqaʿat
qiddushin)*.[35] The halakhic specifics of this situation would require a too lengthy and too
intricate digression from the theme of this chapter. Suffice it to say, in summary, that
such annulment is based on the Talmudic principle that "whoever marries does so on
condition that the marriage meets the standards of rabbinic law *(adaʿata de-
rabbanan)*."[36] Furthermore, I have found an actual case in a classic halakhic source
describing how this principle was put into practice in the interest of the Jewish family in
general and the alleviation of the suffering of pious Jewish women in particular.[37]

The traditionalists must be willing to modify Jewish divorce procedure, when there
are cogent halakhic grounds, in the interest of demonstrably Jewish ethical values. If
not, they cannot fault the majority of liberal Jews who look with grave suspicion at a
system which in effect rewards husbands in violation of rabbinic law *(hote niskar)* and
punishes women who adhere to the law.[38] If some liberals are willing to accept the
objective norms of Halakhah pertaining to personal status in the interest of authentic
Jewish unity, then traditional Jews must be prepared to objectively interpret and apply
Jewish law in a way that is informed by Jewish ethical concerns, and override practices
whose basis is only customary *(minhag)* and which are now counterproductive to the
integrity of the whole halakhic system.[39] They will also have to overcome the fear of
being branded by those to the right of them as transgressors or worse.

Finally, the question of the use of rabbinical annulment is based on the very idea of
community which we are seeking here and now. For the concept of rabbinical annulment
implies that the common good *(tiqqun haʿolam)*, in this case the very integrity of Jewish

marriage, takes precedence over individual rights whose exercise is not in the interest of this common good.[40] The effect of such common good can only be in a unified community worthy of the commitment of its members, a moral consensus if you will. It is the very fragmentation of contemporary Jewish life which troubles us all, the absence of authentic community over and above party affiliations. The scandal of Jewish divorce is a symptom of this very alienation. Therefore, the solution of this problem not only requires the revival of a long dormant halakhic institution through intellectual ingenuity; it also requires the type of community which would have the moral power to revive other aspects of Jewish tradition which sustain community and minimize alienation. Thus this question of Jewish divorce law, requiring for its solution more traditionalism from the liberals and more liberalism from the traditionalists, speaks to the heart of what we are striving to begin here and now.

4. *The Halakhic Question of Community*

Heretofore I have been dealing with the acceptance of objective halakhic criteria by both liberals and traditionalists for the sake of authentic community, as well as reinterpretation of Halakhah by halakhic principles in order to eliminate practices which mitigate against authentic community. However, at this point in our inquiry a new problem arises, namely, the problem of *subjective halakhic criteria*. I am referring to the fact that not only does the Halakhah specify *what* is required for a valid divorce or conversion, it also specifies *who* may effect these procedures and *who* may not. It is at this level that our respective theological and halakhic differences become most problematic. Indeed, based upon a literal reading of the rabbinic sources, certain Orthodox rabbis, especially in the State of Israel, have invalidated the divorces and conversions conducted by non-Orthodox—or even more liberal Orthodox—rabbis, asserting that these rabbis are intellectually and morally disqualified from exercising these rabbinical functions.[41] Because of this attitude many liberal Jews, even with traditional leanings, have argued that it is pointless for them to adhere to objective halakhic norms in these areas effecting personal status in the interest of *kelal Yisrael* inasmuch as most traditionalists will invalidate what they do on subjective grounds anyway.

The question of testimony and adjudication, which is essential to both divorce and conversion proceedings, is based on the more fundamental question of community. It is

much more than a merely incidental problem on the way to community. This point is
brought out by the late Professor Samuel Atlas of the Hebrew Union College-Jewish
Institute of Religion in New York, who was one of the most outstanding scholars of both
rabbinics and philosophy in American Judaism.   Professor Atlas defined the role of
witnesses in Jewish marriage and divorce proceedings as follows.

> The very character (teebo) of the institution of marriage and divorce is
> that of a communal institution (mosad tzibburi hu). . . . It is such that
> the community is involved in the marriage and divorce of a woman
> because of the change of her status in society . . . therefore, the
> presence of the witnesses is necessary in that they act on behalf of the
> community (ke-ba'ay koah ha-tzibbur) . . . for the function of the
> witnesses in marriage is to establish the matter (le-qayyem dabar), not
> just to clarify something doubtful.[42]

Professor Atlas' analysis is based on the important distinction between two types of
testimony, what I should call (1) initiatory testimony and (2) confirmational testimony.
In the first type of testimony the witnesses are the very social presupposition for the
legal validity of the act. Without their presence the act is without proper context and is,
therefore, meaningless.[43] In this sense they represent the entire community of Israel. In
the second type of testimony, on the other hand, the function of the witnesses is to
confirm what has already taken place and could have meaning even without them. Their
role is essentially one of publicity (gilluy milta).[44] The standards for the first type of
witness are far more exclusive than those for the second type, because in the first type
the witnesses must unambiguously represent the community in its ideal role as the proper
context for the operation of the law of God.[45] Thus those who actually supervise these
proceedings are required to fulfill even more stringent prerequisites than those for the
witnesses.[46] In the second type of testimony the witnesses merely supply certain factual
data of a subsequent character.

Concerning the greater leniency of this second type of witness the Talmud notes,
"any matter which is merely one of publicity is not one about which people usually
lie."[47] Thus in this type of testimony virtually anyone who is not obviously intellectually
and morally deficient may testify. The question arose as to how far this category of
testimony may be seen to extend. For example, the rabbis had ruled that even one
witness could testify about the writing and sealing of a bill of divorce so that a woman

not remain in a perpetually husbandless state *(agunah)*.[48]   This was clearly a bold departure from earlier legal standards. The Talmud discusses its justification.

> Concerning all testimony called for by the Torah, it is so that one witness is valid for ritual matters *(be'isurin)* . . . but here where we are certain that this concerns the possible transgression by a married woman *(isura d'eshet ish)*, it becomes a matter having adulterous possibilities *(dabar she-b'ervah)* for which there are to be no less than two witnesses. . . . Here the rabbis were lenient because of the case of *agunah.*[49]

The question facing the Talmudic commentators and codifiers was *how* the rabbis legally accomplished this innovation. The twelfth century Franco-German authority, Rabbenu Tam, argued that this was a case where the act of witness was confirmational rather than initiatory, the *get* having already been properly executed.[50]   Furthermore, such rabbinic leniency even extended to the case where one witness, not acceptable for initiatory testimony, was accepted as a witness of the death of a man so that his wife could be free to remarry.[51] Concerning this Maimonides writes,

> Let it not be difficult in your eyes that the sages permitted in grave matters having adulterous possibilities the testimony of a woman or a slave or a maidservant or a gentile giving a simple factual report *(ha-meseeah lefi tumo)* . . . for the Torah did not insist upon two witnesses and the other specifics of testimony except in a matter which could not be determined *(la'amod al boryo)* except by the testimony of these two witnesses.[52]

Thus we see what was in effect a major shift from the more stringent to the more lenient category of testimony in a matter of grave personal status.

5.   *Testimony in Divorce and Conversion Proceedings*

In divorce proceedings there are two functions for witnesses: (1) witnessing the writing and the sealing of the *get (eday mesirah)*. The question became which function is primary and which function is secondary.

The *Mishnah* records that the actual signatures of the witnesses on the *get* is a rabbinic decree in the interest of the common good *(mipnay tiqqun ha'olam)*, namely, to better insure that the validity of the *get* not be subsequently challenged.[53] Although there is Scriptural evidence that the signatures of the witnesses is of primary importance, the Talmud notes approvingly that this is the view of R. Eleazar, who held

that the witnesses of the actual transfer of the *get* are of primary importance, that they
effect the divorce *(eday mesirah kartay)*.[54] Nevertheless, R. Isaac Alfasi *(Rif)* qualifies
this ruling as follows,

> From this we infer that we only require actual witness of delivery where
> there are no witnesses to the sealing of the *get*. However, where there
> were such witnesses to the actual delivery ... although initially
> *(le-katehilah)* we require witnesses to the actual delivery, *ex post facto*
> we do not.[55]

Maimonides, who usually follows Alfasi, notes that such is the law even if the witnesses
to the delivery of the *get* are invalid *(pesulin)* by the more stringent criteria of
witnesses. He also notes *en passant* that a Geonic opinion regards such a *get* as
invalid.[56]

The point that emerges from this discussion is that here we see another shift from
the more stringent standards of initiatory testimony to the more lenient standards of
confirmational testimony. This suggests a possible course of action for those of us who
would like to see the joint participation of traditional and liberal Jews in procedures
involving Jewish personal status.

More often than not today the witnesses of the sealing of the *get* are not the same
who witness its delivery to the woman. There are several reasons for this. First of all, it
is usually the congregational rabbi who arranges for the *get* on behalf of the man or the
woman who is affiliated with his congregation. Since it is rarely the case that a
congregational rabbi is a specialist in this area *(mesader gittin)*, he usually arranges for
the man to sign a proxy authorizing the writing of the *get* in his absence. It is also quite
rare for the husband to actually deliver the *get* to his former wife in person. Most
couples find this direct confrontation to be too painful an experience inasmuch as they
have usually been through an already painful civil divorce procedure. Thus, more often
than not, the rabbi is designated as the agent of the husband to deliver the *get* to his
former wife.

Based on this state of affairs, and basing ourselves on some of the halakhic
developments we have just examined, I would like to suggest the following procedure.
Let a *Bet Din* be established composed of both liberal and traditional rabbis. Let several
rabbis, who clearly fulfill all the intellectual, moral and religious requirements for
initiatory witness (both Scriptural and rabbinic), be designated as the official witnesses

of this *Bet Din*. Let the *gittin* that they have written and signed be delivered only in the presence of a board of rabbis representative of both traditional and liberal rabbis. This would, I think, fulfill defensible halakhic requirements for *gittin* and it would involve both liberal and traditional rabbis in an actual procedure involving the Halakhah of personal status.

Basically the same type of procedure could be set up for conversion. For here again, although initially those supervising conversions are supposed to have a fully traditional life style, we nevertheless see that a convert is considered a convert irrespective of who supervised his or her conversion as long as the proper specifics were carried out.[57] Moreover, if conversions are conducted by a board of rabbis representative of both liberals and traditionalists, and if all these rabbis were to sign the document attesting to the valid conversion, then it would have to be said that the convert converted to *kelal Yisrael* but to no particular denomination therein. Thus anyone who wanted to invalidate such a conversion (or such a *get*) would have to invalidate all the rabbis who were members of that board of rabbis. In such a case the traditional rabbis would have to make common cause with the liberal rabbis who have accepted the objective halakhic norms of personal status. In other words, the price of such halakhic unanimity in American Judaism is greater objective stringency on the part of the liberals and greater subjective leniency on the part of the traditionalists.[58]

6. *Subjective Unanimity in Testimony*

The procedure suggested above does enable a halakhic modus vivendi to be possible between traditionalists and liberals on two vital procedures concerning personal status. Nevertheless, it still does not reach the heart of our problem, which is how to establish an authentic community going beyond the party affiliations which at present characterize American Judaism. The procedure suggested above does not reach the heart of our problem because it is based on the tendency to give greater emphasis to confirmational testimony in the development of the Halakhah. However, as we have seen, although greater emphasis can be placed on this type of testimony, and this can provide a solution to some of our halakhic problems, it is still initiatory testimony which is the essential function of witness *(ed)* in the constitution of the Jewish community as a witness of the covenant *(edah)*.[59] It is testimony on this level which is essential for the normative function of the covenantal community. The question here is whether we can function as witnesses in the primary sense in situations having halakhic consequences for the personal status of Jews.

Concerning subjective prerequisites for being a valid witness Maimonides writes,

> One who is invalidated (nifsal) because of a transgression: if two witnesses testify that he did a particular transgression, even though they did not forewarn him about it and he was not punished for it—such a person is invalid (pasul) for testimony. How does this specifically apply? —When one transgressed norms which Jews commonly accept (she-pashat be-Yisrael) as transgressions.[60]

Earlier, in the preceding chapter, Maimonides makes a distinction between those who are invalid for testimony because of their transgression of Scriptural law and those who are invalid for testimony because of their transgression of rabbinic law. In the former case since their very public action is so immediately recognizable as being in violation of Jewish law, it can be assumed that the average Jew will understand why their testimony is invalid. In the latter case, however, the average Jew must be publically informed (hakhrazah) that such a person is invalid as a witness.[61] This distinction is based on clear Talmudic precedent.[62] But, whereas our text of the Talmud, as well as our text of Alfasi, indicate that such public announcements on one's status as a violator of rabbinic law be made in a rabbinic court (Bet Din), Maimonides' text states that it be done in "the synagogues" (batay kenesiyot). Now one could interpret this to simply mean that such announcements be made in a prominent public place.[63] However, I believe that Maimonides' choice of "the synagogues" adds something. The synagogue (bet ha-kenesset), as opposed to the house of study (bet ha-midrash), is characterized as the place where the Written Torah is read and taught.[64] It is precisely here, as opposed to a Bet Din or Bet Midrash frequented by scholars familiar with rabbinic law[65], that it can be assumed that the people are familiar only with the basic Scriptural transgressions but are unfamiliar with the developments of rabbinic law. Thus if this type of announcement is not made, the Scriptural category (mid'Oraita) for valid witnesses alone seems to apply.

Furthermore, elaborating on the Talmud, Maimonides writes,

> One who has neither knowledge of Scripture nor of Mishnah, nor who practices common propriety (derekh eretz) is assumed to be wicked and

is invalid for testimony. For whoever has descended to this level it can
be assumed (hazaqah) that he transgresses in the majority of cases he has
the opportunity to do so.[66]

Maimonides even goes further and rules that as long as one is engaged in the practice of

mitzvot and charity and whose public behavior is respectable, such a person's testimony

is to be accepted.[67] Thus we see that the basic criteria of witness are adherence to

Scriptural law and publically respectable behavior as a human being and as a Jew.

On those grounds I believe a traditional-liberal consensus—in the primary sense of

initiatory witness—is an halakhic possibility in American Judaism today. And this leads

us back to a point I made at the beginning of this chapter. It will be recalled that I

compared our situation today to that which pertained between the Pharisees and the

Sadducees—although we seem to be more cordial than they were to each other.[68] What I

attempted to show was that on key questions involving the Jewish people as a whole the

Pharisees seem to have attempted to establish some sort of consensus by their concept of

"a matter on which the Sadducees would agree." It will be recalled that the Talmud

considers such matters to be a common knowledge even in elementary schools. Now we

know that in Talmudic times most elementary schools were conducted in synagogues.[69]

This was not only a matter of locale, it was also a matter of curriculum: the synagogue

was the place where Scripture was read and expounded to both adults and children. And

such is still the case today. Is not the presence of the Sefer Torah and its being read and

expounded by whatever pronunciation or cycle of readings, by whatever method of

teaching and by whatever curriculum, the very point that all our synagogues have in

common? As such this point in common, plus our common acceptance of the objective

normative criteria of the Halakhah of personal status, plus our common respect for each

other's moral, intellectual and religious integrity as part of kelal Yisrael—all of this

enables us to begin to normatively constitute a community worthy of our covenantal

status.

The last matter with which I would like to deal in this paper is the question of

whether or not we traditionalists are required to publically disqualify in the synagogues

those who do not accept all the institutions of rabbinic law (hakhrazah)? If this is an

halakhic requirement, then everything we have attempted to halakhically accomplish

heretofore would surely be in jeopardy. For it would clearly involve the traditionalists among us in condemning the liberals among us. Everything we abhor in contemporary Jewish life we would be required to do: issue bans (herem), engage in public name-calling, etc., etc., etc. Only recently American Jews have been exposed to the nauseating spectacle of warring Hasidic groups in New York, whose public antics necessitated the intervention of the police. Who among us wants to be part of anything which is even remotely similar to all this?

I would suggest that condemnations are permissable only when it can be assured that the overwhelming number of Jews are fully observant of Jewish law, Scriptural or rabbinic, and that only a tiny minority openly flaunt these publically accepted standards as an act of defiance and separation from the normative community. In this context condemnations were at times necessary in order to show that the integrity of the community had to be taken seriously. However, today we cannot assume that such a normative consensus exists in Jewry. Therefore, to engage in such public condemnation, with all the ill will it entails, can only serve to make the cause of Jewish law and observance look like one more partisan interest. For this very problem there is Talmudic guidance. When the Torah commands us "to surely admonish (hokheah tokheah) your neighbor" (Leviticus 19:17), the Talmud notes,

> R. Ilaa said in the name of R. Eleazar ben R. Simon that just as one is commanded to say something which will be heard, so is he commanded not to say something which will not be heard.[70]

In other words, if we are commanded to refrain from admonition which could be confused with personal controversy, how much more should we refrain from admonition which could diminish the very repute of the Torah in the eyes of the people.[71]

In examining the Halakhah concerning the vital questions of covenant and community we notice that sometimes the Halakhah presupposes an already existent community and sometimes it attempts to establish one. Our interpretation of the Halakhah has led us to emphasize it as the criterion for the establishment of community. For us community lies mostly on the horizon. We must find the halakhic means to enhance not diminish community among all Jews.

WOMEN IN THE RABBINATE?

1. *Introduction*

The question of whether or not women may become rabbis has become the subject of intense controversy of late.[1] This question is not one which simply arose out of a particular situation *(ma'aseh she-hayah)* where an immediate normative ruling was called for; rather, it is one where an entire contemporary ideology—Feminism—confronts the entire Jewish tradition. As such the practical question of rabbinical ordination for women is not limited to a random occurrence or even a set of random occurrences; rather, it arises from a new theory confronting an old tradition.

Indeed, the question of rabbinical ordination for women epitomizes a confrontation which in the broadest sense is political. Feminism is asking the Jewish religious community to reconstitute its political order. A political order consists of institutions which structure relations between the participants in the particular order. Authorities are those persons in the political order who determine the meaning of these institutional structures for the participants, that is, they legislate, administer, and, especially, judge.[2] If Judaism is the constitution of the political order of the Jewish religious community, then the authorities in this political order, certainly since the destruction of the Second Temple in 70 C.E., and probably earlier, have been the rabbis. Inasmuch as women have been excluded from the rabbinate, they have been excluded from authority in the Jewish religious community. The demand of Jewish feminists that women now be included in the rabbinate can only be considered revolutionary. Furthermore, this demand epitomizes the confrontation between Feminism and Judaism in that revolutions always seek a radical change in the existing authority more than anything else, because the designation of authority in the community more than anything else determines the character of the political community. Such terms as "patriarchy," "democracy," "aristocracy" and "theocracy" are all definitions of the character of various political communities by designating the primary authority in each of them.[3] Certainly the more perceptive Jewish feminists are well aware of how revolutionary their project in truth is.[4] The political question is: Can traditional Judaism sustain such a revolution? In the conclusion of this chapter I will suggest how a feminist revolution can be so sustained; but, I doubt whether many Jewish feminists will agree that my suggestion is sufficient.

They will probably regard it as too conservative. Before that sugggestion can be cogently put forth, however, the halakhic, historical, theological and philosophical questions pertaining to the ordination of women as rabbis must be first dealt with, albeit too briefly here.

2. *Halakhah and History*

The halakhic question of how legally insuperable is the traditional exclusion of women from the rabbinate is one which can only be comprehensively answered if we look at how political roles are determined in a society governed by Halakhah.

One can see four basic political roles in an halakhic society: (1) private participants; (2) domestic participants; (3) public participants; (4) authorities.

Private participants in the society are persons who are permitted to practice its rites qua individuals, but whose practice has no public significance. Generally, women have been exempt from those rites which are to be performed at a specific time.[5] However, there has also been a general tendency in the history of the Halakhah to allow women to practice whatever rites they choose over and above what they are obligated to practice.[6]

In the area of domestic participation in society the role of women was greatly enhanced in the history of the Halakhah. They were basically elevated from the level of chattel to the level of free persons with definite rights in the marital union.[7] However, all of the development in the area of Jewish matrimonial law was based on the fundamental premise that a woman's essential role in life is to be a wife and mother, and this purpose of the law pertaining to her was invoked in the reinterpretation of various specific legal impediments which arose from time to time.[8] One can see most halakhic development pertaining to women as being in the interest of protecting women from the exploitation by men which, of course, destroys true marital mutuality.[9]

It is in the area of public participation in society where one can see the great halakhic divide between men and women. The true dignity of women was seen in their domestic rather than their communal role, since "all of the honor of the princess is within (*penimah*)" (Psalms 45:14).[10] Indeed in her domestic role it could well be argued that the woman is the dominant participant, "the cornerstone of the house" (Psalms 113:9),[11] a point to which I will return when examining the claims of Jewish egalitarianism.

It is only when we have reached this point in our inquiry that the halakhic question of women rabbis can be seen in proper sequence.

Because a woman is not considered a public participant in society she is not counted as a member of the quorum required for public worship.[12] (Whether or not women may themselves constitute their own quorum is a topic of current halakhic debate.[13]) Not being obligated for regular public worship she cannot very well be a public participant in its constitution.[14] Her role is that of either spectator or private participant. Thus it follows from all of this that a woman may not lead a congregation in public worship or read the Torah for them.[15] For the same reason a woman may not be the celebrant of a wedding in that the recitation of the nuptial blessings (birkat hatanim) may only be done by one of the men who is part of the quorum required for their recitation.[16] Although these are not necessarily rabbinical functions, they are usual ones.[17] Indeed, a rabbi who could neither publically read the Torah, nor lead public worship, nor celebrate weddings, such a rabbi would be practically disenfranchised in any Jewish congregation governed by Halakhah.

We are now at the point where the essential definition of a rabbi comes to the fore. *A rabbi is one who alone may be an authority in a religious court (Bet Din) dealing with matters of personal and familial status.* Although rabbis do many other things such as preaching, teaching, counseling and pastoring, none of these activities is essentially rabbinical. They may be done by virtually any other qualified Jew. If one is willing to eliminate the essential rabbinical role and concentrate only on the common ones today, as is the case in the Reform rabbinate, then one has in effect made the title "rabbi" lose its only specific distinction. As such, it is so far removed from its traditional matrix as to become a homonym. If this is the case, then the rabbinate becomes so amorphous a vocation that it could be argued that no serious traditional Jew—male or female—could hardly aspire to it.

The authoritative role of a judge is related to the role of a witness as a public representative of the society as a whole. The latter is the *conditio sine qua non* of the former. As the *Mishnah* states, "whoever is fit (kasher) to judge is fit to witness; but there are those who are fit to witness and are not fit to judge."[18] The Halakhah is clear, with the exception of areas where a woman's testimony is indispensible and without which domesticity would be impossible, a witness (ed) may only be a man.[19] A judge,

moreover, requires the requisite learning over and above the gender and moral requisites

of a witness.[20] The exclusion of women from the role of witness is considered explicitly

Scriptural (gezerat ha-Katub) and is, therefore, beyond repeal; a fortiori the exclusion of

women from the essential rabbinical role of judge (dayyan).[21] Jewish legal proceedings

where women functioned as either witnesses or judges are invalid, and the consequences

for those dependent on these proceedings for clarification of their Jewish status could be

tragically irreversible.[22]   Hence at the halakhic level the feminist challenge to

traditional Judaism finds itself at an absolute impasse.[23]

3. Theology

Theologically, the feminist challenge to Judaism is its voluntarism. Should not a

person who wants to be an authority and has the moral and intellectual abilities to be an

authority, should not such a person be allowed to be one? However, this would only be

possible if the Jewish covenant with God were initiated by its human participants. If

that were the case, then women could elect to be public participants in the covenant and,

therefore, could be eligible to qualify as authorities.   The logic of the type of

voluntaristic theology espoused by the Jewish feminists was made in the first attempted

internal revolution against established Jewish authority, that of Korah and his group. In

challenging the authority of Moses and Aaron Korah states, "you have too much, for the

entire congregation all of them are holy (qedoshim) and the Lord is in the midst of them"

(Numbers 16:3). In other words, why have the others been excluded from positions of

authority held by Moses and Aaron alone?[24] Moses' answer is, "tomorrow the Lord will

make known who is His and who is holy and He will draw him near; and whom He chooses

(yibhar bo) He will draw near to Himself" (16:5). The logic of Moses' answer is as

follows: Just as God chose the people of Israel in general from all the other peoples, so

has He chosen Moses and Aaron from all the other leaders. The covenant and the various

statuses it contains are not voluntary from the human position. Humans, to be sure, can

choose to either obey or disobey God; however, the obligation is prior to their choice.

Their choice is a subsequent response.[25]

Ultimately, the status of being a Jew—with the exception of converts at the time of

their conversion—is an involuntary matter.[26] One can neither choose to be a Jew nor choose not to be one from the Divine position. "Even if a Jew has sinned he is, nevertheless, a Jew."[27] Even an apostate, although denied virtually all the privileges of being a Jew, is, nevertheless, considered a Jew subject to the full yoke of the commandments.[28]

All of this, theologically, follows from the presupposition of the covenant, namely, God as Creator. For, if God can choose one universe over other possible and actual universes,[29] and if God can choose one small species—homo sapiens—to create in His image, and if God can choose one small people—Israel—to be the recipient of His Torah, then why can God not choose men rather than women to be authorities in a society governed by that Torah? Here again the modern mind and temperament are faced with the scandal of the particularism of Judaism. Now it is faced with the particularism of Jewish sexism. Earlier in the modern period it was faced with the scandal of Judaism's particularism in such areas as the Hebrew language, the Sabbath, the dietary laws, and the Land of Israel[30]—the last being a form of our scandalous particularism which so many in the world still find so hard to face. Clearly the inner meaning of Jewish particularism is not democratic; but, as Josephus pointed out quite correctly, Judaism is theocratic not democratic: the rule of God not the rule of humans.[31] This does not mean, of course, that there are not democratic elements in Judaism, but one could hardly argue that they are primary.[32] Hence at the theological level the feminist challenge to Judaism meets an impasse every bit as absolute as the halakhic one we just examined.

4. Philosophy

By demanding a categorical egalitarianism in Jewish religious life Feminism is making a philosophical assertion. It is asserting that absolute equality between men and women in the Jewish community is a desideratum, a moral imperative. Nevertheless, no such egalitarian commandment can be found in Normative Jewish Tradition. Moreover, I know of no Jewish feminist who has argued convincingly for the philosophical cogency of egalitarianism per se, much less for Jewish egalitarianism.[33] Let us now briefly examine just how equality has functioned in Jewish tradition.

The Torah writes, "let there be one law (mishpat ehad) for the sojourner (ka-ger) and the native-born (ka'ezrah), for I am the Lord your God" (Leviticus 24:22). The Talmud interprets this verse to mean: "a law equal (ha-shaveh) for all of you."[34] Here equality is used to justify a monetary interpretation of the *lex talionis* inasmuch as mutual

mutilation can never be truly equal. Only money, being an entity whose value is

abstractly stipulated, can fulfill this ideal requirement.[35] The first characteristic of

equality in Jewish tradition, then, is abstractedness.

The *Mishnah* interprets this same Scriptural verse as mandating equal measures to be

followed in both civil and criminal legal proceedings.[36] And, although the subject of this

verse, the sojourner or resident-alien *(ger toshab)* is not mentioned in this interpretation,

he is implied in it. For the resident-alien was a private participant in Jewish society.

Despite the fact that he could neither witness against Jews nor judge them, he was

guaranteed the protection of Jewish civil and criminal justice if he publically agreed to

live by the seven Noahide laws.[37] As Hermann Cohen correctly pointed out, this was the

equivalent in ancient Israel of secular citizenship *(Staatsbuerger)*.[38] Thus the second

characteristic of equality is that it seems to be limited to the realm of civil and criminal

responsibilities. In this abstract, formal, realm persons are in effect desexualized *(das

Man)*, that is, their sexual identities are bracketed. In this realm they are all

homogenized, all regarded as the same. In the fullness of life, however, to which the

Torah addresses itself, sexual identity as difference *(hetero-*sexuality) is constantly

recognized and affirmed.

Concerning the civil and criminal equality of men and women the Talmud teaches,

"Scripture equated *(hishvah ha-Katub)* women and men (1) for all punishments of the

Torah ...[39] (2) for all civil matters *(dinin)* in the Torah ... (3) for all capital

punishments *(meetot)* in the Torah."[40] In its discussion of the rationale of this earlier

statement the Talmud notes the following. (1) The first equation is the rule because God

has identical compassion for women and men enabling both to atone *(kapparah)* by being

punished;[41] and this in spite of the fact that men are obligated for many more

commandments *(bar mitzvah)* than are women *(lav bat mitzvah hi)*.[42] (2) The second

equation is the rule because God has identical concern for a woman's livelihood *(hayuta)*

which would be impaired by a lack of civil rights; and this in spite of the fact that men

are more likely to be involved in business than are women. (3) And the third equation is

the rule because the loss of human life, be it female or male, is heinous to God; and this

in spite of the fact that men being obligated for more commandments should perhaps

have the right to ransom their lives *(kofer)* in the case of a crime punishable by death.[43] Thus the third characteristic of equality is that its operation in the area of civil and criminal rights and responsibilities is irrespective of gender. However, as we have already seen, these rights and responsibilities are those of a private participant in society, and any attempt to infer that they have public significance as well was usually rejected by subsequent halakhists.[44]

Although in the full religious life of the Jewish community women and men do not share the direct equality of civil and criminal rights and responsibilities, nevertheless, there is a certain proportional equality if one views the respective roles of women and men in their totality.[45] Ironically enough, egalitarian logic at this very point in Jewish history has actually upset this proportional equality and thus has diminished rather than enhanced the importance of the Jewish woman.

We have seen earlier how the primary role of the Jewish woman is that of a domestic participant in Jewish life. Moreover, she is not only *a* domestic participant, she is *the* domestic determinant by virtue of a simple fact: it is the Jewish woman and the Jewish woman alone who confers unambiguous Jewish identity on her Jewish children.[46] The Jewish man only confers subsequent infra-Jewish status on his children.[47] Whether or not this was always the case in Judaism can be debated by historians,[48] but the fact remains that this has been the unchallenged normative Jewish position until very recent times.

However, the same egalitarian logic which so eagerly pursues *Gleichshaltung* in the public sphere by breaking down the barriers between men and women, this same logic breaks down the primary domestic position of the Jewish woman as the conferer of Jewish identity on posterity. It is no historical accident that the Reform Movement, which a short time ago (twelve years in the context of Jewish history is a very short time indeed) began to ordain women as rabbis, has recently decreed that the Jewish identity of a child may be determined *either* by his or her Jewish mother *or* by his or her Jewish father. This is no historical accident because it is a further and more radical consequence of the very same egalitarian logic which called for the ordination of women as rabbis. Considering the non-normative way the Reform Movement has always approached Jewish tradition, this further consequence of their egalitarianism cannot be faulted as either inconsistent or insincere. Those who reject this current Reform position can only do so if they also reject the philosophically grounded egalitarianism upon which it is based. Those non-Reform liberals in contemporary religious Jewry—and here I particularly mean many of the leaders of the Conservative Movement—who want women as rabbis but recoil at the thought of the more radical rejection of matrilineal descent, are philosophically as well as historically naive if they believe they can coherently affirm both egalitarianism and the traditional halakhic criteria of status. And these criteria are only intelligible if seen in the context of the theological and philosophical principles I have just presented.

Philosophically this is the very crux of the question. For Jewish feminists assume that absolute equality is both self-evident and Jewishly authentic. From what we have seen, heretofore, neither assertion is true.

5. *Conclusion: A Suggestion*

Although the basic demands of the Jewish feminists have no adequate foundation in traditional Judaism—halakhically, historically, theologically, or philosophically—they do reflect a sincere and sustained cry for some way of recognizing the participatory and authoritative role Jewish women do play in the secular Jewish community and now desire to play in the religious community as well. The sincerity and intensity of this cry call for some deeper thinking. One cannot simply argue from the tradition and expect the answer to be obediently accepted. This would be as the rabbis used to say about inadequate responses to good questions, "to push away with a straw."[49] The political dynamics involved in modern protest movements—and Feminism is the ideological basis of what we used to call a short time ago, "Women's *Liberation*"—just do not operate so simply. Clearly Jewish Feminism is not going to disappear or retreat into silence.

Since in my own thinking I have just recently accepted this inevitability, my traditionalist response to it is admittedly awkward.

Judaism, it seems to me, can sustain a feminist revolution if that revolution is a genuine development into a new historical situation. In such a revolution, actually *evolution* is a more apt name for it, old institutions are not destroyed but new institutions are added to the whole of Jewish life. In the emergent process both the old and the new institutions assume their respective roles of importance without either engineering the abolition of the other. A new economy of relations is gradually worked out. One can see this is the evolution which Pharisaism and Rabbinic Judaism effected in

Jewish history.

It is clear from an unbiased reading of Scripture that the whole institution of the Oral Torah itself is not something Scriptural. The prima facie meaning of the verse, "you shall not deviate *(lo tasur)* from the matter *(ha-dabar)* they will tell you" (Deuteronomy 17:11) simply is that Scriptural law needs to be interpreted in adjudication. Furthermore, the chief religious authorities were the hereditary priests as it states, "when you come to the levitical priests and to judge who will be in those days" (17:9). Nevertheless, the rabbis used this verse as the Scriptural support for *their* authority to create new religious institutions, something explicitedly prohibited by the same Deuteronomic code.[50]

The new institution of the rabbinate *(hakhamim)* gradually overtook in importance the older hereditary priesthood without, however, abrogating the specific functions of the priests. This can be seen in the following *Mishnah*.

> How is the infected house inspected? "And he whose house it is shall come and tell the priest saying, 'there appears to me there is something like an infection in the house'." (Leviticus 14:35) Even if he is a rabbinic scholar *(talmid hakham)* and knows that it is definitely an infection, he may not decree and say 'there appears to me an infection in the house,' but 'something *like* an infection *(ke-nega)* appears to me in the house.'[51]

In other words, the priest is not to be denied his Scriptural privilege of declaring a house to be infected. However, the implication of this *Mishnah* is that the rabbinic scholar is the one, by virtue of his greater learning, who is in the fullest sense the more authoritative figure. What we have in the Pharisaic-Rabbinic evolution is the shift from the authority of heredity to the authority of learning and teaching. On the specific level of the priest's Scriptural privilege nothing has changed, but in the full economy of Jewish religious life everything has changed.[52] A parallel to this same phenomenon is the assertion of the *Mishnah* that in the later days of the Second Temple the rabbinic scholars had to give the High Priest a cram course in the laws of Yom Kippur so that he could properly perform his Scripturally ordained duties.[53] As the Talmud noted elsewhere, "the words of the student and the words of the teacher, to whose words do we listen?!"[54] Finally, there is the famous *Mishnah* which states that the life of a bastard (one having a very low Jewish pedigree from birth) takes precedence over the life of the High Priest (one having the highest Jewish pedigree), if the bastard is a rabbinic scholar and the High Priest is an ignoramus *(am ha'aretz)*.[55] "The stone which the builders rejected has become the cornerstone of the house." (Psalms 118:22)

I mention all of this because at the level of learning, and authentic Jewish evolution is always a learning and a relearning *(midrash hakhamim)*, distinctions of pedigree and gender recede into the background. This comes out in the following way. When the *Mishnah* rules that women may neither serve as witnesses nor as judges, the medieval Tosafists saw the Scriptural Deborah as a seeming counter-example to this rule, as it says, "and she judged *(ve-hi shoftah)* Israel at that time" (Judges 4:4).[56] Their answer was that this was either a special Divine dispensation, or "she did not judge but taught them the laws" *(melamedet lahem ha-dinim)*.[57] In other words, her role was intellectual rather than judicial. Nevertheless, it is clear where the true spiritual authority lay. In pre-war Eastern Europe, for example, although the *rav* or *dayyan* made the regular halakhic judgments in the Jewish community, his was not always the true spiritual authority. Among *Hasidim* this authority was in the hands of the *rebbe*, who rarely made specific halakhic judgments. Among *Mitnagdim* (especially in Lithuania) it was often the *rosh yeshiva.*

Ironically enough, there are fewer halakhic impediments to learning from women than in teaching them.[58] Therefore, my conservative suggestion is that Jewish feminists become our best scholars and teachers, that they master the traditional sources and reinterpret them in the light of their unique experience and insight. It is for them to create a new house of study *(Bet Midrash)* about which the Talmud says, "it is impossible that there be a *Bet Midrash* without something new *(be-lo hiddush).*"[59] Out of this *Bet Midrash,* which Bialik, no doubt paraphrasing this Talmudic passage, called "the creative house *(bet ha-yotzer)* of the soul of the nation,"[60] could come a renaissance of Jewish learning and insight in our age of incredible Jewish ignorance and shallowness.

Whether our Jewish feminists choose the harder road of Jewish creativity which brings forth the new without destroying the old, or whether they choose the easier road of revolutionary nihilism which destroys the old and ultimately replaces it with further destruction, this is a choice they and they alone must make. If they do choose the harder road of learning and reverence *(Torah ve-yirah),*[61] then I for one am willing to say that "from all my teachers I have been enlightened" (Psalms 119:99)[62] and that this traditionalist is willing to become their student. What will practically emerge from all of this? I can only answer as did the rabbis in Lydda at a time of even greater Jewish uncertainty, "greater is learning [than even doing] because it ultimately leads to the deed."[63]

ALCOHOL AND DRUG ABUSE IN THE PERSPECTIVE
OF JEWISH TRADITION

1. *Introduction*

It is clearly evident that alcohol and drug abuse, "substance abuse" for short, is a course of action anyone who values life and well-being would choose to avoid consistently. Substance abuse obviously falls under those norms which prohibit causing ourselves physical, mental or emotional pain and deterioration. The Scriptural prescription, "you shall be very careful with your lives" (Deuteronomy 4:15) has been continually reiterated throughout the history of Judaism.[1]

Although the above norm is immediately evident, two additional points require further analysis. First, the term "substance abuse" raises the question: Is all substance *use* necessarily *abusive*? Is there a definable difference between acceptable use of alcohol and drugs and unacceptable use, that is *ab*-use, of them? Second, if there is indeed such a definable difference between substance use and substance abuse in Jewish tradition, then we should attempt to discover how the tradition determines this difference and how it speculates about the underlying reasons for it. These questions, then, call for both halakhic and theological analysis.

2. *A Proposed Ban on Marijuana Use*

Eleven years ago in a collection of papers entitled *Judaism and Drugs*,[2] it was reported that a group of Orthodox teenagers asked three leading Orthodox halakhists—Rabbis Moshe Feinstein of New York, Immanuel Jakobovits of London, and Aaron Soloveitchik of Chicago—if Jewish law permits or prohibits the use of marijuana. All three of these learned rabbis were unanimous in responding that marijuana use is prohibited by Jewish law.[3] Since new prohibitions sooner or later require justification in the classical sources of Judaism,[4] the three rabbis based their opinion on three points. (1) Marijuana use interferes with the study of the Torah and the performance of the commandments.[5] (2) Marijuana use leads to "slavish sensuousness," which is prohibited in Numbers 15:39 ("you shall not stray after your heart and after your eyes, following which you are lusting"), and which destroys free will.[6] (3) Marijuana use is a violation of Deuteronomy

22:8 ("you shall not place anything dangerous in your house"), which in rabbinic tradition is interpreted to be a prohibition of anything likely to be harmful.[7] Thus they conclude, "The fact that it is not now harmful to a person does not preclude the chance that it may one day be . . ."[8]

All of this sounds reasonable and, indeed, the way these three rabbis responded to the question indicates that they considered their conclusion to be rather obvious. Nevertheless, a rather powerful counterpoint was raised by Professor Benny Kraut (at the time a student at Yeshiva University). He wrote, "The fundamental flaw . . . is that no distinction is made between the 'pothead' and the occasional 'social' user."[9] Later on he notes that all the arguments against marijuana use per se could be used against alcohol use of any kind.[10] This point is a *reductio ad absurdam* since there is no prohibition against alcohol use per se in Jewish tradition, as we shall soon see.[11] Finally, he candidly states that he has always had difficulty understanding the rule that on Purim one is to become so drunk that he can no longer distinguish between "cursed Haman and blessed Mordecai."[12]

Kraut's counterpoint clearly indicates that there is a difference in Jewish tradition between substance use, which is permitted, and substance abuse, which is by definition prohibited. Let us now see how this distinction was maintained concerning alcohol and, then, attempt to determine whether or not the same distinction can be made in the case of the use of a substance like marijuana, whose advocates argue, is not at all dangerous if used moderately.

3. *Alcohol Use in Jewish Tradition*

The use of alcohol plays an important role in traditional Jewish life. Most of the ancient texts refer to wine; however, this is the case mostly because wine was the alcoholic beverage most widely used in the Land of Israel by our ancestors. It does not seem, in almost all of their rulings, that the use of alcohol is necessarily limited to wine by the rabbis.[13]

First of all, the use of alcohol is considered a legitimate pleasure in this world. Thus the Talmud notes that the Scriptural *Nazir*, that is one who took a vow to abstain from alcohol (among other things) is required to bring a sin-offering for "having sinned because of the life" (Numbers 6:11). The ostensive meaning of the Scriptural text is that the

Nazirite had sinned because of contact with a human corpse, something the Nazarite vow precludes. Nevertheless, R. Eleazar Ha-Kfar, quoting R. Judah the Prince, states that in addition to this ostensive meaning of the text, the seeming redundant words "because of the life" (al ha-nafesh) also mean that the Nazirite had sinned against himself by "painfully removing (ha-metza'er) himself from wine."[14] And this text is used as the prime example of a general rule prohibiting the denial of any legitimate bodily pleasure. Although there were definitely those in rabbinic tradition who advocated asceticism, including teetotalism, the preponderance of rabbinic tradition seems to have regarded ascetism as unnecessarily harsh.[15] Teetotalism seems to have been advised only for those who doubted their ability to "hold their liquor" and who feared what they might do when drunk.[16] In Judaism, alcoholism may very well be the abuse of the *privilege* to enjoy alcohol in moderation. Now in Scripture we do have the example of the teetotaling Rechabites. However, the admiration for them expressed by the prophet Jeremiah was not for their teetotalism per se but, rather, for their overall adherence to their ancestral traditions, of which abstention from alcohol was most prominent (Jeremiah 35:5ff.).

Second, alcohol was considered helpful in alleviating certain emotional symptoms, especially the immediate sadness of mourning. Thus the Talmud notes that originally ten cups of wine were drunk in the house of mourning. As time went on more cups were added until intoxication became common. When this happened the original practice of ten cups only was reinstituted.[17] In another passage wine seems to have been recommended for mild depression, which is an insight going back to Scripture, namely, "wine gladdens the human heart" (Psalms 104:15).[18] Along these lines it is worth noting that the Talmud indicates that a portion of wine and a narcotic was administered to criminals just before their execution in order that they lose consciousness and not suffer a painful death.[19]

Finally, wine is a ritual requirement in such Jewish ceremonies as *kiddush, habdalah* and weddings. Thus the Talmud interprets the Scriptural commandment "Remember the Sabbath day to hallow it" (le-qadsho—Exodus 20:8) as "remember it over wine at its beginning."[20] Although the late Professor Louis Ginzberg of the Jewish Theological Seminary of America proved that unfermented grape juice may be used in all of these rituals, it should be noted that he made this point during National Prohibition in the 1920's, when criminal elements controlled the "sacramental" wine business. However, even he clearly admitted that fermented wine was certainly the usual and preferred substance throughout Jewish history.[21]

4. Alcohol Abuse in Jewish Tradition

As much as the traditional sources advocate the personal, social and religious value of alcohol, so do they warn about its detrimental effects if used immoderately. Thus the Talmud records that R. Kahana noted that a frequent word for wine, *teerash*, could also be vocalized *teerash*. Now *rosh* means "head," whereas *rash* means "poor."[22] In other words, the one who uses wine intelligently and responsibly maintains proper self-control, whereas the one who surrenders to intoxication loses what he has. Hence the personality of the drinker determines whether or not his drinking will be beneficial. In Scripture the prophet Isaiah castigated "the drunkards of Ephraim ... who are overcome by wine" (Isaiah 28:1).

Intoxication was not in any way considered an exalted human state and the euphoria, which so often accompanies it, was not to be confused with religious bliss.

In Scripture the two sons of Aaron, Nadab and Abihu, are described as "bringing strange fire before the Lord which He had not commanded them" (Leviticus 10:1). For this they died at the hands of God. Now the obvious question is: What was their specific sin for which they died? Noting that immediately following this episode God tells Aaron and his sons that they may not drink "wine and liquor" (10:9) when on duty in the Sanctuary, a *midrash* assumes that this very juxtaposition indicates that "the two sons of Aaron only died because they entered the Sanctuary intoxicated *(shetuyay yayin)*."[23] Nevertheless, God himself says of them, "through those close to Me *(bi-kerobay)* will I be sanctified" (10:3). This undoubtedly troubled the author of the *Zohar* because in one place he queries, "We are taught that they were drunk, but would one give wine to drink on such an occasion, or could one suppose that they were so arrogant that they become intoxicated?!"[24] The answer given is that they were attempting to delve into the sources of sin, not to practice it, but to understand it in order to improve the world.[25] The same motivation is ascribed to the drunkenness of Noah. The author of the *Zohar* elsewhere condemns the loss of self-control which comes with drunkenness as being incompatible with true mystical insight *(sod)*.[26] In these passages it seems that the *Zohar* is attempting to dispel any mystique of alcoholism. Intoxication is precluded from authentic mystical ecstacy.

On a more mundane level intoxication is considered to be incompatible with the role of a teacher of Torah. The Scriptural verse we have been examining, "wine and liquor you shall not drink, you and your sons, when you come to the Tent of Meeting" (Leviticus 10:9) continues with an extension of this prohibition. Not only does it apply to their ritual roles as priests at the altar, but also to their role as religious authorities and teachers in the larger social setting, "to instruct authoritatively *(u-le-horot)* the people of Israel in all of the laws which the Lord your God has spoken through Moses" (10:11). Summarizing considerable rabbinic discussion of this norm, Maimonides generalizes as follows, "Just as it is prohibited for a priest to enter the Sanctuary because of intoxication, so is it prohibited for anyone, priest or layman, to offer normative instruction when drunk . . . unless he is instructing on a point we can assume is obvious to everyone already."[27] Thus the intellectual and moral insight associated with Torah are not to be diminished by intoxication.

The rabbis were also concerned with the effect of alcoholism on one's personal responsibility. A distinction is made between ordinary drunkenness, where there is still some degree of awareness and self-control, and the "drunkenness of Lot," where all self-control and indeed awareness is lost.[28] In the former state one is considered fully responsible for the civil and criminal consequences of his or her acts, only being prohibited from formal prayer. In the latter state one is considered exempt from any responsibility at all. Here we see that there seems to be a fundamental difference recognized between alcoholism as a disease, which overcomes all sense of freedom and responsibility, and drunkenness as a state which can too easily be rationalized by one using it as a cover for acts for which one is culpable. Here the rule of the *Mishnah* that "one is always responsible *(mu'ad le'olam)*" surely still applies.[29] In the case of the alcoholic the root problem is not what he or she does when drunk but, rather, his or her drinking itself. For the drinking itself the alcoholic is culpable and must seek help in overcoming all its self-destructiveness. Indeed Lot, whose drunkenness seems to be the paradigm for the judgment of the genuine alcoholic, is considered elsewhere by the Talmud to be a transgressor.[30] Without this feeling of guilt for his or her alcoholism, how can the alcoholic possibly be motivated to overcome it?

5. *Acceptable and Unacceptable Drinking*

One could say that the difference between acceptable and unacceptable drinking is
that intoxication should be avoided. Although each person's tolerance of alcohol differs
and, therefore, each person must discover his or her own level of tolerance, the Talmud,
nevertheless, did establish certain quantitative standards for estimating the *average*
level of tolerance.[31] However useful such standards are in helping us apply norms
pertaining to drunkenness, they themselves do not tell us why drunkenness is to be
avoided by Jews. For the answer to such an essential question cannot come from simply
measuring behavior. In a Jewish perspective we must see why the state of drunkenness is
antithetical to the state of human existence the *mitzvot* intend.[32] Since this state of
human existence is one lived in the community of observing Jews *(kenesset Yisrael)*,[33]
we must understand why the authentic constitution of this community precludes
drunkenness.

This is brought out in the attempt to understand the Torah's discussion of the
juvenile delinquent—the *ben sorer u-moreh*—the "wayward and rebellious son" in
Deuteronomy 21. The Torah prescribes execution for such an offender at the insistence
of his parents. Now there was a considerable body of rabbinic opinion that believed this
harsh rule was never applied and never would be applied. These rabbis thought that the
whole commandment should be one for us to "interpret and receive reward," namely, we
should attempt to find in it anthropological, ethical and theological insights, not legal
norms per se.[34]

In the Scriptural text the parents of this juvenile delinquent accuse their son of
being "a drunkard *(sob'e)*" (21:20). The *Mishnah* attempts to present a quantitative
criterion for the amount of alcohol consumed which would make one such a drunkard.
However, it also notes that were this alcohol consumed at a "sacred event" *(haburat
mitzvah)*, then the boy would not be executed.[35] The Talmud analyzes this as follows,

> R. Abbahu said that he is not guilty until he eats in a group who are all
> drunkards ... We are thus informed that even if all of them are
> drunkards, because he is engaged in doing a *mitzvah,* he would not be
> completely carried away.[36]

Later on the Talmud suggests that such a "sacred communal event" might even be
something as commonplace as publically comforting the mourners, which is not even

strictly Scriptural in origin.[37]

Now what we see from all of this is that it is participation in an authentic Jewish communal event, a true *haburat mitzvah,* that can elevate even a group of drunkards from a drunken orgy to a community pleasing to God.[38] (One can debate, however, to what extent many of our contemporary "shivahs" and "simhahs" are *haburot mitzvah.*) Such an occasion must preclude drunkenness because it is characterized by Toraitic discourse which requires one's full attention.[39] In theological terms it means that the body, that complex organ of sense and sensuousness, participates in a spiritual reality and is, therefore, limited, transformed and, indeed, intensified by it. For why is the juvenile delinquent's drunkenness so feared?—Because of its ultimate consequences *(needon al shem sofo),* which are seen as his being violently estranged from both God and man.[40] Indeed, according to the Talmud elsewhere, all of us are capable of such estrangement were it not for the sanctifying mitzvot, which are compared to a life-giving potion *(sam hayyim).*[41] The problem, then, is not the substance abused but, rather, the level of social and religious estrangement of the substance abuser.

In the Aggadah, that genre of Jewish expression where the rabbinic mind engaged in such profound and imaginative speculation, we see the interpersonal understanding of intoxication at work. In the cases of Noah and Lot, the two earliest examples of drunkenness in Scripture, the rabbis saw their intoxication as occasions of sexual regression and perversion. And in both cases this combination of intoxication and sexual perversion involved estrangement from kith and kin. Scripture explicitly presents Lot's drunkenness as that which enabled his daughters to commit incest with him (Genesis 19:31ff.). In the Talmud Noah's drunkenness is seen either as an occasion for homosexuality or mutilation.[42] Concerning Noah the Talmud imagines God speaking to him as follows,

> The Holy-One-blessed-be-He said to Noah, 'Noah! Did you not learn from Adam that it was only wine which caused his problem?' Now this is according to R. Meir who said that the tree from which Adam ate was the vine, for there is nothing which brings lament *(yelalah)* to man more than the vine.[43]

In other words, the Talmud sees the very beginning of the human predicament as an attempt to regress into a purely sensuous reality with a simultaneous repression of the spirit, the spirit which seeks God and other persons.[44] Thus the Talmud continues its reflection on drunkenness, elaborating on the Scriptural verse wherein the mother of Lemuel (usually seen as another name for King Solomon) admonishes him with the words, "Do not (al) go to the kings to drink wine, to the rulers where there is liquor" (Proverbs 31:4). She said to him, 'what do you have in common with kings, who drink wine and become drunk and say, why do we need God (El)?! ' "[45] Drunkenness is the result, not the cause, of the drinker encapsulating himself or herself in a windowless world, a world closing out everyone else either outside or above. The motivation in today's parlance is to be "stoned," or in the words of a famous Simon and Garfunkel song, "I am a rock; I am an Island. A rock feels no pain and an island never cries." It is like those who drink "the drink called loneliness" in Billy Joel's recent, moving, song, "Piano Man." As a midrash says, "All this happened to Noah the righteous . . . how much more could it happen to the rest of humanity!"[46] In our attempts to treat substance abuse it is this very heart of darkness that we must penetrate in order to understand its loneliness and its pain. We must hear that loneliness and that pain however it cries out to us.[47]

6. Can There Be A Halakhic Ban On Marijuana Use?

At the beginning of this paper I raised the question of whether or not there can be a legitimate use of marijuana, whose adherents claim is far less harmful than cigarette smoking, when used in moderation.

In terms of strict halakhic precedent, if the claims of the supporters of marijuana use are indeed true, then the only objection one could offer against its use is that, at present, it is illegal in the United States, and we Jews are required to obey the civil and criminal law of the state.[48]   Nevertheless, laws do change (for example, National Prohibition was repealed in 1933 after over a decade of widespread violation), and one could still be an advocate of the use of marijuana without being an actual user of a substance which is illegal at the present time. In fact, I have been able to find two related precedents which indicate that the inhalation of mildly stimulating substances is actually a part of Jewish religious life.

The Mishnah speaks of the burning of certain pungent spices after a meal and that every individual enjoying them was to utter a blessing, thanking God for the pleasure it brought him or her.[49]   In the Talmud's discussion of this Mishnah, Rab, an important authority, indicated that the sense of smell is the most spiritual of the senses. For smell is associated with breath, and it is breath which denotes the life of both the body and the soul.[50]   Indeed, ordinary experience teaches us how stimulating smell is to the imagination, to our capacity for phantasy.

Moreover, the *Mishnah* requires the use of pungent spices in the ritual of *habdalah*, when we officially end the Sabbath.[51] Now *habdalah* involves wine, a torch, and spices. Wine is used because it also iniated the Sabbath at *kiddush*.[52] A torch is used to signify that human labor, of which lighting a fire is the prime example, is now permitted, just as it was prohibited on the Sabbath.[53] Spices are used, according to R. Samuel ben Meir (*Rashbam*), an important twelfth century French halakhist, "because of the loss of the additional Sabbath soul."[54] (According to ancient Jewish folklore a Jew receives an extra soul on the Sabbath only.[55]) In other words, in today's parlance, spices are used for a mild "high" after the exhilaration of the Sabbath has gone, leaving us depressed. — I have heard similar reasoning used to justify the benefits of marijuana use!

Does this mean that after all my characteristic conservatism, both halakhic and theological, I am now giving a *hekhsher* (permission) for marijuana use by Jews? Clearly, on grounds of strict halakhic precedent, this could be done with, I dare say, more cogent halakhic reasoning than put forth for the halakhic prohibition of marijuana which we examined earlier in this paper. Nevertheless, I think the question involves some deeper historical and theological issues, on which I have been reflecting in this paper. It was clearly such issues that motivated the great halakhists of the past when they were faced with new situations. The decrees (*taqqanot* and *gezerot*) they made were arrived at with the full knowledge of their power and responsibility to innovate if need be, based on general principles rather than specific precedent, for there were no such precedents.[56]

I am opposed to permitting the use of marijuana, or even advocating the repeal of secular laws prohibiting its use, for the following reason.

Alcohol use has a long tradition going back to the very beginnings of our history. During that history the use of alcohol has been both socialized and sanctified. As we have seen from both the Aggadah and the Kabbalah, where the Jewish imagination engaged in deep and moving speculation, the mystique of alcoholism was removed. Alcohol was not in itself worthy of praise, but only as a means of including the senses and their drive for pleasure into the transcendent realm of the spirit. Only the process of history, spanning hundreds of generations, could achieve this. In the case of marijuana, on the other hand, we have no such historical process of socialization and sanctification. It has not yet stood the test of history. We do not yet know if it enhances true community. Perhaps it inhibits it. Furthermore, marijuana is more than a substance today. It has become *the symbol* of a whole drug culture, a culture based on the hedonistic imperative, "If it feels good, do it!" Can anything be more antithetical to Judaism, with all its emphasis on sacrifice and discipline?[57]

In the past our sages outlawed practices, which in and of themselves were not objectionable, because of their association with cultures they considered antithetical to Judaism. The most prominent example of this is the ban on the use of gentile wine *(stam yaynam)*. Two reasons are given for it. (1) It may very well have been used in connection with idolatrous rites *(yayn nesekh)*.[58] (2) It led to the type of social interaction which could then lead, in some cases, to intermarriage and total assimilation.[59] This power of legislation is available to halakhic authorities in any generation. It seems to me that marijuana, although probably not objectionable as a substance *per se,* is *very objectionable* because of the hedonistic drug culture it represents and symbolizes today.

Judaism is inconsistent with hedonism, not because it opposes bodily pleasure—quite the contrary, it often requires it—but because hedonism mystifies the body, seeing its pleasure as the end of all human life and striving.[60] Hedonism tells us that the *summum bonum,* the highest good, is to fulfill our body's desire for pleasure, and the highest duty is to love ourselves as bodies. Judaism tells us that the highest good is "the nearness of God" (Psalms 73:25-28) and the highest duty is "to love the Lord your God" (Deuteronomy 6:5).[61] The problem of substance abuse is the problem of what does human desire in truth intend. Judaism, in contradistinction to hedonism and all its cultures, to all its idolatries, teaches that "before you O' Lord is my whole desire, and my cry is not hidden from You" (Psalms 38:10).[62]

JUDAISM AND CONTEMPORARY BIOETHICS

1. *The Interest in Normative Ethics*

An essay on Judaism and bioethics implies that bioethics, as a method of inquiry, is interested in Judaism and that Judaism lends itself to such an interest. Before any specific issues can be systematically examined, this relation between an *interested* method of inquiry and an interesting datum must be constituted.[1]

Ethical inquiry can be conducted in three distinct ways corresponding to three distinct fundamental questions. Ethical inquiry of the analytic variety asks: *What* is ethics? It apprehends an area of human discourse conventionally called "ethics" and seeks to delineate its boundaries and designate its content. Its scope is essentially descriptive. Ethical inquiry of the metaphysical variety, on the other hand, asks: *Why* is there ethics? It seeks to understand ethics in the context of something more fundamental than the ethical area with which the analytic spectator is concerned. It attempts to constitute the apodictic background out of which ethics is to subsequently emerge.[2] Finally, ethical inquiry of the normative variety asks the practical question: *How* is one to act?

Normative ethical judgments are made in the context of historical situations or cases. The assessment of the facts in the case will influence the judgment by suggesting the application of one norm or several.[3] In the formulation of a judgment a specific set of human circumstances is described. The circumstances contain either an element of conflict or an element of lack between individual or collective members within society. Hence a resolution of the conflict or lack *is called for.* An ethical judgment is the response to this call for resolution. The social inadequacy of *what is* leads to the judgment of *what is to be done.*

Now if the normative ethical judgment in one situation is taken to have broader significance than its specific application in the case for which it was initially formulated, then it becomes a general prescription, a *norm.*[4] This process of application involves analogy. Thus a new situation B is considered similar enough to the old situation A to warrant the application of norm C in both situations. Norm C in situation B is based on its precedent in situation A. Only historical experience can enable this process of analogous application to be effective, because only historical experience can enable one to see situations in the context of a normative continuum. Analogical reasoning is essentially an exercise in estimation. Thus the normative effectiveness of ethics requires an acceptance of historical experience and continuity. The use of this historical experience is required if ethical concepts are to be adequately schematized. We will see how this analogical reasoning functions in the Jewish ethical tradition when we analyze a specific ethical paradigm from it.

Clearly the normative question is the one which is most often asked today. As such it is the question which concerns a greater number of thoughtful people in our society than either the analytic or the metaphysical questions. For the analyst looks at ethics after the fact, and the metaphysician looks at ethics before the fact, but practical ethical concern begins *within* the ethically significant situation. Therefore, the normative question is the *terminus a quo* of ethical inquiry because it is the most practical. In ethics, theory is ultimately for the sake of practice.

This search for a wider number of precedents by contemporary ethical inquiry seems to be the result of the wider range of situations calling for ethical judgments. In areas of bioethical concern the explosion in medical research and treatment has led to a great number of new and increasingly complex cases. Very often these new and complex cases do not appear to have much in common with the older, more simple cases wherein traditional ethical principles were explicated. Because of this a wider range of precedents is called for so that these principles may be adequately schematized in the new cases. In other words, we need precedents which approximate in some way or other the new cases so that we may continue to apply ethical principles by the process of analogy.

Moreover, the gradual decline of what may be called "medical absolutism," namely, the assumption that all dilemmas concerning proper medical practice can be solved by value-free "scientific" criteria, has contributed to a renewed respect for the wisdom of the past embodied in historical traditions. The most evident social manifestation of the attempt to qualify medical absolutism is the current rise in the number of medical malpractice suits before the courts. If medical practice is seen to require ethical controls, then the data of ethical precedents will be seen as at least equally important for medical judgment as the data of scientific experimentation.

Finally, the recognition of the ever-present danger of subjective fallibility in medical practice has led to a renewed emphasis on personal responsibility. Here again, this recognition has led to a renewed respect for those historical traditions which have emphasized personal responsibility for individual action. Thus, words like "sin" and "transgression" seem to be reentering contemporary ethical discourse. The use of such words and the concepts they name requires a renewed ethical interest in the religious traditions which are their cultural matrix.

Considering the rich history of normative ethics in Judaism, it is no surprise that this historical tradition is of increasing interest to many normative ethicians today, especially bioethicians. It is also no more surprising that several contemporary Jewish theologians are addressing themselves to this general ethical interest. I do not believe that this interest nor the response to it would be nearly as intense if current ethical discussion were primarily of the analytic or metaphysical variety. This is not because Judaism has nothing to offer these types of ethical inquiry, but, rather, because neither of these types of ethical inquiry is very much concerned with historical traditions. Analytical ethical inquiry in our day seems to be concerned with the analysis of "ordinary" language about ethical concerns. As such it is rather horizontal in its horizon of interest. History is essentially beyond its scope. On the other hand, metaphysically inclined ethical inquiry strives to construct ethics *sub specie aeternitatis*, that is, to understand ethics within some "perennial" philosophy or other. History is essentially beneath its scope.

2. *Religious Response*

Despite the fact that Judaism, along with other religious traditions, can provide a rich and varied number of precedents for contemporary ethical inquiry, it cannot simply be regarded as a historical source. This would only be possible if Judaism were exclusively an entity of the past. There have been times when Christianity or Islam or Secular Humanism has tried to reduce Judaism to the role of a "fossil"; however this has always been belied by the continuing life of the Jewish people and the continuing development of Jewish thought. Therefore, if philosophical ethicians are interested in Jewish tradition as a living tradition with its own interiority, then they must ask Judaism, either through its texts or through its teachers, three questions. (1) *What* aspects of Jewish tradition are ethically valid for the non-Jewish world? (2) *Why* are these aspects of Jewish tradition ethically valid for the non-Jewish world? (3) *How* are these aspects of Jewish ethical teachings to be applied to non-Jews? Thus we see that the analytic, metaphysical, and normative questions which we discovered at the beginning of this chapter characterize ethical inquiry in general, now characterized ethical inquiry into Judaism in particular. This is so because Judaism is a living tradition and its teachings should not be regarded simply as information to be taken by the outside world but as a gift which this tradition presents itself. The giving of such a gift presupposes an understanding of how the tradition itself makes such a giving possible. This understanding is a process of philosophical inquiry. Therefore, if the philosophically interested ethician wishes to truly receive from Jewish tradition, rather than merely pick from it, he must ask of Jewish tradition the same questions he asks in his general ethical inquiry. Which particular questions he begins to ask will most likely be determined by his own immediate situation. We have seen that in current ethical discourse the question is most likely to be the normative one, namely, how does Judaism apply to current cases? Nevertheless, this question cannot exclude the analytic or the metaphysical questions about Jewish ethics without losing an appreciation of the inherently Jewish matrix of what has been given.

Jewish theologians responding to this general ethical interest should be at least equally precise in their method of presentation. Although they are understandably flattered that after so many centuries of obscurity their views are finally being sought by the non-Jewish world, they should, nevertheless, remember that the tradition itself recognized that there are times when it can speak directly to the non-Jewish world and other times when it can only speak indirectly, even metaphorically.[5]

Throughout Jewish tradition I detect three distinct approaches to the problem of the relevance of Judaism to universal ethical concerns.

The first approach may be termed "dogmatic." It is based on the assumption that Judaism has something to say concerning universal ethical questions precisely because Jews should teach, if not actually politically enforce, certain of their own minimal moral laws among all humankind. This approach was explicitly stated by Maimonides. He writes, "And so Moses our master commanded by Divine revelation to force all humanity to accept the commandments commanded to the sons of Noah. And whoever does not accept them is to be executed. Whoever accepts them is called a 'resident-alien'."[6]

This is the approach taken by certain Jewish traditionalists today. When interest is expressed in Jewish ethical teaching they simply enunciate those aspects of Jewish tradition which apply to non-Jews. However, the presupposition for this simple enunciation is that the non-Jewish inquiry is based on an acceptance, at least a tacit acceptance, of the authority of Jewish law. Thus Maimonides indicated in one of his legal responsa that Jews are permitted to teach Scripture to Christians, but not to Muslims, because only Christians accept the revealed authority of the Hebrew Bible.[7] By so responding he was reinterpreting the earlier Talmudic prohibition of teaching Torah to non-Jews, namely, the Torah can only be taught to those who accept its revealed authority.[8] Christians are now excluded from this class of non-Jews. Nevertheless, one can hardly assume that current non-Jewish interest in Jewish ethical teaching is founded on any such acceptance of the authority of Jewish law. Therefore, based upon the very criteria of this traditionalist approach, it is questionable whether Judaism has anything to offer current ethical inquiry, with the exception, perhaps, of the ethical inquiry conducted by certain Christian fundamentalists. Most ethical inquiry today cannot be characterized as approaching Judaism with the attitude described by the prophet, "And many nations will go and say, 'Come let us go up to the mountain of the Lord, to the house of the God of Jacob, and He will instruct us in His ways and we shall walk in His paths' " (Micah 4:2). Furthermore, it should be recognized that most current ethical inquiry is conducted within the context of a pluralistic democratic society. The very foundations of such a society preclude the religious authority of one segment of the population over another, not only by means of overt political coercion but, also, by means of covert historical triumphalism.

The second approach might be termed "apologetic." This approach is based on the assumption that Judaism's ethical teaching is essentially the same as that of either liberal Christianity or Secular Humanism. Jewish apologists used to like to speak of the Jewish ethical "genius" and the "mission of Israel" to teach monotheistic ethics to the world.[9] The problem with this approach as the basis for the giving of Jewish ethics to the world is that it is essentially redundant. At most it simply reconfirms the consensual ethical principles held by the majority culture at any particular point in history. Jewish apologetics responds to non-Jewish ethical inquiry something like this. "We already have said what you are now saying; indeed we said it better." However, if this is the case, then the intrusion of Judaism into what is in fact an ethical *fait accompli* is actually a diluting element. It adds nothing to ethical discourse except reconfirmation or obscure applications, when intellectual effort would be far better spent in searching either for metaphysical foundations for ethical principles now only held by informal consent or for further normative applications of these principles. In other words, apologetics, as I have defined it here, is tedious. Furthermore, it adds an element of chauvinism which is itself ethically objectionable, perhaps even more so than the dogmatic triumphalism just described above.

The third approach to ethical inquiry into Judaism, and the one I wish to advocate in this chapter, might be called "phenomenological." In this approach the inquirer enters into the intelligible structure of Judaism and attempts to see the *method* of ethical judgment *at work*. Only this approach enables the inquiring ethician to ask all three fundamental ethical questions. Thus he asks: *What* is universally relevant in Jewish ethics? *Why* is one obliged by it? *How* is it to be applied? Of course one might very well object to this approach with the same objection raised against the dogmatic approach, namely, it presupposes an acceptance of the authority of Jewish tradition. However, further examination will indicate that this is not precisely true.

Ethical discussion in Judaism involves three distinct areas of interpersonal relationship: (1) the relationship between God and the Jews, (2) the relationship between Jews and their fellow Jews, (3) the relationship between Jews and non-Jews.

The ethics of the first area of relationship might be termed "covenantal"; that is, the relationship between God and the people of Israel, revealed in Scripture and developed by tradition, is the context for a series of mutual obligations. It presupposes God's election of Israel and Israel's acceptance of that election. A universal method in inquiry cannot be *ethically* interested in this area of relationship because it has no *practical* meaning outside of the religious Jewish community.

The ethics of the second area of relationship might be termed "ethnic"; that is, the relationships among Jews are the context for a series of mutual obligations. Such obligations presuppose membership in the Jewish people, if not as a religious entity then, minimally, as an ethnic entity. A universal method of ethical inquiry here also cannot be ethically interested in this area of relationship because it has no practical meaning outside the ethnic Jewish community.

In the area of relationship between Jews and non-Jews, however, we discover a subarea which can be relevant to the ethically interested non-Jewish inquirer.

Now the area of relationship between Jews and non-Jews can be divided into three subareas: (1) ritual, (2) political, (3) personal.

In the ritual subarea the constitution of the relationship between Jews and non-Jews is based upon the prior relationship between the Jews and God. Here the ritual status of non-Jews is defined by their *not* being members of the covenantal community but as being still related to God. As such the ritual import of their interaction with Jews is determined by their specific proximity to or remoteness from the Jewish relationship with God.[10]

In the political subarea the relationship between Jews and non-Jews is constituted on the basis of the prior relationship between Jews themselves. Here the political status of non-Jews is defined by their *not* being members of the Jewish community taken as a political entity but being, nevertheless, not totally unrelated to the political workings of the Jewish community. As such the political import of the interaction with Jews is determined by their particular empathy or enmity toward the Jewish people.[11]

It is now clear that neither the ritual nor the political subareas of the general relationship between Jews and non-Jews is relevant to the ethically interested non-Jewish inquirer. For in both these subareas there is no real mutuality of judgment; in both the non-Jews are judged but they themselves make no judgment. In other words, the non-Jews are not active participants in the process of ethical judgment which Jews are to make about them. This does not in any way imply that the whole area of relationship itself is not ethically significant. For Jews there is a definite and objective ethical structure for dealing with non-Jews on the ritual or the political level. However, non-Jews, by not being members of the Jewish community in either the covenantal or the ethnic sense, cannot very well be participants in the process of ethical judgment here.

3. *Noahide Law*

In the area of relationship between Jews and non-Jews, specifically in the subarea of personal interrelationships having no immediate ritual or political overtones, we finally locate the one specific context wherein general ethical inquiry into Judaism is truly possible. For at this level we discover ethically interesting data dealing with man qua man, data which, at least theoretically, involve human participation in the process of judgment, irrespective of whether or not one is a member of either the covenanted or the ethnic community of Israel.

This area of relationship between humans qua humans was outlined by the rabbinic sages, if not fully constituted by them, in the doctrine of "Noahide law." This doctrine proclaimed that all human beings, who are by Scriptural definition "sons of Noah," are bound by seven basic norms, namely, the prohibitions of (1) anarchy, (2) blasphemy, (3) idolatry, (4) murder, (5) sexual promiscuity (that is, adultery, incest, and homosexuality), (6) theft, and (7) brutality to animals. Furthermore, this law was considered to have preceded historically in Sinaitic covenant. Thus, although Jews were bound by the Sinaitic covenant to observe 613 laws, these subsequent laws were not seen as contradicting the earlier seven Noahide laws. Indeed, in those cases where the subsequent development of Jewish law seemed to contradict these basic human norms, the Jewish law was revised on the assumption that it would be immoral to let such a contradiction with the basic Noahide law stand. A late Talmudic principle summarizes this whole approach by stating, "There is nothing prohibited to the gentiles which is permitted to the Jews."[12] Moreover, it was recognized that the gentiles did not and could not limit their norms to the seven basic Noahide laws.[13] Here, as in the development of Jewish law, the only requirement was that the basic Noahide law not be contradicted. However, the inevitable process of historical specification of these basic laws, as well as the addition of new laws and customs, was recognized and accepted. Thus, for example, differing criteria in the areas of incestuous relationships, marriage and divorce, witness, and property were specifically noted and accepted in the Talmud and its related literature.[14] Hence we see that Noahide law was conceived of by the rabbis as the necessary (but not sufficient) foundation of morality, whether Jewish or non-Jewish. This common moral foundation is not obliterated by the subsequent religious and ethnic distinctions within humankind. As such it is the area wherein Jewish tradition provides data of universal ethical interest and significance.

It would be misleading of me, however, not to mention that my characterization of the significance of the doctrine of Noahide law is not and has not been accepted by many Jewish theologians. There have been those who have insisted that this doctrine presupposes non-Jewish acceptance of either the Jewish doctrine or revelation or the political right of Jewish authority to include non-Jews in its domain.[15] To refute these assertions, or even to show that they only represent one theological strain within Judaism, would take me far beyond the parameters of this chapter. Such a discussion would involve a minute analysis of Jewish law and theology. Suffice it to say, the interpretation of the significance of the doctrine of Noahide law, which I have presented here, represents a line of Jewish interpretation having enough precedent in the history of Judaism to be plausible. It was expressed best by the person who I believe was the greatest Jewish philosopher in modern times, Hermann Cohen: "The concept of the Noachide is the foundation for natural law not only as an expression of the objective law but also as the determination of the subject of the law. . . . The precepts required of the Noachide are moral precepts. The belief in the Jewish God is not required."[16] Although I differ from Cohen's Kantian approach to Judaism, especially to Jewish ethics, I think he was correct in characterizing the noncovenantal (in the Jewish sense of "covenant") character of Noahide law and the Noahide in Jewish theology.

4. *Noahide Reasoning*

Our discussion heretofore has led us to an answer to the analytic question: What is universally significant in Jewish ethics? We can now answer that it is the subject matter of Noahide law. It has been necessary to reach the answer to this question by a precise and explicit methodology. Only such a methodology can lead to answers which avoid the extremes of dogmatism and apologetics, both of which speak in the name of Judaism chauvinistically, thus making themselves irrelevant to ethical inquiry in a democratic society.

Next we must turn to the normative question. How does Noahide law prescribe for non-Jews? A full examination of this general question would take us far beyond the parameters of this chapter. One specific presentation of such a universal ethical norm, as enunciated by Jewish tradition, should be sufficiently illustrative. It deals with what is no doubt one of the most important normative questions ethics can deal with: How do we establish priority when two lives are threatening each other?

In the *Mishnah* we read, "If a woman is in hard labor, the fetus is to be cut up in her womb and brought out limb by limb, because her life takes precedence over its life. If the greater part of the fetus' body has already come out, it must not be destroyed because *one independent life is not to be pushed aside for another independent life.*"[17] Maimonides indicates in his discussion of this case that the principle enunciated is one "to which reason inclines" and, therefore, he does not seek to ground it in either a specific Scriptural verse or a rabbinic tradition or edict.[18] As such it is rational and universally binding. The rule is presented in the context of a specific case to which it is applied. We must now see how the rule applies more generally, how it functions as a general norm not just a specific judgment. As the case has been interpreted, prenatal life is seen as clearly different from postnatal life. In cases of unavoidable conflict postnatal life takes precedence over prenatal life. The factor of physical independence seems to be the criterion of distinction.[19] All life, both physically independent and dependent, is designated by the general term, *hayyim*. Physically independent life is specifically termed *nefesh* as in Genesis 2:7, "And He blew into his nostrils the breath of life and the man became a living being *(nefesh hayyah)*." The reason, then, it seems that the mother's life takes precedence over that of her unborn child is that while both are "living" *(hayyim)*, only she is a *nefesh*, a physically independent living being. In a later Talmudic passage the fetus is considered to be a "limb" of its mother and, hence, may be amputated as one would amputate any other life-threatening limb.[20] After a majority of the child's body is out of the mother's body, however, it itself is considered to be as much of a *nefesh* as is the mother. Her precedence ceases and both are now equally proximate to us as human persons.

In a later text the Babylonian Talmud considers the life-threatening fetus to be "like a pursuer."[21] The principle of the pursuer applied here was originally presented in another passage in the *Mishnah* where it is stated that a victim may be saved from either his or her mortal pursuer even if this requires that the victim or a bystander kill the pursuer to prevent the mortal assault on the victim.[22] The reasoning behind this principle seems to be as follows. Lives are taken to be equal in value, that is, they are all considered to be equally proximate to our moral concern. The pursuer forfeits his right to life by threatening another life. The balance of equality is broken if the pursuer is successful in his assault upon the victim. What the victim by acting in self-defense, or the bystander by acting as a rescuer, is doing is to affirm this threatened equality. To protect the pursuer, or to ignore him, would be to practically approve of the act about to be done.[23] As the sage Rava said to one contemplating murder to satisfy the order of a tyrant, "How do you know that your blood is redder? Perhaps the victim's blood is redder than yours!"[24] The life of the victim is considered to have priority over the life of the pursuer when only one life can be saved. This is presented as a rationally evident principle.

A number of scholars questioned why this principle was introduced in the discussion of abortion. Can the fetus be considered as a "pursuer" in that it is not conscious or rational and, hence, not morally culpable? R. Ezekiel Landau, an eighteenth-century Bohemian authority, answered that the introduction of this additional principle limited abortion to life-threatening situations alone.[25] Without it one might assume that the life of the fetus has no protection at all. The analogy with the pursuer grants fetal life a greater dignity and protection. That is, just as a pursuer only forfeits his life by his pursuit which can only be stopped by killing him, but would otherwise retain his right to life, so does a fetus have a right to life except when it becomes a threat to the life of its mother, a threat that can only be prevented from becoming lethal by killing it. Earlier, in a nonlegal context, the prenatal humanity of life was expressed by a Roman sage, Antoninus, in a dialogue with a second-century C.E. rabbi, Judah the Prince.[26] The rabbi agrees with the Roman sage and finds scriptual support for his view in Job 10:12. Two generations earlier the Palestinian sage R. Ishmael had ruled that feticide merited the punishment for murder, based on his exegesis of Genesis 9:6.[27]

This addition of the factor of pursuit qualifies the principle, "One life is not pushed aside for another life."[28] Whereas the basic principle seems to define equality in terms of the physical proximity of the lives before us,[29] the qualification indicates that the life of a victim of assault has a *moral proximity* over the life of its pursuer. It requires our most immediate attention. This same type of reasoning is used to justify one's saving his own life even if that will deny life-sustaining materials to someone else. One is not himself considered a pursuer in this situation because he is not actively threatening the other person's life; he is only saving the most proximate life—his own.[30] With this qualification we can see how the law developed from a simple distinction between prenatal and postnatal life into a more complex distinction between proximate and inapproximate human life, first in the physical sense and then in the moral sense. Thus, in the final analysis the principle *one life is not to be pushed aside for another* is qualified, not only in the case of abortion, but in any threatening situation where a victim is clearly identifiable.

Here we see the importance of analogy in normative Jewish ethics, an importance I have already indicated characterizes the historical component required by normative ethics in general. This designation of the fetus who threatens its mother's life as "like a pursuer" is an explicit use of analogy. The problem with analogy, however, is that there are as many or more points which distinguish the two cases compared as there are those which identify them. How, then, does one decide whether the difference or the identity is to be emphasized?

An important medieval gloss on the Talmud states that normative analogies are made by selection, that is, they are made by subjective means.[31] This acknowledgment reveals a number of important points about the analogical method of normative Jewish ethics as developed in Halakhah.

1. Although there is a factor of subjective selection, that selection is limited to precedents already found within the normative continuum. Thus, selection presupposes the primacy of the tradition and cannot function over and above it. This enables Halakhah to be both stable and flexible because the *internal* possibility of analogical reasoning indicates that Halakhah is an *open* system.

2. The use of analogy enables the halakhic system to be more sensitive to the ambiguities of human experience to which it must address itself. In the question of abortion which we have just examined, we have the ambiguity inherent in the conflict between two lives. A simple deduction from the principle that postnatal life has priority over prenatal life might indicate that postnatal life may destroy the prenatal life for any or no reason. The introduction of the principle of the pursuer indicated that only when the postnatal life is unavoidably victimized by the prenatal life can it defend itself even if the only such defense is to kill its "pursuer." This analogy is required because of the essential ambiguity involved in a conflict between two lives within one body. So, analogy here and elsewhere is sensitive to the phenomenology of morally complex situations.

3. Finally, the use of analogy by means of subjective selection, if it is not to be arbitrary, must look to criteria beyond the strict precedents of the law itself. These criteria are either theological or philosophical. In cases involving relationships between Jews the criteria will be theological, that is, one's understanding of the covenant will

have to constitute the general background for a specific ethical judgment. Thus, for example, Maimonides permits a convert to Judaism to recite the liturgical formula "God of *our* fathers," basing his judgment on the recognition that the convert's acceptance of the covenant between God and Israel makes him *as much* a son of Abraham as a native-born Jew.[32] The theological recognition of the common covenantal involvement enabled Maimonides to select an earlier norm which permitted this recitation and to reject another earlier norm which prohibited it. In the case of abortion, dealing as it does with a universally human situation, we have seen how the philosophical criteria of the value of life and moral proximity were operative in the legal analogy developed.

As an example of how Jewish normative reasoning operates, using rationally evident principles that are by no means limited to Jews, the development of this law indicates that normative conclusions in cases of complex moral conflict are not simply deduced from one principle. Rather, the analysis of the situation calls for the use of several principles. In the attempt to dialectically correlate these several principles a coherent conclusion emerges. This type of dialectical normative reasoning characterizes the method of Halakhah, whether the case concerns the relationship between God and the Jews, between Jews themselves, or between the Jews and non-Jews. We have now seen such a dialectic at work in the subarea of interpersonal relationships where covenantal or ethnic identity is not an issue. By delineating this area and showing how it functions normatively, we can see that Judaism offers the non-Jewish world an ethical exemplar without requiring anything more than practical ethical interest and concern on the part of the non-Jewish world.

5. *Metaphysical Considerations*

If one defines normative ethics as a self-sufficient system, then it is possible that Jewish normative ethics can be seen to fit this definition. And, moreover, I have both delineated and specifically described an area of Halakhah which is universally significant in the ethical sense; that is, it deals with man qua man as both the subject and the object of an area of law.[33] Nevertheless, such a characterization of Jewish normative ethics is only correct if we assume that Judaism is simply a form of "revealed legislation." My late, revered teacher, Professor Abraham J. Heschel, called this outlook "religious behaviorism."[34] Clearly Judaism, even on the most empirically evident level, is more than a system of behavior. It contains ideas as well as norms. Therefore, we must ask the metaphysical question: Why is there universal ethics in Judaism? In other words, what grounds this type of normative ethics?

Most traditionalists would answer this question with the reply: Jewish ethics, whether specific or universal, is an expression of the will of God. Such an answer is a correct statement about the way ethics has been presented in Jewish tradition. Norms are either presented as explicit Divine commandments revealed in Scripture, or as inferences from Scripture, or as specifically humanly legislated decrees generally sanctioned by Scripture. However, several outstanding classical Jewish theologians, most notably Maimonides, argued that a revealed source does not preclude rationality.[35] Indeed assuming that revealed law is the product of Divine wisdom precludes ascribing it to Divine caprice.[36] A noncapricious will is by definition rational. Furthermore, the rationality of those universal laws, which do not involve a specific covenant with the people of Israel, is most readily discoverable. Hence, a theological metaphysics of morals does not necessarily entail a theological epistemology of morals in all cases. Therefore, such a simple dogmatic assertion as we have just heard does not limit the rational character of Jewish ethics defined as universal in scope, as long as its general acceptance itself does not preclude rational explanation.

Nevertheless, despite the fact that such an assertion of Divine authority does not compete with the rationality of the area of ethics Judaism accepts as universal, it is not metaphysically satisfying. It is not because it itself is an ethical assertion. It provides a general prescription, a *Grundnorm*, to ground all of the specific norms found in the ethical system.[37] But such a provision does not and cannot answer the basic metaphysical question: Why is there ethics? Metaphysical inquiry seeks a transethical foundation for ethics, a *conditio per quam*.

In the areas of ethics dealing with Jews in their relationship with God and with each other, metaphysical inquiry has attempted to constitute the covenantal relationship between God and the people of Israel as the foundation presupposed by the promulgation of God's commandments in the Torah. Such inquiry has had to deal with the specific character of the relationship between God and the people of Israel. The commandments of the Torah specifically addressed to Jews explicitly involve this relationship and, indeed, are meaningless if it is not taken into constant consideration.

If the covenant at Sinai is taken to be the relational context for specifically Jewish ethics, what then constitutes the relational context for universal ethics in Judaism? Two approaches to this question can be located in Jewish theology.

The first approach to this question attempts to see the covenant between God and the Noahides in Genesis 8-9 as functioning similarly for non-Jews as the covenant between God and Israel functions for Jews. Just as God covenanted with the people of Israel and the Sinaitic law was revealed to concretize that covenant, so God earlier covenanted with the Noahides and the Noahide law was revealed to concretize that covenant.[38] However, the problem with this interpretation is that whereas the covenant with Israel is the necessary context for the Sinaitic law, as indicated by the numerous admonitions to remember the exodus from Egypt wherein this covenant began to become manifest to the whole people of Israel, the covenant with Noah and his progeny plays no such necessary role for Noahide law. None of the Noahide laws in any way involves the recognition of an historical event. Furthermore, whereas Israel's acceptance of the covenant is an indispensable element in its effectiveness, the acceptance of Noahide law by the gentiles is not explicitly mentioned in Scripture.[39] Therefore, although the term *berit* (covenant) is mentioned in both the context of the Noahide relationship with God and the Israelite relationship with God, the respective contexts wherein this word is used indicate very different meanings.[40]

The second approach to this question about the relational context for universal ethics in Judaism, and by far the more widely explicated approach, sees this relational context to be expressed in the doctrine, "Man is created in the image of God." Indeed, Scripture itself presents this doctrine of the *imago Dei* as the metaphysical grounding for the prohibition of bloodshed and its punishment. "Whosoever sheds the blood of a human being, his blood shall be shed by a human being, *because in the image of God He made man*" (Genesis 9:6; my italics). In the history of Jewish theology there have been basically three interpretations of the meaning of this metaphysical doctrine.

The first interpretation, formulated by Jewish theologians beginning with Philo, sees the image of God as being man's intellect.[41] This is what he shares with God and this is what distinguishes him from the animals. Such a doctrine was earlier put forth by Plato, Aristotle, and the Stoics.[42] Their doctrine undoubtedly influenced this interpretation of the *imago Dei*. Aside from the question of whether the human distinction from animals is only one of degree rather than one of kind, we must see whether such an interpretation adequately explains the doctrine of *imago Dei* as the metaphysical ground for universal ethics in Judaism.

I believe it is inadequate because, whereas God's intellect is unlimited, human intellect is limited due to human finitude: "My thoughts are not your thoughts" (Isaiah 55:8). Therefore, intellect does not constitute a relationship of mutual presence *between* man and God. All this interpretation can assert is that man's intellect is somehow *derived from* God's intellect. However, without a special mutuality we get back to creation in general, namely, the assertion that all being is somehow contingent on God. As such we cannot constitute the human distinction from the rest of creation because such an assumption does not indicate how the relation between human and Divine intellect is any different from the relation between all created being and Divine Being. And since this relation between created and Uncreated Being cannot be intelligibly constituted, as Maimonides astutely observed,[43] the interpretation which sees the *imago Dei* as being intellect cannot function as an intelligible metaphysical ground for ethics, anymore than the doctrine of *creatio ex nihilo* can function as an intelligible metaphysical ground for cosmology.

The second interpretation of the doctrine of man created in the image of God sees the image of God as being man's freedom.[44] This is what he shares with God and this is what distinguishes him from the rest of creation. However, here again whereas God's freedom is unlimited, man's freedom is limited by the world which precedes his emergence. Only God can say, "I will be whatever I will be" (Exodus 3:14).[45] If God freely wills that man be free, then that can only mean that human freedom is entirely different from Divine freedom and cannot limit it in any way.[46] Here again we do not have a relationship of mutual presence. Here again we get back to creation in general and are unable to distinguish the creation of human freedom from the creation of anything else in the universe. This is why Kant and his Jewish followers, who saw rational autonomy as the ground of ethics,[47] would not constitute the relationship between man and God as being in any way metaphysically prior to the relationship between man and man. For them man creates his own autonomy. God at best simply endorses it and enables it to emerge in history.[48]

These two interpretations of what the doctrine of *imago Dei* signifies—the first designating human intellect and the second designating human freedom—are not only inadequate to explain the uniqueness of the human relationship with God, they are also inadequate to explain the fullness of human existence itself. For both involve a reduction of existence to essence.

To assert that the intellect is the *imago Dei* is to theologically reassert Aristotle's philosophical assumption that "man is the only animal who posesses rational speech *(logon)*."[49] Thus the value of everything in human existence which is not rational is determined solely by its potential for rational use. Its value is, then, clearly relative and subordinate. Such a metaphysical assertion is inadequate to ground an ethical system which regards human life as inviolable, even if it has not the capacity for ratiocination and rational communication *(logos)*. Thus, such an assertion cannot ground, for example, the traditional prohibitions of abortion, infanticide, or the euthanasia of the comatose, the catatonic, or the severely retarded.[50] Persons who are the objects of these acts are not rational by any definition of that term. This does not mean that this metaphysical assertion necessarily leads one to advocate these practices. However, by being unable to ground their prohibition this metaphysical assertion leaves room for further assertions which do lead to the permission of these practices, or even advocate them. And these subsequent assertions do not contradict the prime assertion that humanness is rationality and, therefore, can function in harmony with it.

To assert that freedom is the *imago Dei* is to theologically reassert Aristotle's philosophical assumption that "man is a political being by nature."[51] In this way the value of everything in human society which is not a free political participant is determined solely by its political potential. Here, too, the nonpolitical aspects of human society are clearly relative and subordinate. Such a metaphysical assertion is even more inadequate than the first to ground certain fundamental, traditional ethical norms. For whereas the assertion that humanness is rationality regards ratiocination and rational communication as the *conditio per quam* of human life, the assertion that humanness is freedom means that the value of human life is determined by the degree of its participation in human society. Freedom is clearly a political idea, that is, it manifests itself as the presupposition of legislation.[52] Only free beings are the subjects of law. Now it is conceivable that one can be rational but politically useless—a paraplegic or a terminal cancer patient, for example. It is inconceivable, however, that one can be politically useful without being rational. Therefore, human freedom, as a politically determined reality, is even more restrictive than human rationality which is a verbally determined reality. Hence, if freedom is what makes one human, then the ethical prohibition of treating another human being as a thing rather than a person has no grounding. This is why the Roman Code of Justinian acknowledged that slavery was sanctioned by the *ius gentium* because it was present in every society *(consensus gentium)* but was, nevertheless, contrary to the natural law itself.[53] What was recognized here is that human freedom is determined by an external relation, namely, one's status in society. Rationality, on the other hand, is determined by an internal relation, the relation between mind and body. This distinction between rationality and freedom was missed by Kant, who saw no difference between a rational person's relationship with himself and his relationship with society.[54] Therefore, the assertion that human freedom is humanness allows for the permission of even more acts that traditional ethics has prohibited than the older assertion that humanness is rationality.

It should be noted, furthermore, that both of these assertions are extremely vulnerable to the critiques of Feuerbach and Freud, who see God as an idealized human projection.[55] For both assertions see immanent human characteristics as finite participants in an infinite Divine reality. However, since the mode of participation is never constituted it is easier to interpret such assertions as occasioned by human feelings of finite helplessness, since one is able to describe the human desire for infinity. Participation in Divine reality is not required for an intelligible description of either human rationality or human freedom. Hence one can see how the theological assertions that the *imago Dei* is either rationality or human freedom so easily lend themselves to the atheistic assertion that, in truth, God is the *imago hominis*.

The third interpretation of the doctrine that man is created in the image of God asserts that humanness is man's whole presence before God and man's apprehension of this presence. As the early rabbinic sage, R. Akiba, put it, "Beloved is man who is created in an image *(tzelem)*; by additional love was this made known to him as it is said, 'in the image of God He made man'."[56] Whereas the other two interpretations of this Scriptural doctrine reduce humanness to a predominant factor within human existence,[57] this transcendent definition asserts that man's uniqueness is God's intimate knowledge of him and his awareness of this relationship and his ability to respond directly to God. God knows man in his whole existence and, unlike man, does not have to abstract any qualities from that whole existence. "Man sees appearances, but God sees the heart" (1 Samuel 16:7); and the rabbinic tradition emphasizes that "heart" refers to both the cognitive and the noncognitive, the volitional and the nonvolitional, aspects of human existence.[58] Thus the image of God does not refer to human properties but to the possibility of a God-initiated relationship of mutual presence between God and man. It is the context of man's response to the commandments of God. This was best brought out, I believe, by the 19th century Hasidic master, R. Menahem Mendel of Vishnitz, when he commented on the use of the plural in Gen. 1:26, "Let *us (na'aseh)* make man in *our* image according to *our* likeness": "God said to man, 'let us make man in our image according to our likeness.' ... to make the whole man *(adam ha-shalem)* ... you and I must make him. First there must be an awakening below and afterwards it is aided above."[59]

Here we find expressed the idea that humanness consists in the capacity for a relationship with God. Man's true dignity, his inviolable sanctity, comes from his being capable of being in the presence of God and being called to respond to God's revelation to him. From this follows the most basic norm—human blood is not to be shed. The norm follows from this basic metaphysical assertion because to violate it is to practically contradict the *truth* of human existence. It further leads us to conclude that, since a human person's existence in its entirety is uniquely present before God, only the absence of breath, the *conditio sine qua non* of both independent physical life and rational discourse, indicates the "passing away" of that presence. "And the Lord God formed man of the dust of the earth and He breathed the breath of life into his nostrils and man became a living being" (Genesis 2:7).[60] To limit the definition of human life only to the manifestation of rationality or freedom indicates that the *conditio per quam* of humanness is either man's relationship with himself or with society. On the other hand, the doctrine of the image of God asserts that man is an inseparable mental and physical presence and that one cannot be abstracted from the other. And, moreover, since in cases of doubt the benefit of the doubt should always be in favor of human life,[61] one should not be regarded as dead, that is, passed away from human life, unless the signs of *both* mental and physical life are clearly absent.[62] This principle of the benefit of a doubt can also be extended to prenatal life as well. For, in the absence of conflict with a fully present human life, a life as soon as it is conceived by an act of intercourse between two fully present human beings should be inviolable. This metaphysical criterion, then, enables all human life, from conception to mental and physical death, to be included within the basic norm: Human blood is not to be shed.

6. Conclusion

I have tried to show, at least in outline, that Judaism is indeed of interest to the philosophical ethician—that it gives itself to his analytic, normative, and metaphysical inquiry. I have also tried to indicate an approach to this interest, working from within the classical texts of Jewish tradition, an approach which attempts to be phenomenological rather than dogmatic or apologetic. By participating in this process of inquiry, by enabling the ethical riches of Jewish tradition to show themselves to an ethically concerned seeker, Jewish theologians are thereby fulfilling Moses' admonition, "See, I have imparted to you laws and norms, as the Lord my God has commanded me. . . . Observe them faithfully, for that will be proof of your wisdom and discernment to other peoples, who on hearing of all these laws will say, 'Surely this is a great nation of wise and discerning people' " (Deuteronomy 4:5-6).[63] According to one rabbinic tradition the Israelites were commanded to write the Torah, or at least its most universal teachings, on stones in all the languages of humankind.[64] However, it was the non-Jews themselves who came to take what they believed pertained to them. The dialogue between Judaism and the ethically interested world is a relationship of careful giving and equally careful taking.

THE THREAT OF NUCLEAR WAR: JEWISH PERSPECTIVES

1. *Introduction*

For the past thirty-nine years, since we have been aware of the threat of nuclear war, an enormous body of diverse opinion has emerged concerning this question. It would seem that this diverse body of opinion, however, can now be reduced to two basic viewpoints. (1) Nuclear war would necessarily involve the extinction of human civilization, if not all life on this planet. (2) Nuclear war, while undoubtedly more destructive than any other war heretofore in human history, would not necessarily involve the destruction of human civilization or the destruction of all life on this planet. For the first point of view nuclear war is truly eschatological, that is, it marks the absolute end of human existence, no future beyond it being conceivable. For the second point of view, on the other hand, the difference between nuclear war and conventional war is one of degree—even vast degree—but not one of kind. Wars have been a continual part of human history, but they have not transcended human history by providing it with an absolute limit. —So these people say.[1]

It would seem, then, that this dispute is in essence empirical, and that it can be ultimately resolved on the basis of enough evidence and the testimony of enough expert specialists. If this is the case, it is becoming more and more plausible to agree with the viewpoint which holds that there is a fundamental difference in kind between nuclear war and conventional war, that nuclear war would most certainly entail the end of the world as we humans now know it. This point of view is presented in the pastoral letter, "The Challenge of Peace: God's Promise and Our Response," drawn up by the National Conference of Catholic Bishops in 1982. My references are to the first draft of October, 1982, but the points I discuss are reiterated in the final version as well.

2. *The Theology of the Pastoral Letter*

I would like to examine, some of the presuppositions of the document, which is an articulate expression of one major viewpoint in the debate over nuclear war. These presuppositions, being in essence theological, involve questions which are far deeper than the empirical question about the probable effects of nuclear war on our life and civilization in this world. As such, it will be even more difficult to address these questions than the already difficult empirical question I have just mentioned. In the context of this theological reflection on a major social and political question—if not *the* major social and political question—of our age, I hope to bring some small light from the insights of Jewish tradition.

If I have read the pastoral letter correctly, it presupposes two points. (1) Although man is not the creator of his world, man has the power to totally destroy it. (2) The affirmation of the absolute value of human life is a rationally self-evident principle. Despite the erudite citations from Scripture and Roman Catholic tradition, both of these points are presented in such a way as to be within the discipline known as "natural theology," a discipline which for many Catholics found its most profound expression in the writings of St. Thomas Aquinas. These points are presented as principles which, using a Talmudic expression, "if they had not been written, they should have been written."[2]

Nevertheless, these two points raise important theological problems, which indicate that they might not be so indisputable after all.

I was amazed that the pastoral letter, which is an essentially theological document, and which refers to "God's Promise", never once mentions that Divine promise to Noah after the Flood, namely, "I will uphold my covenant with you, and all flesh will never again be cut off by the waters of the flood; there will be no flood again to destroy *(le-shahet)* the earth." (Genesis 9:11)

Now one could of course argue two exegetical points which would evade this problem. (1) The text only speaks about a flood *of water*. Perhaps other forms of destruction are excluded. (2) The text only speaks about God's restraint of his destructive potential, not man's restraint of his own. However, neither of these evasions is very convincing.

Even though there is one rabbinic opinion which holds that the Divine promise does not preclude "a destruction *(mabul)* of fire and sulphur", most rabbinic treatments of this text see it as the manifestation of God's first promise to humankind. This promise, then, is the paradigm for all subsequent Divine promises. Thus Isaiah states, "for this which I have promised is like the waters of Noah to me" (Isaiah 54:9).[3] God's first promise would not have been very heartening if it implied that some form of destruction other than a flood was not included in it. Surely God was addressing a more widespread human fear than hydrophobia! Global destruction is global destruction, and the fear of global destruction is the fear of global destruction, irrespective of the means of global destruction.

Concerning the attempted distinction between God's promise not to destroy the earth again and man's ability to do so, one must remember that the first destruction of the earth, the Flood, was seen by Scripture as the direct consequence of human sinfulness. Thus the very verb used in the Divine promise not to destroy the earth again —shahet—is used to describe the very state of affairs which led to the first destruction. "And God saw that the earth was indeed corrupt (nishhatah), for all flesh had corrupted (hishheet) its way on earth." (Genesis 6:12) And the preceding verse (6:11) tells us what that corruption was, namely, "the earth was filled with violence."

Therefore, it would seem that careful exegesis surely indicates that it is Scriptural doctrine that man's sinfulness can never again cause global destruction. Surely the counterpoint offered by this recurrent Scriptural doctrine must be taken with utmost seriousness by Jewish and Christian theologians who look to the Hebrew Bible as the word of God, however we might use the secular tools of philology, archaeology and history to aid us in our sacred exegetical tasks.

The second presupposition of the pastoral letter is that the affirmation of the absolute value of human life is a rationally self-evident principle. However, this too is open to theological criticism.

Scripture states the following about the affirmation of human life. "See I place before you today life and good, death and evil . . . the blessing and the curse. You shall choose life that you and your progeny will live" (Deuteronomy 30:15, 19). Note that a choice between good and evil, blessing and curse, is not presented. It seems practically impossible that one would affirm anything other than what he or she believed to be good and blessed, at least for him or herself, no matter how misguided the subsequent choice of means might be. Aristotle was right when he said that such affirmation is presupposed by any choice.[4] The choice between life and death, however, is not self-evident in this sense. Many people have chosen death believing it to be both good and blessed. Did not Jonah beg God to die saying, "My death is better (tob) than my life" (Jonah 4:8)? Did not Socrates argue that:

> The state of death *(to thethnanai)* is one of two things: either it is virtual
> nothingness . . . or a change and migration of the soul from this to
> another place. And if it is unconsciousness *(mēdemia aisthēsis)* . . . death
> would be a wonderful *(thaumasion)* gain.[5]

Did not Freud argue that:

> The attributes of life were at some time evoked in inanimate matter . . .
> The tension which then arose in what hitherto been an inanimate
> substance endeavoured to cancel itself out. In this way the first instinct
> came into being: the instinct to return to the inanimate state.[6]

Therefore, it seems as though the categorical identification of human life with good
is not something which comes from reason and experience but, rather, from revelation.
If human life as the *imago Dei* is sacred and thus intrinsically good, it is because of its
capacity for a relationship with God, not because of such inherent properties as intellect
and will, which can easily be shown to be non-existent when inoperative.[7] Indeed, in the
creation account in Scripture the goodness of the whole created order is not declared by
creation itself about itself but, rather, it is declared by God about *His* creation. "And
God saw all that he made and it was indeed very good" (Genesis 1:31).

Nevertheless, no matter how correct my Scriptural exegesis and theology might be,
it would seem as though it leads to some rather unacceptable moral conclusions. (1) If
God will never again allow man's sinfulness to destroy life on earth, then it would seem
that nuclear war and conventional war are in essence the same. Thus all the old rules
about "just war," rules which assumed that human history always transcends wars, are as
operative as they ever were.[8] All the attempts to see nuclear war as something *sui
generis* are thereby rejected by this theology. (2) If the rule to always choose life as good
is revealed rather than rational, then how can people of faith convince those of no faith,
or of faiths not based on Scriptural revelation—the majority of the people of the
earth—that nuclear war is inherently evil because it threatens all of human life? Jewish
tradition was wary of even the most cogent exegesis if it led to results unacceptable to
the moral consensus of the community.[9] Surely there is an international consensus, a
consensus gentium, that nuclear war is evil and that everyone should affirm the goodness,
if not the sanctity, of all human life.

3. *Warning About Imminent Destruction and Human Responsibility*

At this point in our reflection we must examine what the threat of global destruction, or any mass destruction, means in theological terms.

It seems to be the purpose of that growing number of people, who advocate that nuclear war would quickly end in global destruction, to warn everyone else about these dire consequences. Hopefully, this warning will inspire masses of people to force those to whom they have given political power to reverse the nuclear arms race and eventually ban nuclear weapons altogether. The rabbis saw Noah's purpose in taking a long time to build the Ark in public as being similar, namely, to warn his fellow humans about the coming disaster.[10] *Nihil volitum nisi praecognitum,* that is, one cannot will what he does not know. Only true information will lead to correct choice.[11] This presupposes, then, that such knowledge will heighten the sense of human moral power to affect a clear change in the course of historical events. However, I seriously question whether our experience corroborates this judgment. Since the nuclear destruction of Hiroshima and Nagasaki in 1945, the obvious consequences of nuclear war have become evident to almost everyone. Yet has this led to a feeling of moral power, or a feeling of moral impotence? Do we now feel more in control of historical destiny or less in control of it? It seems to me that the latter is the case, that the more we talk of the imminence of nuclear war and holocaust the more we impress on ourselves how little power we really do have over the course of human events. Afterall, nuclear holocaust could come as the result of mechanical failure in a computer! This is the effect of becoming preoccupied with doom.

Come and see how Scripture judges the effects of such thinking and talk.

> My Lord God of hosts summoned on that day weeping and mourning, baldness and the wearing of sackcloth. But instead there was joy and gladness, the killing of cattle and the slaughter of sheep. "Eat meat and drink wine! Eat, drink for tomorrow we die!" (Isaiah 22:12-13)

In other words, the threat of imminent destruction does not necessarily lead to greater social responsibility and personal care for the genuine needs of others. Rather, more often than not it leads to the very opposite, to greater narcissistic preoccupation with immediate self-gratification and raw hedonism. Surely our own experience these past thirty-nine years confirms the truth of Scripture's description of the attitude of the people of ancient Jerusalem on the eve of their doom. Have we not seen an unending emphasis on narcisistic self-indulgence, on individual pleasure?

Now why do I cite this fact as a disturbing one? It is not because I adhere to any Manichean or quasi-Manichean notion that the body is evil and its pleasures sinful per se. How could I as a theologian rooted in the Hebrew Scriptures adhere to such a notion when the chief expression of God's love for his people is seen through the intense eroticism of Song of Songs?[12] Furthermore, a prominent rabbinic tradition regarded the Nazarite's vow of abstinence from the legitimate pleasure of wine, for example, as being itself sinful.[13] Asceticism per se found few adherents in my tradition.[14]—No, it is not any such dualistic metaphysics which causes my discomfort and concern. Rather, it is the fact that the emphasis on pleasure as an end to itself too often diverts human attention from the real needs of others, attention which requires sacrifice and at times suffering for the sake of what is good for all. Along these lines I would like to share with you a rabbinic treatment of the "eat, drink and be merry" passage we just saw in Isaiah.

> At a time when the community is in a state of sorrow one should not say, 'I will go to my house to eat and drink and it will be well with my life! Concerning such a person Scripture states, 'But instead there was joy and gladness . . . and what is written thereafter? 'There was revealed in my ears the Lord of Hosts saying that this iniquity will not be atoned even until they die.' (Isaiah 22:14) This is the quality of ordinary people (midat baynonim—people who fear death [Rashi]). But concerning the quality of the wicked it is written, 'Come I will buy wine. Let us get drunk together with liquor. And tomorrow will be the same as today.' (Isaiah 56:12) And what is written after that? 'The righteous one perishes and no one considers that because of evil the righteous one was taken away.' (57:1)—But let one be in sorrow with the community.[15]

Here we see a prophecy that well describes what two generations living with the imminent threat of nuclear war have experienced. The belief that the end of the world is not only possible but highly probable has not engendered a greater sense of human community. Rather, by emphasizing that there is no secure future it has enabled many to conclude that any sacrifice for the future is an exercise in futility, that the only security is the enclosed present of the physical senses. Is it not the hope for a future which enables community to develop toward the common horizon of what is yet to come out of a shared present? "Thus says the Lord, 'stop your voice from weeping and your eyes from tears, for there is reward for your effort . . . and there is hope for your future,' says the Lord." (Jeremiah 31:15-16) Indeed, after the cessation of the flood the new humanity emerging from the sons of Noah had to hear the following before they could be given law and thereby be required to act responsibly again.

> And the Lord said to himself, 'I will not ever again curse the earth because of man, for the inclination of man's heart is bad from his youth, and I will not smite all life which I have made. Furthermore, all the seasons of the earth: planting and harvest, cold and heat, summer and winter, shall not cease.' (Genesis 8:21-22)

Or, as one of the most astute students of politics in recent times, the late Professor Hans J. Morgenthau, wrote conversely, over twenty years ago,

> The significance of the possibility of nuclear death is that it radically affects the meaning of death, of immortality. It affects that meaning by destroying most of it . . . Thus nuclear destruction destroys the meaning of death by depriving it of its individuality. It destroys the meaning of immortality by making both society and history impossible. [16]

Is it not this despair of the future, with its narcissistic implications, which diverts so much of the time, energy and money, especially of our youth, away from the building of true community into such things as drugs, games, and depersonalized, irresponsible, sex? [17] I raise all of these points because it does not seem to me that the affirmation of the probability of nuclear destruction leads to a sense of personal and social power and freedom needed to radically change the course of human events. Rather, it seems more often than not to lead to the sense of powerlessness and meaninglessness about which T.S. Eliot wrote over fifty years ago in "The Hollow Men,"

> *This is the way the world ends.   This is the way the world ends.   This is the way the world ends.   Not with a bang but a whimper.* [18]

Furthermore, no matter how much we may protest to the contrary, the emphasis on nuclear destruction has actually stimulated the development of the so-called "conventional" weapons. For no one can argue that they would lead to global destruction. All they can do is destroy part of our world. After all the talk about the global destruction of nuclear war, the old-time conventional weapons sound better and better. It is here where the danger lies, it seems to me. By making nuclear weapons and the probability of nuclear war something *sui generis*, we have accomplished two rather dubious results. (1) We have increased the sense of international despair, which mitigates against reasoned and free responsibility. (2) We have diverted instead of confronted the perpetual problem of human sinfulness and aggression by concentrating on only one symptom of it—albeit a terrifying symptom-instead of dealing with the many symptoms of it, let alone the deeper causes.

The belief that man can indeed destroy his world is emphasized by the pastoral letter in these words.

> We can threaten the created order. For people of faith this means we read the Book of Genesis with a new awareness; the moral issue at stake in nuclear war involves the meaning of sin in its most graphic dimensions. Every sinful act is a confrontation of the creature and the Creator. Today the destructive potential of the nuclear powers threatens the sovereignty of God over the world he has brought into being. We could destroy his work. (312)

While I am sympathetic with the moral concern that inspired such a statement, I cannot accept its theology. I do not believe, basing myself on Scriptural revelation, that man has the power to so threaten the sovereignty of God. In fact, I believe that the Divine promise to never again permit global destruction mitigates against such arrogant delusion, delusion which lies at the heart of sin. For the moral task of Scripturally based theology today should be to convince humankind that its desire to engage in nuclear war is futile because of our creaturely limits. All such attempts to magnify the human power to wage war against God have had the results of increasing, not decreasing, sin and its destructive manifestations. Did not the very first rejection of God's sovereignty and authority begin when the first woman, and then the first man with her, believed that they could "be like God" (Genesis 3:5), thereby replacing his sovereignty and authority with a new equality between heaven and earth? Furthermore, rabbinic tradition saw that one of the motivations of the builders of the Tower of Babel was to wage war against God. And it was precisely this group, seeking as they did international unity based on delusion of their own power, who experienced disunity, dispersion, and the loss of the power of effective communication.[19]

I am at least as desirous that the threat of nuclear war be ended as those with whose theology I cannot agree. However, I believe that we should not be emphasizing the power of the war-makers to destroy the entire planet and with its God's kingship. Rather, I believe we should emphasize that they only have the power to destroy themselves, that in truth "the victory is the Lord's" (I Chronicles 29:11)—with or without them. It is more frightening for people to believe that their destructive power will destroy themselves but that the world will go on without them, than to believe that they can bring the whole world down with them as Samson said, "let my life die with the Philistines" (Judges 16:30). This theological point comes out in the rabbinic treatment of the scriptural verse uttered by King David, "were it that I believed that I will see the goodness of the Lord in the land of the living" (Psalms 27:13). The rabbis were surprized that pious King David was so lacking in faith that he seemed to deny belief in God's ultimate sovereignty and providence. However, they put the following in his mouth as a means of explanation. "Master of the universe! I am certain that You indeed recompense the righteous in the future, but I do not know whether my portion is among them, lest my sin prevent it."[20] In other words, the sinner is more likely to change when he is told by the people of faith of the ultimate futility not the ultimate efficacy of his sinful power. I think that this is both better theology and better psychology.

4. *Halakhah and Social Priorities*

Heretofore the insights from Jewish tradition I have attempted to show you have all been from that tradition in its aggadic manifestation, that is, that aspect of our tradition which deals with attitudes and suggestions about attitudes, rather than with specific norms. For Halakhah which does deal with such specific normative questions, cannot be invoked when dealing with the question of global destruction, because this theme is one with which the human imagination alone has dealt, but it is not within the realm of actual human experience. We have no specific normative precedents for dealing with the question of global destruction. Where there are no precedents there is no Halakhah.[21] Nevertheless, if we are not to believe that God will break his promise and permit global destruction, then we do have normative precedents for dealing with the question of how to control human aggression and where the priorities of society are to lie.

The Talmud presents the following example of a halakhic treatment of social priorities.

> In Ammon and Moab the tithe for the poor is to be given even during the
> Sabbatical year, as an earlier authority indicated: Many towns were
> captured by those who left Egypt but were not captured by those who

left Babylonia. For the sanctification of the land in the first instance was only established for that time (le-sha'atah) but not for the future. They excluded these towns from the latter conquest in order that the poor might rely on them during the Sabbatical year.[22]

To see the relevance of this passage we must explain it. During the Sabbatical year, when the land was to lie fallow, the people were to basically live off of produce they had already accumulated during the previous six years (Leviticus 25:3). Now all of this was well and good if one had sufficient means to do such long-term planning. The poor, on the other hand, might more often than not be in great difficulty, especially if there was not enough food around. Therefore, the rabbis reasoned that Jewish society limited its own sovereignty and limited the results of its military power. In other words, it decided that the needs of the most helpless, the most vulnerable people in its population, took priority over the fruits of military success and the ultimate concerns of territorial integrity and political security.

The historical background of this type of legal enactment can be seen in the differing approaches to national destruction taken by the Zealots and the Pharisees, respectively, in the first century of this era.

The Zealots chose national sovereign pride over national life without it. At least according to Josephus, they chose suicide at Masada as their only option. Josephus put the following soliloquy in the mouth of their leader, Eleazar ben Jair.

> Let our wives thus die not dishonoured, our children unacquainted with slavery; and when they are gone, let us render a generous service to each other . . . in keeping with our initial resolve, we preferred death to slavery (thanaton thelomenoi pro douleias).[23]

The Pharisees, conversely, chose national life over national pride. Thus the Talmud notes that when Jerusalem was to be destroyed the Pharisee leader, Rabban Johanan ben Zakkai, bargained with the Roman commander, Vespasian, asking for "Yavneh and its sages."[24] By so doing he saved at least a remnant of Jewish life and community rather than opting for more death and destruction. And, indeed, subsequent Jewish tradition attempted to mitigate as much as possible against heroic martyrdom.[25] The lives of the people were to take precedence over their pride and even their full national political sovereignty.

The lesson to be learned from this normative precedent and the historical situation

of the first century Jewish community should be clear by now. The nuclear arms race
has not only threatened us with great destruction in the future, it has already led in the
present to the neglect of the immediate human needs of all the nations in the world. For
the more we spend in time, money and energy on the arms race, the less we spend in
dealing with poverty, crime, alienation and all of the human ills which plague us more
and more. Instead of making all of our arguments for arms freezes, arms reduction, and
preventing nuclear war hang on the question of future nuclear holocaust, let them hang
on the more immediate question of where do our present priorities lie, and where should
they lie.[26]

Along these lines I find the attitude of the current Reagan administration to be
morally wrong because the needs of the insatiable military establishment are seen as
prior and immediate, whereas the truly wretched in this land are told to wait and be
patient and ask for less. Indeed, the prophet Samuel warned the people of Israel, who
wanted a king so as to achieve military superiority, that in the end "you will be his
slaves" (I Samuel 8:17).[27] Our current government policies of giving more and more to
the military and less and less to the needy are morally wrong and based on theological
error, for they assume that our security lies "in chariots and horses" (Psalms 20:8) instead
of in the righteousness of God which bids us "to loosen the bands of wickedness and untie
the cords of the yoke; to free the oppressed; to share your bread with the hungry, and to
take the suffering poor into your home . . . " (Isaiah 58:6-7). If we demand that the social
and political priorities in this nation be changed, we will then see an automatic decrease
in the arms race and a lessening of the threat of nuclear war. There is just so much
money we can spend. The question is where it is spent first. We have erred in being
more concerned with our future safety than with our present needs. "The secret things
belong to the Lord our God, but what has been revealed is for we and our children to do
now, all the words of this Torah." (Deuteronomy 29:28)

5. *Conclusion*

The last issue I would like to consider is the assumption that it is self-evident that
human life is absolutely good and, therefore, always to be affirmed. Earlier I questioned
that assumption. For whereas we are not commanded by God to choose good, inasmuch
as we could not choose what seemed to us to be bad, we are commanded by God to

choose life. The problem that this presents is that it seems to limit absolute concern with the sanctity of human life to those who base their faith on Scriptural revelation. As we all know, the majority of the people of the world either base their moral choices on totally secular realities, or on sacred realities which are not those of Scriptural revelation. In other words, does not our theology limit our moral effectiveness in an international world, in this "global village."[28] This is certainly an important problem for people of faith who wish to address issues which are not formally religious.

Nevertheless, I believe it is more humanly realistic, as well as more theologically correct, to assume that the absolute sanctity of human life is by no means self-evident. If it were, it would be hard to accept the miserable and dangerous situation human beings find themselves in this last part of the twentieth century, a situation epitomized by the threat of nuclear war. When we assume that it is self-evident that all human life is sacred, we are actually engaging in a very dangerous type of Utopian thinking. Utopian thinking assumes that if only humankind would acknowledge the obvious, the human condition would be quickly and radically improved. Utopianism is dangerous because it totally underestimates the obstinancy of the human heart, the difficulty of the human condition, and the complexity of human history. All three of these factors work against the sanctity of human life.

The obstinancy of the human heart is its pride. "The heart is most devious; who can know it?" (Jeremiah 17:9) This pride all too frequently prefers the works of human hands to the existence of human life itself. For humankind's propensity for idolatry is precisely its preference for its own works over those of God, of which human life is in His image and likeness. "Their idols of silver and gold are the works of human hands. . . . All who make them will be like them; all who trust in them." (Psalms 115:4, 8) Indeed, the Talmud queries that if one is to love God "with all your life (be-khol nafshekha)" (Deuteronomy 6:5), is it not obvious that one should love God "with all your possessions (be-khol me'odekha)?" Why does the obvious inference have to be specifically mentioned in Scripture? The answer is that some people, maybe most people, prefer their possessions to their own life, and certainly to the lives of others.[29] In ancient Jewish legend one of the sins of the builders of the Tower of Babel was that they were more upset over the loss of a brick than over the death of a worker.[30]

The difficulty of the human condition is seen in the fact that no one moral issue is ever isolated from a plethora of related issues. The attempt to see the threat of nuclear war as something *sui generis* is a simplistic avoidance of the true complexity of the human condition. It is becoming one more example of "one issue politics" which in our day so quickly retreats into fanatical sectarianism. The threat of nuclear war is related to many other issues and cannot be adequately addressed without dealing with them as well. It is related to the whole question of technology. What is man's proper relation to the works of his hands? Is man the master or the steward of the earth? It is related to the whole question of man's relation to his own body. Does man look to his own progeny or to the work of his hands for his authentic future? If we are concerned about there being no future for this generation of the earth's children, what have we been doing or not doing to provide them with an authentic present? Rabbinic tradition states that the sin of the two and one half tribes who did not want to go into the Promised Land with the rest of the people of Israel was that they stated "we will build sheep-pens for our flocks and, then, cities for our children" (Numbers 32:16).[31] Their priorities were out of order and, indeed, they were a society far more violent than that of the rest of the people.[32] The problem of nuclear war is connected with the whole difficulty of the human condition and its propensity for violence and destruction. Thus our efforts can never be total solutions for "the work is not for you to finish, but you are not free to neglect it either."[33]

The complexity of human history indicates that whatever problems we are indeed able to even somewhat alleviate are more than a simple matter of making a reasonable decision. Human beings have a history of self-destructiveness going back to the first event outside of the Garden of Eden, the fratricide of Abel by Cain. Now according to one rabbinic comment they fought over the love of a woman.[34] This is an extraordinary insight, for it focuses the whole history of human aggression and destructiveness on our inescapable feeling of being unloved, or not being loved enough. In modern times W. H. Auden stated it powerfully in his great poem, "September 1, 1939."

> The windiest militant trash important persons shout
> It is not so crude as our wish: What mad Nijinsky
> wrote about Diaghelev is true of the normal heart;
> For the error bread in the bone of each woman and
> of each man craves what it cannot have,
> Not universal love but to be loved alone.

And Auden goes on to say,

> There is no such thing as the State and no one exists
> alone; Hunger allows no choice to the citizen or the
> police
> We must love one another or die.[35]

Yes, we must love one another or die. But the people of faith know that "you shall love your neighbor as yourself" is an imperative only because "I am the Lord" (Leviticus 19:18).[36] There is nothing more unnatural than being required to love our neighbor whom we more often fear than love. *Bellum omnium contra omnes* in Hobbes' words, universal conflict, is the true "state of nature."[37] It is a matter of grace over nature. Unlike the Utopian who simply assumes universal love and goodwill as facts, people of faith regard them as messianic desiderata, something for which we can hope and even work, but not something we can truly accomplish ourselves, something we must pray that God will "write on their heart' (Jeremiah 31:32). By affirming our messianic hope for the coming of God's kingdom of peace we work to prepare our own hearts at least as much as we work to change the world. We resist the simple solution of Utopianism and thereby save ourselves from the despair which overcomes the idealists when they realize that their dreams are only dreams. We believe human history has a goal and is not an endless trail of disappointments.

> Happy is the person whose strength is in You,
> with the highways in his heart.
> Passing through the vale of tears, they are
> watered with blessings by the early rain.
> They go from strength to strength until ap-
> pearing before God in Zion. (Psalms 84:6-8)

To do our best to limit the threat of nuclear war, or any war, is one of the tasks we must do on the highway. It cannot be avoided by any one of the travellers to Zion. God requires as much—no more, but no less.

THE LOGIC OF THE COVENANT: AN ESSAY IN SYSTEMATIC JEWISH THEOLOGY

1. *Introduction*

The very term "systematic Jewish theology" as applied to rabbinic thought to some would, no doubt, seem to be a chimera, or in the language of the rabbis themselves "something which never was and never will be."[1] For if the main components of classical Jewish thought, especially as expressed in rabbinic literature, are Halakhah and Aggadah, then it would seem that Aggadah, even when it is theological expression and not just folklore, is, compared to Halakhah, decidedly unsystematic speculation—imaginative and subjective—and that the systematic manifestation of Judaism is Halakhah. Although systematic theologies of Judaism have indeed been presented, both by rationalist philosophers and kabbalists, they derived their structure if not at least some of their substance as well from nonrabbinic sources. The rationalist and kabbalistic theologians of the Middle Ages were not reasoning the same way the rabbis did. Thus the great modern historian of Jewish thought, Gershom Scholem, although he considered Kabbalah closer to rabbinic thought than medieval philosophical theology, nevertheless wrote about both of them, "Undoubtedly both the mystics and philosophers completely transform the structure of ancient Judaism."[2] Even the great categorizing works of such modern students of rabbinic theology as Solomon Schechter, George Foote Moore, Isaak Heinemann, Max Kadushin, Louis Finkelstein, and Ephraim Urbach, have not themselves produced systematic theology out of the rabbinic sources, but have rather located—with great insight to be sure—certain recurrent rabbinic themes and rabbinic methods of expression.[3] Only my late revered teacher, Professor Abraham Joshua Heschel, attempted to do more than this. Unfortunately, his untimely death prevented him from carrying his project in rabbinic theology further than outlining and documenting some of the main themes. His magnum opus in rabbinic theology is also his unfinished symphony.[4]

However, if Halakhah is where Jewish thought was and is still most systematic, then could not one look for at least more systematic content in those expressions of Aggadah which are more closely related to Halakhah? Indeed it would appear that those *aggadot* having an halakhic connection have shown themselves to be more systematic than those whose relation to Halakhah is more remote. This can be seen in two different genre of *aggadot.*

There are *aggadot* which are a posteriori reflections on specific *mitzvot*, namely, the genre of Jewish theology known as "reasons for the commandments" *(taʿmay ha-mitzvot)*. In these reflections the theologian attempts to discover what purposes various *mitzvot* fulfill.[5]

Certain *aggadot*, however, took the form of a priori reflections on what are the conditions which made the giving of the Torah by God and the receiving of the Torah by Israel possible. Although the word "covenant" *(berit)* in rabbinic nomenclature is usually limited to its specific denotation as "the covenant of circumcision" *(berit millah)*,[6] it is clear that this type of reflection is covenantal theology in that covenant designates the relationship between God and Israel of which Torah (and within it the *mitzvot*) is the authoritative expression. In this chapter I shall attempt to show some of the systematic theologizing the rabbis did engage in concerning the covenant. I shall attempt to show that this type of theologizing was more systematic than other types of aggadic thinking, not only because it deals with the religious foundations of Jewish law, but also because it incorporates certain halakhic concepts which pertain to interhuman relationships and applies them, by analogy, to the relationship between God and Israel. Just as there is no hiatus in the halakhic continuum from the rabbinic period to our own day, I hope to show that the same can be said for a theological tradition which is both systematic and the source for further systematizing even unto our own day.

2. *The Prescriptive Covenantal Model*

Although the covenant is always assymetrical in that God and His human creatures are never truly equal, there are great differences in degree in the various theories about the constitution of this assymetrical relationship.

The most radical statement of this assymetry is the following *aggadah.*

> 'And they stood at the foot *(be-tahtit)* of the mountain' (Exodus 19:17).
> R. Abdimi bar Hama bar Hasa said that this teaches us that the
> Holy-One-blessed-be-He turned the mountain over them like a trough and
> said to them that if you accept the Torah it is well and good; if not, this
> will be your grave.[7]

This statement presents a model of the covenant including the following points: (1) God as omnipotent, unaffected, Lawgiver; (2) the Torah as pure heteronomy; (3) Israel as passive recipients of the Divine Law; (4) terror of imminently disastrous consequences as the motivation for obedience. The passage just quoted is not at all atypical, but most succinctly expresses a whole theology having much precedent and many parallels. Regarding (1) note: "The Holy-One-blessed-be-He said that I have made a law and have decreed a decree *(gezerah gazarti)* and you are not permitted to violate My decree."[8] Regarding (2) note: "I want to do many things, but what can I do? My Father in heaven has decreed *(gazar)* for me such and such."[9] Regarding (3) note: "I have never stated anything which I did not receive as a tradition *(sham'ati)* from my master (going all the way back to Sinai)."[10] Regarding (4) note: "The attributes of the Holy-One-blessed-be-He are not (in essence) beneficial *(rahamim)* but are decrees *(gezerot)* alone."[11]

Nevertheless, the other rabbis who are recorded as discussing this theological notion of covenant were not at all satisfied with it. And if one looks at cognate rabbinic texts, it can be shown that all four points outlined above are disputed.

The first criticism of this theology, placed by the editors of the Babylonian Talmud immediately after this statement, pertains to the fourth point, that is, terror as the motivation for obedience. "R. Aha bar Jacob said that this is a great protest *(moda'a raba)* against the Torah." Here the law of human agreements is applied, by analogy, to the agreement between God and Israel. The term *moda'a* is a technical legal term used to signify the abrogation of a contract because one of the parties was coerced into accepting it.[12] If one is not held responsible for acts done contrary to the Torah done under compulsion, then by inference, one should not be obligated to obey the Torah and its commandments accepted the same way.[13] Later on the Talmud presents a criticism of capricious acceptance of the Torah, which like terror, is an unreasoned response devoid of true insight.[14]

This leads to the criticism which pertains to the third point, that is, the passivity of Israel as the recipients of the Torah. "Rava said that despite this the generation during the days of Ahashuerus accepted it willingly *(qibbluha)* as it is written, 'the Jews upheld *(qiyyamu)* and accepted it' (Esther 9:27)."[15] The import of this statement and its maker should not be overlooked. The maker of the statement was the fourth century C.E. Babylonian sage, Rava, who can be seen as one of the strongest proponents of rational jurisprudence in rabbinic thought.[16] What he is emphasizing here is that the Law as a whole cannot be based upon irrational ascent by Israel. The verse he chose in its immediate context denotes the acceptance by the Jews of the new holy day of Purim as decreed by Mordecai and Esther. Purim, it should be recalled, has no explicit foundation in the Written Torah.[17] It is the example par excellence of the power that the rabbis themselves have to innovate new institutions, a power whose legitimisation required a novel interpretation of the ban on adding to the commandments of the Torah (bal tosef).[18] In the context of the Talmud's discussion elsewhere of the validity of Purim in general and the book of Esther in particular, the earlier Babylonian sage, Samuel, uses this very verse in this very interpretation as his proof text, one which Rava himself found to be more convincing than any other.[19] Thus there is no doubt that Rava was familiar with this seminal interpretation and applied it to the more basic theological concern, namely, the acceptance of the Torah by the Jewish people. Indeed the verse itself speaks of a time when the Jewish people were in exile, separated from the usual politico-religious coercion of their sovereign pre-exilic theocracy, and when they nevertheless reaccepted the Torah willingly.[20] This willingness, probably more than anything else, made the reconstitution of Judaism in the Land of Israel by Ezra and his associates possible. It was in and through their reconstitution that the Oral Torah, entailing much human interpretation and innovation, came into full flower.[21] Thus Rava's refutation of the designation of Jewish acceptance of the Torah as something essentially passive is based on the whole indispensible connection between the Written and Oral Torahs in rabbinic doctrine.

If the Jewish people are not simply the passive recipients of the Law but active participants in its promulgation, interpretation and supplementation, then the second point is challenged, namely, that the Torah is pure heteronomy for the subjects of the Divine will.[22] Finally, the first point is also challenged, for if the Jewish people are participants in the Torah's formulation, then the Torah is not simply a Divine fiat, further indicating God's remote control of the world, but it is rather a realm in which God and Israel participate and interpenetrate each other's lives. On the basis of the prescriptive model of covenant, which we have just been examining, there is no real interpersonal relationship between God and man in the Torah and there is, therefore, no love to be practiced or experienced on either side of such a master-slave situation characterized by terror.[23]

3. *Covenant As Mutual Participation*

The most evident place to begin examining rabbinic treatments of the *mitzvot*, as mutual God-man participation in a realm constituted between them, is from the human side of the relationship, for the *mitzvot* are ostensibly addressed to man. In the following *midrash* the *mitzvot* are depicted as answering Israel's need to be identified as God's child.

> A king's son said to him, 'Make me visibly identifiable *(siymuni)* in the midst of the country that I am your son.' His father said to him, 'If your request is that all should know that your are my son, then wear my royal purple garment *(purpura)* and place my crown upon your head; then all will know that you are my son.' So did the Holy-One-blessed-be-He say to Israel, 'If you desire that you should be identified as my children, engage in the Torah and its commandments and all will see that you are My sons.'[24]

Even though the initial motivation for this request seems to be a desire that others know about Israel's special relationship with God, the underlying psychological motivation can be seen in the fact that only when something is evident to others are we ourselves convinced that it is true.

The primacy of this intimate self-awareness is brought out by this *aggadah*.

> Beloved is Israel whom the Holy-One-blessed-be-He surrounded with *mitzvot: tefillin* on their heads and arms, *tzitzit* on their clothing, *mezuzot* on their doors. . . . At the time when King David entered the bathhouse and saw himself naked he said, 'Oh me, standing naked without *mitzvot* !' But when he remembered the circumcision in his flesh, he regained his composure.[25]

Thus, although God's word is the substantial starting-point of revelation, it must be occasioned by Israel's expression of their need for it. In this sense revelation is responsive. This comes out in the following aggadic examination of an halakhic practice.

> R. Simon ben Pazzi said, 'How do we know that the translator of the Torah reading *(Meturgaman)* is not permitted to make his voice louder than that of the Torah reader himself *(ha-qore)*? Scripture states, "Moses spoke and God answered with a voice *(be-qol)*" (Exodus 19:19). But it does not state with whose voice; nevertheless, "with a voice" means with the voice of Moses.[26]

First of all, the prima facie meaning of Exodus 19:19 is that Moses addresses God and God responds to what seem to be his requests. The question which the commentators here discuss is: Who in this *aggadah* corresponds to the reader of the Torah in the *halakhah,* and who corresponds to the translator?[27] The question can be answered, it seems to me, if we look at a later version of this passage in *Midrash Rabbah.*

> R. Luliani said in the name of R. Isaac that it is stated in Scripture, "Moses spoke and God answered with a voice." It does not state 'God spoke and Moses answered with a voice' . . . with Moses' own voice He spoke with him *(immo).*[28]

In other words, God spoke through the voice of Moses *both* in terms of the Torah's text *and* its interpretation. The Torah, then, becomes, as it were, an indistinguishable intermingling of human request and Divine response—of God's word and man's interpretation.[29] The subsequent *halakhah* reflects this in the ruling that the voice of the translator and the voice of the reader are to be equally audible.[30]

4. *God's Covenantal Involvement*

Man's greatest need is seen in his need for God to become intimately involved in his life on earth, for God to respond to him as he responded to God in the covenant. As such, the logic of strict omnipotence must be bracketed and a logic of interdependence must be substituted for it. Not only was the Torah "not given to angels,"[31] but in so doing God has involved Himself in the mortality and impurity of flesh and blood on earth.

> R. Simon said that God's love for Israel is great in that He revealed Himself *(she-nigleh)* in a place of idolatry, in a place of filth, in a place of impurity in order to redeem them . . . The Holy-One-blessed-be-He said, How can I redeem them? It is impossible to leave them alone. Better I should go down and save them, as it says in Scripture, "And I will go down to save them from the hand of Egypt" (Exodus 3:8). When He brought them out He called Aaron to purify Himself as it states in Scripture, "and he will purge the holy Sanctuary" (Leviticus 16:33); "and he will purge *(ve-khipper)* the Holy-One *(ha-Qadosh)*" (Leviticus 16:16).[32]

As the Talmud notes, interpreting this last verse, "He who is with them in the midst of their impurities" (Leviticus 16:16) refers to "the *Shekhinah,* which even during the time they are impure is still manifest *(she-sharuy)* among them."[33]

If God is willing to descend from His omnipotence in order to relate to Israel, then some of His *mitzvot* can be seen as ways of making this dependence apparent. A late *midrash* constructs a parable where a king's friend, with whom the king is to dine, is ashamed of his meagre possessions compared to that with which the king is accustomed. In order to make his host more comfortable—that is, in order that there be some mutuality and the host not be overwhelmed by his royal guest—the king sets aside his own possessions and only uses the meagre ones of his friend.[34] An earlier version of this *midrash* sees this as the reason why God commands Israel to kindle light in the sanctuary even though He certainly does not need it. It is they who need to act *as if* He does.[35]

5. *God's Practice of the Commandments*

Along the lines of the prescriptive model of covenant, which we examined earlier, at the time of revelation God is active and man is passive. After the time of revelation, however, the roles are reversed, that is, man is active—either obeying or disobeying the commandments—and God is passive or absent from this human activity, which now must be man's own doing if he is to be held responsible for it.[36] In the phenomenological sense of this covenantal model the doing of the *mitzvot* themselves here and now does not afford an experience of God and man mutually *being-together.*

Even when the *mitzvot* are conceived of as being opportunities for man to respond to God's presence with us, the aggadic texts we examined heretofore make that presence seem to be a matter of almost Divine condescension. It is perhaps like an adult playing a child's game in order to share time with the child, but the child being nevertheless aware that this adult has not penetrated the world of children. Such an adult appears even more out of place to the child with whom he is playing than to other adults who might be convinced that such a magnanimous gesture works. Following this analogy further we might say that the only mutuality possible is when the adult allows the child, for as much time as the child can take, to enter into the adult world with him. The adult does this by making himself accessible enough to the child to be an object of imitation. The following *midrash* expresses the notion that the *mitzvot* are the means of *imitatio Dei* because they enable man to do what God has revealed that He himself had already done.

> R. Eleazar said that ordinarily *(be-noheg she-ba'olam)* a king of flesh and blood makes a decree *(gozer gezerah)* and if he wants to uphold it he does; if not, it is upheld by others. But, with the Holy-One-blessed-be-He it is not so; rather He makes a decree and He Himself upholds it first. Thus it is written in Scripture, "before the aged you shall rise and you shall honor the presence of the elderly, and you shall fear the Lord" (Leviticus 19:32)—I am the One who first upheld the commandment to stand before the aged.[37]

The version of this teaching in the Palestinian Talmud states, "what is the basis for this?   'And they shall keep My charge (mishmarti); I am the Lord' (Leviticus 22:9), namely, I am He who has kept the commandments of the Torah first."[38]

The force of this teaching is that God binds Himself to Israel in ways which are meant to be exemplary.

> R. Abin bar Ada said in the name of R. Isaac that we know that God put on tefillin as it says in Scripture, "the Lord swore . . . by the strength (uzzo) of His outstretched arm" (Isaiah 62:8) . . . these are tefillin as it says in Scripture, "the Lord gives strength (oz) to His people" (Psalms 29:11). And we know that tefillin are Israel's strength as it is written in Scripture, "and all the peoples of the earth will see that the Name of the Lord is called upon you and they will fear you" (Deuteronomy 28:10) . . . R. Nahman bar Isaac said to R. Hiyya bar Abin, 'what are written in the tefillin of the Master-of-the-universe?' He said to him, "who is like Israel, a singular nation on earth" (I Chronicles 17:21).[39]

What emerges from this is that God has bound Himself to Israel even before they bound themselves to Him. Response and imitation are in essence the same.

> A baraita taught, "this is my God and I will glorify Him (ve'anvehu)" (Exodus 15:2) means beautify yourself (hitna'eh) before Him with mitzvot: a beautiful sukkah, a beautiful lulab . . . Abba Saul says that "I will glory Him" means to be like Him (hevay domeh lo): just as He is gracious and merciful, so you be gracious and merciful.[40]

The view of the first anonymous rabbi is that man's response to God is a response to precepts, whereas Abba Saul's view is that it is a response to personal example. The connection between this aggadah and the one before it is that Abba Saul alludes to the passage "the Lord, the Lord, a merciful and gracious God" (Exodus 34:6), which is God's response to Moses' request that He reveal Himself over and above His outward actions, namely, "do show me Your glory" (Exodus 33:18). God says, "I will pass all My goodness by your face . . . My back you will see, but My face will not be seen" (Exodus 33:19, 23). Concerning this another aggadah states, "R. Hana bar Bizna said in the name of R. Simon Hasida that this teaches us that the Holy-One-blessed-be-He showed Moses the knot of His tefillin."[41]

In a midrash which comes later in the sequence discussing God's prior upholding of the mitzvot, the mitzvot are seen as being the means of Israel's unique self-actualization in intimate relationship with God.

"And My commandments you shall keep and do them (vasitem otam)"
(Leviticus 26:3). R. Hama bar R. Hanina said that if you keep the Torah I
[God] will consider it as if you yourselves made them and made yourselves (attem). R. Hanina bar Pappi said [God said to them], 'if you keep
the Torah, I will consider it as if you both made yourselves and made
them [the commandments].'[42]

Only a response of imitation could enable one to experience the mitzvot as
co-creation along with God's creation of one's own self. The Halakhah too recognized
that the self-motivation which results from the internalization of the mitzvot is as
important an incentive as revelation itself.

R. Gidal said in the name of Rab, 'How do we know that one may take an
oath (she-nishba'in) to uphold the commandments?' —Because it says in
Scripture, "I take an oath and then I will uphold your righteous
ordinances" (Psalms 119:106). But has he not already been foresworn and
does it not stand from Mount Sinai? —This lets us know that it is
permitted for one to motivate himself (le-zeruzay nafshsayh).[43]

6. Human Judgment and Divine Compliance

If through the covenant God subjects Himself to the practice of the mitzvot, then
the question of where disputes concerning the meaning of the mitzvot are decided is the
next issue to be dealt with in apodictic sequence. This comes out in one of the most
famous and oft-quoted aggadot, concerning an halakhic debate between R. Eliezer ben
Hyrkanus and R. Joshua ben Hananyah.

R. Eliezer said to them again, 'If the halakhah is according to my view,
God (Shamayim) will so attest.' A heavenly echo (bat qol) came forth and
declared, 'Why do you hold a position against that of R. Eliezer? the
halakhah is always according to him.' R. Joshua stood up on his feet and
said, "It is not in heaven" (Deuteronomy 30:12) ...' R. Jeremiah said
that the Torah has already been given from Mount Sinai and we do not
regard a heavenly echo as being authoritative, for You already wrote at
Mount Sinai, "Incline after the majority" (Exodus 23:2). R. Nathan
happened to meet Elijah. He said to him, 'What did the Holy-One-
blessed-be-He do at that time?' He said to him that He smiled and said,
'My children have vanquished Me indeed (nitzhuni)![44]

Both R. Eliezer and R. Joshua affirm that the Torah has been fully given at Mount
Sinai. There are no new mitzvot in the Scriptural sense.[45] The question between them is
whether halakhic disputes are decided in heaven or on earth. The term "vanquish"

(*nitzuah*) is crucial here. Earlier in the presentation of this incident, when R. Eliezer brought forth other supernatural phenomena, R. Joshua dismissed them out of hand saying, "if scholars vanquish (*menatzhim*) each other in Halakhah, what business is that of yours?[46] Such phenomena are clearly irrelevant to the situation at hand. However, when God Himself endorses the view of R. Eliezer, but the law is decided according to R. Joshua nevertheless, then not only is R. Eliezer vanquished but so is God, as it were. The Torah has been fully given, therefore there is no room for man to institute a new Law. And, since the Torah has been fully given to man on earth, there is thus no room for God to determine subsequent interpretation.[47] The very act of human interpretation requires both imagination and courage. Both in terms of revelation before and, especially, other-worldly reward and punishment afterwards, man is clearly subject to the power and authority of God. But, by binding Himself to a Law He has given to man on earth, that is to Israel, God is now subject to man's interpretation and judgment concerning these mutual *mitzvot.* God's happiness in this dependence is brought out in this *aggadah.*

> R. Kahana said in the name of R. Ishmael ben R. Jose that it is written "For the Leader (*la-mnatzeah*), a song of David" (Psalms 13:1) in Scripture as if to say, 'sing to Whom is vanquished and is happy about it.' Come and see that the way of the Holy-One-blessed-be-He is not like that of flesh and blood. Flesh and blood when vanquished is sad, but when vanquished the Holy-One-blessed-be-He is happy.[48]

The covenant means that God has initiated a relationship with man to which both are then mutually subject. Within the context of this relationship God has chosen to be affected by man. This is essentially an act of Divine self-limitation (*tzimtzum*), which the later kabbalistic theologians developed considerably.[49] This is why God responds to human pleas not to annul this self-limitation, which would destroy the human covenantal participant. God is implored to remain faithful to the covenant, to remain within the relationship, even when man has attempted to transcend it by turning away from God to idolatry in all its forms.

This notion is developed in the aggadic treatment of Moses' dialogue with God regarding the sin of the Golden Calf. Like all persuasive discourse the dialogue entails an explicit logic. The *aggadah* develops the logical implication of this imagined dialogue by placing it in an halakhic context inasmuch as the covenant was taken to imply God's own lawfulness.

Because He said, "let Me alone and I will destroy them" (Deuteronomy 9:14), Moses said, 'this matter depends on me.' He stood up and strengthened himself in prayer and sought mercy . . . R. Abbahu said that were it not written in Scripture it would be impossible to utter it. It teaches us that Moses grabbed the Holy-One-blessed-be-He like a man grabbing another by his garment. He said to Him, 'Master-of-the-universe, I will not release You until You have compassion and forgive them!'[50]

So far we see a general expression of the aggadic notion that Israel will not allow God to remove Himself from the convenantal relationship. In the continuation of this discussion, however, a crucial halakhic element is inserted, which deepens our insight into the exact character of the covenantal relationship.

"And Moses implored (va-yehal) the presence of the Lord" (Exodus 32:11) . . . Rava said this means until he released (she-hittir) Him from His vow (nidro).[51] It is written here "and he implored," and it is written elsewhere in Scripture, "he did not break (yahel) his word" (Numbers 30:3) —and a master stated that this means, 'he did not break it but others may do so for him.' . . . Remember Abraham, Isaac and Israel Your servants to whom You took an oath (nishba'ta) by Your own self (bakh)" (Exodus 32:13). What does "by Your own self" mean? R. Eleazar said that Moses said to the Holy-One-blessed-be-He, 'Master-of-the-universe, if You had taken an oath for them by heaven and earth, I would have said that just as heaven and earth will be destroyed (betelim), so will Your oath be destroyed. Now that You took an oath for them by Your great Name: just as Your great Name lives and endures forever and ever, so does Your oath endure forever and ever. . . .' "And the Lord said that I have forgiven according to your word (salakhti ki-debarekha)" (Numbers 14:20). . . . It was taught in the school of R. Ishmael . . . in the future the nations-of-the-world will say, 'happy is the disciple whose master agrees with him!'[52]

The dialogue consists of three steps: (1) God proposes to destroy the people of Israel for their sins; (2) Moses pleads that this would be inconsistent with God's own covenantal commitment; (3) God accepts Moses' plea and limits His full reaffirmation of absolute omnipotence, for such a reaffirmation would make relationship impossible. Now this aggadah figuratively employs the halakhic institution of the release from vows (hattarat nedarim) in the following way. (1) God's proposal is taken to be a vow (neder), namely, a promised action. (2) Moses attempts to release God from this vow by showing that God's proposal is inconsistent with His covenantal commitment (shebu'a). This is precisely how one is released from any ordinary vow, namely, not by the person who made the vow, in that he lacks the insight and objectivity to distinguish between his words and his true intent, but rather by another concerned and authorized person who can make this distinction in the best interests of all involved. (3) God accepts Moses' releasing Him from His vow by reaffirming His initial promise which He made in the form of an oath. This is precisely like Israel's Sinaitic obligation which precludes subsequent oathes which are themselves inconsistent with it.

Vows can be cancelled in one of two ways. The first type of cancellation is called *hattarat nedarim*, that is, "release from vows." Here the person who has made the vow requests a rabbinical authority to show the inner inconsistency of his vow, how the words uttered are inappropriate for the end intended.[53] The second type of cancellation is called *hafarat nedarim*, "nullification of vows." Here, on the other hand, we see the prior right of one person to approve or disapprove the vow of someone under his authority before it is translated into action. The former type of cancellation necessarily involves rational analysis, a psychological examination of motivation. The latter type of cancellation, conversely, simply requires the exercise of authority and does not necessarily require any rational analysis whatsoever.[54] Clearly the former not the latter is a paradigm for theology as a rational enterprise.

As the *aggadah* presents it, God grants man the privilege of *hattarat nedarim* namely, the privilege of counsel. However, He does not grant man the power of *hafarat nedarim* because this would be based on the following erroneous analogy: man is to God as a husband is to his wife. But, halakhically, the husband initiates the relationship with his wife.[55] Indeed, in the Aggadah as a whole, in the erotic analogy of husband and wife, God is the husband and Israel is the wife since it is God, not Israel, who substantially initiates the covenant.[56]

Israel has the privilege of releasing God from His vow to destroy them, if it can be shown that this vow is inconsistent with the original covenantal oath taken at Sinai. This aggadic point can only be properly understood if the halakhic points it presupposes are explicated. These points are: (1) the difference between an oath (*shebu'a*) and a vow (*neder*); (2) the difference between cancelling a vow by privileged fiat (*hafarat nedarim*) and cancelling a vow by juridical reasoning, showing an inner inconsistency between word and prior intent (*hattarat nedarim*).

The Talmud notes an essential difference between an oath and a vow in that "with vows one prohibits (mitasar) an article (heftza) from himself . . . with oaths one prohibits himself (nafshayh) from an article."[57] Although it looks like these two definitions are interchangeable, a deeper examination indicates that they are fundamentally different. In a vow the primary concern is with the external object and then the person's relation to it. Thus one may actually vow not to have anything to do with an object associated with a mitzvah—for example, a sukkah—and the vow is valid because it is primarily concerned with an external object, which in and of itself is not the subject of a prior obligation as is the person. However, in an oath the primary concern is with the person himself and only secondarily with the external object to which he is related. Thus if one takes an oath not to personally practice a certain mitzvah for which he is obligated, that oath is null and void ab initio because it contradicts the prior personal obligation which is the foundation of the covenantal response of Israel at Mount Sinai, a response expressed in the oath, "all that the Lord has spoken we will do" (Exodus 19:8).[58] In this important sense an oath is of greater importance than a vow precisely because it is a more personally relevant act.

Translating this halakhic teaching into the aggadic scenario of the long Talmudic passage we just examined, we see that God's personal choice to covenant Himself with Israel—as in an oath—takes precedence over any vow to disassociate them from Himself. Moses, as the paradigm of all subsequent sages, identifies what is primary and what is secondary in God's relationship with His people and confronts God with it as a rabbinic authority would confront one who took a vow which, if carried out, would alienate him from those nearest to him, those from whom he never meant to be so alienated. It is man in the process of theological reflection who uncovers this inner logic.

Concerning the cancellation of a vow by fiat as opposed to nullification of a vow through rational analysis, the Talmud notes, "a sage releases (mattir) but not a husband; a husband nullifies (mefar) but not a sage."[59] The point distinguishing cancellation from nullification is retroactivity. Nullification of a vow is the power to cancel its being fulfilled; it is a procedure of prevention located between a word and the act it intends. Here there is no retroactivity. Release from a vow, what we call cancellation, on the other hand, is the power to show retroactively that the vow should have never been uttered, let alone put into practice, because it contradicts prior intention.[60] In the case

of a vow taken by a human being such intention can even be tacit. We may assume, for
example, that the person had previously wanted a normal marital state by the very fact
that he married and, therefore, could not have possibly meant to prevent contact with his
wife, which would be the result of following his impulsive vow.[61] Applying this halakhic
model to the theological reality with which this *aggadah* deals, and using the analogy of
marriage so often used in Aggadah, we might say that Moses (and his rabbinical
successors) functions as a rabbinical authority attempting to show an angry husband (God)
that he did not mean to separate himself from his wife (Israel) despite his impulsive vow
to the contrary. Moreover, in this case God's intention is not tacit but explicit. Moses
reminds Him of the oath He took to be personally involved with Israel forever.[62] This is
the prime reality from which God cannot be released because nothing prior to it is
acknowledged which could possibly be the basis for any such release. In other *aggadot*,
when the angels challenge God's choice of Israel as the recipient of His Torah as being
contrary to His omnipotent interests, He retorts by indicating that the Torah (by
implication the Torah to which He is already personally committed to practice Himself)
is itself meaningless without the irrevocable bond with Israel.

> At the time when the Holy-One-blessed-be-He sought to give the Torah
> to Israel the ministering angels . . . said, 'Master-of-the-universe, it is
> for Your happiness, Your honor, Your glory, that Your Torah be in
> heaven.' He said to them, 'no satisfaction *(shuqah)* comes from you . . . it
> is written in it, "when a person dies in a tent" (Numbers 19:14). Is there
> any death among you?'[63]

The logic of oathes is also invoked to convince Israel that from their side of the
covenantal relationship it is just as irrevocable.

> And so we find that when Moses had Israel take the oath he said to them,
> 'it is not with your consent *(al da'atkhem)* that I adjure you but with God's
> consent and my own.' . . . he could have said to them, 'uphold 613
> commandments.' Now according to your [Moses'] theory you should have
> said to them, 'with my consent *(al da'ati)*', but why say to them, 'with
> God's consent *(al da'at ha-Maqom)*'? —So that there could be no nullifca-
> tion *(hafarah)* of their oath.[64]

The text becomes clearer when we see it in relation to the following famous text, a text
from a later period.

> R. Simlai interpreted that 613 commandments were transmitted to
> Moses. R. Hamnuna said, 'what is the meaning of the Scriptural verse,

"Moses commanded a Torah to us as an inheritance" (Deuteronomy 33:4)? The numerical value *(gematria)* of the letters in *Torah* is 611. "I am the Lord" and "there shall be no other gods" (Exodus 20:2-3) they heard directly from the mouth of God *(mi-pi ha-Geburah).*[65]

In other words, the whole Torah is of Divine origin, but most of it was transmitted through Moses to Israel indirectly. In reaffirming the covenant forty years later on the plains of Moab, Moses reminds the people that because their original covenantal oath pertained directly to God, there is no prior basis for ever nullifying it. Any appeal to human authority and tradition aside from revelation can be refuted.[66]

7. *Conclusion*

What we have seen from this brief examination of some seminal aggadic texts is that God's irreducible covenantal oath to remain with Israel in a relationship constituted by the Torah is the foundation for any Jewish theology. It cannot be derived from any prior idea. In the development of this idea we have seen how systematic theology was formulated by the rabbis and how it lends itself to further systematic efforts long after their time. This systematic effort is largely possible because of the incorportion of concepts from the most evident system within Judaism—Halakhah. The point of contact between the two disciplines is that both are conceived in relational terms. Moreover, this relational reality, on both levels, Halakhah and Aggadah, calls forth an examination of relational logic for the sake of judgment: in Halakhah for the sake of practical judgment; in Aggadah for the sake of theoretical judgment.[67] The tendency to look at Judaism as a "pan-halakhic" phenomenon (in Professor Heschel's magnificent characterization of a certain form of Jewish fundamentalism[68]) is often made on intellectual grounds, namely, the "real" Jewish intellect is almost exclusively halakhic. In an earlier study I attempted to show how Aggadah participated in the very intellectual formulation of Halakhah. One cannot understand the latter without the former.[69] Here I have tried to show how *aggadot* dealing with the covenantal foundation of Judaism could not have been logically formulated without the intricate incorporation of halakhic content. Halakhah provides Jewish thinkers with the means for a systematic inquiry into the revealed acts of man—an exciting and rewarding challenge to heart and mind. Aggadah, with the help of Halakhah, provides Jewish thinkers with the means for a systematic inquiry into the revealed acts of God—an even more exciting and rewarding challenge to heart and mind.[70]

NOTES

Chapter One

[1] A leading exponent of this school of thought, Dr. J. David Bleich, typically writes, "Let it be stated unequivocally: *Jewish law does not change* . . . I must either accept this principle or reject the halakhic process in its entirety." "Halakhah As An Absolute," JUDAISM, 29.1 (Winter, 1980), 31, 32. Cf. B. *Abodah Zarah* 35b-37a.

[2] A leading exponent of this school of thought, Dr. Eugene Mihaly, typically writes, "Our reliance is not a static monolithic Halakhah, the endless minutiae which absorbed within themselves and largely reflected antiquated social views, archaic science, transient myths, dated 'tool-worlds' and fluctuating historic circumstances." "Halakhah is Absolute and Passé," *ibid.*, 75.

[3] See Bleich, *op. cit.*, 30-31; also, his *Contemporary Halakhic Problems* (New York, 1977), xvii.

[4] M. *Kiddushin* 1.7.

[5] *Shulhan Arukh: Orah Hayyim*, 589.6.

[6] See B. *Baba Kama* 5b and *Rashi* and *Tos.*, s.v. "le-hilkhotayhen;" B. *Niddah* 51b re Lev. 11:9; C. Tchernowitz, *Toldot Ha-Halakhah* (New York, 1934), 1:102-103. This is why in this system of specifics erudition must be prior to analytical ability, because the sources cannot be reconstructed deductively. See B. *Baba Metzia* 85b; B. *Horayot* 2b and 14a. Cf. M. *Abot* 2.8 and *Abot De-Rabbi Nathan*, chap. 14/end.

[7] See B. *Baba Metzia* 115b and parallels; Maim., *Hilkhot Sanhedrin*, 18.2-3 and *Sefer Ha-Mitzvot*, intro., sec. 4. On the other hand, the view that the general statements in the Written Torah are prior to the specific statements (viz., to *their* specifications) is that of the school of R. Ishmael. See B. *Sotah* 37b and parallels; B. *Shebu'ot* 26a; *Tanhuma: Ki Tissa* (printed ed.), sec. 16 re Job 11:9; A. J. Heschel, *Torah min Ha-Shamayim* (London, 1965), 2:88-89. Nevertheless, the opposing view of R. Akibah was the prevalent one. See *Sifra: Behar*, ed. Weiss, 105a (cf. *Zebahim* 115b). By seeing generalization as subsequent rather than prior, it enabled a far wider range of exegetical and systematic options. See B. *Hagigah* 12a and *Beresheet Rabbah* 1.14 and 22.2; *Abot De-Rabbi Nathan*, chap. 18; B. *Gittin* 67a.

[8] See B. *Erubin* 27a and Jacob Neusner, *Judaism: The Evidence of the Mishnah* (Chicago, 1981), esp., 17ff.

[9] See David Hume, *A Treatise of Human Nature*, 1.14, ed. L. A. Selby-Bigge (Oxford, 1888), 165-166. For the denial that temporal development is deductive, see A. N. Whitehead, *Process and Reality* (New York, 1929), 13.

[10] B. *Kiddushin* 34a-35b. See P. *Pesahim* 8.1/35d re Deut. 16:3.

[11] See Maimonides' comment on M. *Kiddushin* 1.7 and *Hilkhot Abodah Zarah*, 12.3. Cf. B. *Megillah* 23a; *Arakhin* 2b-3a; *Hullin* 2a; P. *Terumot* 1.1/40c and parallels.

[12] B. *Kiddushin* 35a.

[13] See B. *Sukkah* 31a, s.v. "R. Judah." Cf. Rashi thereon. See, also, *Encyclopedia Talmudit*, 10:559ff. For the notion that even 'a fortiori (*qal va-homer*) reasoning is selective rather than logically compelling, see B. *Kiddushin* 4b. Also, see W.V. Quine, "Two Dogmas of Empiricism" in *From a Logical Point of View* (New York, 1963), 42-43.

[14] P. *Pesahim* 6.1/33a.

[15] See B. *Baba Metzia* 86a.

[16]*Teshubot Rashi,* no. 68 re B. *Megillah* 23a, ed. Elfenbein (New York, 1943), 80-81; B. *Kiddushin* 31a, *Tos.,* s.v. "de-la." Cf. B. *Rosh Hashanah* 33a, *Tos.,* s.v. "ha."

[17]See B. *Berakhot* 33a re Ex. 20:7.

[18]See Isserles' note on *Shulhan Arukh: Orah Hayyim,* 589.6. For the factor of women's religious desires being honored, see B. *Hagigah* 16b. For differing views of the current halakhic ramifications of this innovation, see J. J. Weinberg, *Seriday Esh* (Jerusalem, 1966), 3:321-322, no. 104; E. Waldenberg, *Tzitz Eliezer* (Jerusalem, 1966), 9:25-29, no. 2; M. Feinstein, *Igrot Mosheh: Orah Hayyim* (New York, 1970), 2:176-177, no. 2.

[19]See B. *Erubin* 13b and 46b; B. *Yebamot* 14a; also, *Sefer Ha-Hinukh,* no. 496 re B. *Baba Metzia* 59b.

[20]B. *Berakhot* 5a.

[21]See B. *Baba Metzia* 33a.

[22]*Hilkhot Talmud Torah,* 1.11 re B. *Kiddushin* 30a.

[23]*Ibid.,* 1.12.

[24]*Teshubot Ha-Rambam,* ed. Blau (Jerusalem, 1960), 2:333, no. 182. Cf. B. Berakhot 11b and *Hilkhot Tefilah,* 7.10 where he rules that the blessing in this formula is to be said. This formula is, however, absent from certain texts of *Talmud Babli* (see R. N. Rabinovicz, *Diqduqay Sofrim* thereon; also, *Ran* on *Alfasi* thereon and *Rosh,* chap. 1, no. 13). It is also absent from *Siddur Rab Sa'adyah Gaon,* ed. Davidson, Assaf and Joel (Jerusalem, 1963), 358. Blau indicates in his note on this responsum that it is also absent from some Mss. of *Mishneh Torah.* Whether or not Maimonides actually contradicted himself, changed his mind, or had a different text is impossible to ascertain conclusively.

[25]See R. Zechariah Frankel, *Darkhay Ha-Mishnah* (Leipzig, 1959), 20.

[26]See his *Commentary on the Mishnah,* ed. Kappah (Jerusalem, 1976), 1:10-11; *Sefer Ha-Mitzvot,* intro., sec. 2 re *Temurah* 16a, ed. Heller, 8; also, R. Abraham ibn Daoud, *Sefer Ha-Qabbalah,* ed. Cohen, 1; R. Joseph Albo, *Sefer Ha-Iqqarim,* 3.14; A. J. Heschel, *Torah min Ha-Shamayim,* 2:253 ff.

[27]*Hilkhot Mamrim,* 1.1-3. The quote in the text is from M. *Abot* 1.1. See P. *Sanhedrin* 4.2/22a; *Seder Eliyahu Zuta,* chap. 2/beg.

[28]See *Sefer Ha-Mitzvot,* intro., sec. 3; *Commentary on the Mishnah: Sanhedrin,* chap. 10 *(Heleq),* 2:144, prin. 9; *Hilkhot Melkahim* (uncensored ed.), 11.6.

[29]*Menahot* 29b.

[30]"From Sinai" *(mi-sinai)* refers to God who revealed His Torah *at Sinai.* See R. Obadiah Bertinoro's comment on M. *Abot* 1.1.

[31]Rashi (s.v. "nityashbah da'ato"), however, interprets this incident as happening before the giving of the Oral Torah to Moses, the implication being that had Moses already received the Torah he could have predicted R. Akibah's interpretation and would have surely understood it instantly. But it seems contrary to the whole point of the story which emphasizes the creative exegetical ability R. Akibah was to exercize "in the future," a future even Moses could not deduce from the data of revelation. See *Pesiqta Rabbati: Parah,* ed. Friedmann, 64b.

[32]See B. *Sanhedrin* 17a/top and Maim., *Hilkhot Sanhedrin,* 2.1.

[33]P. *Megillah* 4.1/74d. For parallels, see *Vayiqra Rabbah,* ed. Margaliot (Jerusalem, 1956), 3:496-497, nn. thereon.

[34]This is in the sense of *asmakhta* which describes most rabbinic exegesis. See Maim., Sefer *Ha-mitzvot*, intro., sec. 2.

[35]Thus Dr. Robert Gordis, a leading exponent of this school of thought, writes, "Jewish law was never monolithic and unchanged in the past. There are, therefore, no grounds for decreeing that it must be motionless in the present and immovable in the future." "A Dynamic Halakhah: Principles and Procedures," JUDAISM, 28.4 (Summer, 1979), 264.

[36]M. *Gittin* 4.3. See M. *Shebi'it* 10.2.

[37]B. *Baba Batra* 54b and parallels.

[38]B. *Gittin* 36b and *Rashi* thereon.

[39]*Ibid.*, 36b à la M. *Shebi'it* 10.3.

[40]For the notion of innovation contrary to accepted procedure *(hazaqah)* requiring proof, see, esp., B. *Baba Kama* 46a and *Sifre: Debarim*, no. 16, ed. Finkelstein, 27. For an analysis of rabbinic resistance to legal innovation, see David Halivni, "Can A Religious Law Be Immoral?" in *Perspectives on Jews and Judaism: Essays in Honor of Wolfe Kelman* (New York, 1978), 166-167.

[41]See, e.g., P. *Sukkah* 5.4/55a and B. *Sukkah* 53a and *Tos.*, s.v. "im;" also, D. Novak, *Law and Theology in Judaism* (New York, 1976), 2:129 ff.

[42]See Aristotle, *Physics*, 226a35.

[43]See Plato, *Republic*, 338Cff.

[44]See, e.g., Dr. Robert Gordis' affirmation of the authority of "new ethical insights and attitudes" in "A Dynamic Halakhah," 267.

[45]See D. Novak, *The Image of the Non-Jew in Judaism: An Historical and Constructive Study of the Noahide Laws* (New York and Toronto, 1983), xiv-xvi.

[46]Note Dr. Seymour Siegel's assertion that "When the *halacha* cannot adequately express *aggada* it must be modified." "The Meaning of Jewish Law in Conservative Judaism: An Overview and Summary" in *Conservative Judaism and Jewish Law*, ed. S. Siegel and E. B. Gertel (New York, 1977), xxiii. This seems to have been influenced by Dr. Max Kadushin who argued that Halakhah "concretized" value concepts "cultivated" in Aggadah. See *The Rabbinic Mind* (New York, 1952), 89. For a more dialectical view of this relation, however, see A. J. Heschel, *God in Search of Man* (New York, 1955), 336ff.

[47]Along these lines see Hermann Cohen's critique of Moritz Lazarus' *Ethik des Judenthums* in *Juedische Schriften* (Berlin, 1924), 3:1ff.; also, D. Novak, "A Response to Edward Feld's 'Towards an Aggadic Judaism'," CONSERVATIVE JUDAISM, 30.1 (Fall, 1975), 58-61.

[48]Thus, even though the Torah has "seventy meanings" (see B. *Shabbat* 88b re Jer. 23:29), one is condemned for teaching Torah contrary to Halakhah (M. *Abot* 5.8; see M. *Peah* 4.1). Even those who hold that Aggadah can be normative (cf. P. *Peah* 2.4/10a; P. *Horayot* 3.5/48c), only do so when it does not contradict accepted Halakhah. See R. Zvi Hirsch Chajes, *Darkhay Ha-Hora'ah*, sec. 2 in *Kol Kitbay Maharatz Chajes* (Jerusalem, 1958), 1:251.

[49]If ethics is meant to ground Halakhah, then it must have the greater intelligibility of a "metalanguage." See A. Tarski, "The Semantic Conception of Truth" in *Semantics and the Philosophy of Language*, ed. L. Linsky (Urbana, IL, 1952), 349-351.

[50]Thus Cohen entitled his magnum opus on Judaism, *Religion der Vernunft aus den Quellen des Judenthums*. See, esp., 24ff. in S. Kaplan's translation, *Religion of Reason Out of the Sources of Judaism* (New York, 1972).

[51] Although Aristotle, who was the first to use the term "ethics" in the sense of an intellectual discipline, derives ethics *(ethikē)* from *ethos (Nicomachean Ethics,* 1103a20), he, nevertheless, indicates that the business of good leaders is to lead citizens to right action and make them good *(ibid.,* 1103b5). In other words, they are to lead from a reasoned standpoint and not just ennunciate popular opinion.   See Maim., *Moreh Nebukhim,* 2.40.

[52] Actually, neither leniency nor strictness is supposed to be an halakhic end per se. See T. *Yebamot* 1.13; B. *Rosh Hashanah* 14b; B. *Erubin* 6b-7a and *Rashi,* s.v. "de-satran a-hadaday;" P. *Berakhot* 1.4/3b; P. *Nedarim* 9.1/41b.

[53] See B. *Berakhot* 13b, Tos., s.v. "v'amar;" *Encyclopedia Talmudit,* 9:343-345.

[54] See A. J. Yuter, "Mehitzah, Midrash and Modernity: A study in Religious Rhetoric," JUDAISM, 28.2 (Spring, 1979), 147-159; also, G. Bacon, "Da'at Torah ve-Heblay Mashiah," TARBIZ, 52.3 (Nisan-Sivan, 5743/1983), 497-508.

[55] See *infra.,* 29ff.

[56] Hence the seminal rabbinic idea that the Torah precedes creation. See *Beresheet Rabbah,* beg.

[57] The Talmudic suspension of judgment when a clear decision is beyond our reach comes to mind. See, e.g., M. *Baba Metzia* 1.8 and B. *Baba Kama* 96a.

[58] B. *Kiddushin* 54a.

Chapter Two

[1] Note Plato, *Republic,* 331E: "Justice . . . is to give each one what he deserves." In his edition of the *Republic* Paul Shorey quotes the maxim of the Roman jurists, "Iustitia est constans et perpetua voluntas suum cuique tribuens." (Cambridge, MA, 1930) 1:20, note c. The source of the quote is *Digest* I, 1.

[2] See, also, Ezek. 18:2ff. The classical rabbinic expression of this ethical principle in the context of *mamzerut* is in the *Mishnah (Horayot* 3.8/end), "a *mamzer* who is a scholar *(talmid hakham)* takes precedence over a High Priest who is ignorant *(am ha aretz)."* In other words, family pedigree, which the High Priest possessed superlatively, is superceded by personal achievement. See B. *Yoma* 71b.

[3] *Vayiqra Rabbah* 32.8, ed. Margaliot, 754-755.   Cf. *Qohelet Rabbati* 4.3.   See *Debarim Rabbah* 9.4. Re the irrevocability of *mamzerut,* see B. *Yebamot* 22b re Eccl. 1:15.   Re innocent children suffering because of guilty parents, see Maim., *Hilkhot Mamrim,* 3.3 re B. *Abodah Zarah* 26a-26b and B. *Shabbat* 68b.

[4] The dating of the Midrash is the subject of scholarly debate. Leopold Zunz in *Die Gottesdienstlichen Vortraege der Juden* (Frankfurt am-Maim, 1892), 193, dates it in the middle of the 7th century C.E. Mordecai Margaliot, the editor of the critical ed. I use here, in *Mabo . . . Le-Midrash Vayiqra Rabbah* (Jerusalem, 1960) dates it no later than the middle of the 5th century C.E. (pp. xxxi-xxxiii). However, even taking the earlier dating, the radical change in the Halakhah of *mamzerut* came no later than that of the Amora, Amemar (ca. 400 C. E.).   Therefore, the editing of the text comes *after* the radical change (which will soon be examined) was *already* in effect.

[5] B. *Berakhot* 7a and B. *Sanhedrin* 27b. See B. *Moed Katan* 12b-13a and *Tos.,* s.v. "natyybah;" *Bamidbar Rabbah* 19.20; *Seder Eliyahu Zuta,* chap. 6; *Pesiqta De-Rab Kahana,* ed. Mandelbaum, 1:382; *Midrash Tehillim,* 18.3, ed. Buber, 136; *Mishnat Rabbi Eliezer,* ed. Enelow, 95-97. Also, see commentary of R. Isaac Abrabanel on II Sam., chap. 21 and R. Samuel David Luzzatto *(Shadal)* on Ex. 20:5. Re collective guilt, see B. *Shebu'ot* 39a-39b; also, T. *Sotah* 7.2.

[6]This has been a perennial problem in Jewish theology. Thus, e.g., the prescriptions of the Torah presuppose human freedom of choice, but in many places in Scripture there seem to be descriptions of Divine predestination of human acts. For Maimonides, the ethical consideration of human freedom of choice is essential and thus to be literally posited. Contradictory passages about Divine predestination of human acts are to be figuratively reinterpreted. (See *Hilkhot Teshubah*, chaps. 5-6.) Maimonides used the same method of reinterpretation regarding passages in Scripture which seem to ascribe corporeality to God, which he believed contradict the presupposition of Divine transcendence. For Maimonides this metaphysical consideration is essential and is to be literally posited. The contradictory passages describing seeming Divine corporeality are to be figuratively reinterpreted. (See *Hilkhot Yesoday Ha-Torah*, 1.7ff. and *Moreh Nebukhim*, sec. I.).

[7]B. *Niddah* 61b.

[8]See, e.g., Galatians 3:19-25.

[9]B. *Shabbat* 151b. See B. *Berakhot* 18a; B. *Baba Batra* 74a; *Menahot* 41a.

[10]B. *Berakhot* 35b re Is. 64:3. See D. Novak, "Maimonides' Concept of the Messiah," JOURNAL OF RELIGIOUS STUDIES, 9.2 (Summer, 1982), 42-50.

[11]*Vayiqra Rabbah* 13.3, pp. 277-279.

[12]*Urschrift und Uebersetzungen der Bibel* (Breslau, 1857), 54-55.

[13]LXX on Deut. 1:13 uses *phylos* for the Hebrew *shebet*. LXX on Deut. 23:3 uses *ek pornēs* for the Hebrew *mamzer*. This is much less specific than *allogeneis*.

[14]M. *Yebamot* 7.5; T. *Kiddushin* 4.16; B. *Yebamot* 44b and parallels; P. *Yebamot* 1.6/3a and parallels.

[15]M. *Kiddushin* 3.12.

[16]M. *Yebamot* 4.13.

[17]*Sifre: Debarim*, no. 248, ed. Finkelstein, 276-277.

[18]B. *Yebamot* 76b.

[19]M. *Yadayim* 4.4. For *qahal Ha-Shem* as a euphemism for the people of Israel, see Num. 20:4. See, also, Neh. 13:1-3. For the exclusion of female Ammonites and Moabites from the restriction, see P. *Yebamot* 8.3/9c and parallels.

[20]However, no doubt concerned about this, the rabbis transposed the Talmudic ritual of conversion (esp. as on B. *Yebamot* 47a-47b) into the *Midrash Ruth Rabbah* (2.17ff.) to show that Ruth did go through a proper *giyyur*.

[21]P. *Kiddushin* 3.14/64d/bot. For parallels, see R. Aryeh Leib Yellin, *Yefeh Aynayim* on B. *Kiddushin* 68b; also, V. Aptowitzer, "Zekher Le-Zekhut Ha'Em bi-Sifrut Yisra'el," HA-MISHPAT HA'IBRI (1927), 2:9-23.

[22]B. *Kiddushin* 68b. Cf. P. *Sotah* 1.8/17b/top.

[23]*Tos.*, s.v. "binkha," contra *Rashi*, s.v. "ki yasir." After designating what is surely the *peshat* here, Rabbenu Tam then derives the non-Jewish status of the child of a Jewish father and a gentile mother from an *argumentum ex silentio*, viz., since Scripture does not mention the child born of this union, it can be inferred from this that he is not considered a Jew.

[24]*Hilkhot Isuray Bi'ah*, 15.4. In *ibid.*, 12.1 he bases the ban on all intermarriage on Neh. 10:31, although earlier, in his commentary on M. *Kiddushin* 3.12 he accepted the Talmud's exegesis of Deut. 7:4 as the basis of this law. See, also, B. *Abodah Zarah* 36b

where intermarriage with any non-Jew is considered by the rabbis, contra R. Simon ben Johai, as a *gezerah* from the time of Ezra. Cf. B. *Yebamot* 100b re Gen. 17:7.

[25]B. *Yebamot* 44b/bot. For seeming discrepancies in R. Johanan's position, see B. *Yebamot* 45a, *Tos.*, s.v. "yatz'u."

[26]B. *Yebamot* 45b.

[27]*Sifra: Emor*, ed. Weiss, 104c.

[28]*Perush Ha-Ramban al Ha-Torah*, ed. Chavel, 162.

[29]B. *Yebamot* 78b/top.

[30]*Sifre: Bamidbar*, no. 78, ed. Horovitz, 75.

[31]*Vayiqra Rabbah* 32.4, pp. 742-743.

[32]For a sin of the father is mentioned there. Clearly, the father must be a Jew, because if he were a gentile, what is his sin? There is no explicit rabbinic prohibition of a gentile marrying a Jew, only a Jew marrying a gentile. Maimonides in *Hilkhot Isuray Bi'ah*, 12.9 and *Hilkhot Malakhim*, 9.7 rules that there is such a prohibition. However, in the sources cited by his commentators for the possible basis for this B. *Sanhedrin* 57b/bot. is cited; yet this only refers to a gentile having sexual relations with an already married Jewish woman. In *Hilkhot Isuray Bi'ah*, 12.10 Maimonides rules that a gentile woman who had sexual relations with a Jewish man is liable for death, basing himself on M. *Sanhedrin* 7.4 and Num. 31:16. Nevertheless, this is his own rather tenuous inference as pointed out by R. Vidal of Tolosa in *Magid Mishneh* thereto.

[33]See S. Hoenig, *The Great Sanhedrin* (Philadelphia, 1953), 109ff.

[34]B. *Yebamot* 45a and Rashi, s.v. "she-benah pegam;" *Shulhan Arukh: Eben Ha'Ezer*, 4.5.

[35]T. *Kiddushin* 5.4, ed. Lieberman, 294-295.

[36]B. *Kiddushin* 72b.

[37]P. *Kiddushin* 3, end/65a/top.

[38]*Vayiqra Rabbah* 32.7, p. 754.

[39]*Tosefta Kifshuta: Moed* (New York, 1967), 971.

[40]M. *Eduyot*, end. Maimonides stated that in the Messianic Age intermingled gentiles will be separated from the Jewish people, but *mamzerim*, whose families have long been accepted as *kasher*, will be left as is. See *Hilkhot Melakhim*, 12.3 re B. *Kiddushin* 71a/top.

[41]B. *Kiddushin* 70b-71a. R. Joshua ben Levi seems to mean that many wealthy families, whatever their pedigree, already have some "skeletons in the closet," but have in effect "purchased" social respectability.

[42]*Vayiqra Rabbah* 32.5, pp. 748-749. See T. *Kiddushin* 1.4; *Sifra: Qedoshim*, 90d; B. *Yebamot* 37b.

[43]B. *Yebamot* 78b.

[44]P. *Yebamot* 8.3/9c/bot.

[45]This is how my friend, Prof. David Halivni of the Jewish Theological Seminary of America, suggested to me this text be read. I thank him for this insight as well as many others regarding the meaning of various rabbinic texts. Cf. *Sifra: Shemini*, 93d.

[46]B. *Kiddushin* 69a notes that R. Tarfon has not helped the *mamzeret* because even were she to marry a gentile slave, the children of this union would still carry her strain of *mamzerut* since a slave has no pedigree to confer at all *(ebed ayn lo hayyas)*. See B. *Yebamot* 62a and parallels re Gen. 22:5.

[47]M. *Kiddushin* 3.13. See Rabbenu Nissim *(Ran)* on Alfasi *(Rif)*, *Kiddushin*, chap. 3, end, who connects the statement about money purifying *mamzerim* with the *Mishnah*, viz., the rich have money to buy slaves and solve their *mamzerut* problems.

[48]B. *Kiddushin* 69a and P. *Kiddushin* 3.15/64d/bot. For another attempt to limit *mamzerut*, see B. *Makkot* 2a re Deut. 19:19 and Maim., *Hilkhot Isuray Bi'ah*, 5.29; also, T. *Ketubot* 4.9 and P. *Ketubot* 4.8/28d-29a and B. *Baba Metzia* 104a.

[49]B. *Kiddushin* 69a, s.v. "le-khathilah." Rashi bases this on *Targum Onkelos* on Deut. 23:18, which renders "there shall be no male *(qadesh)* or female prostitute *(qadeshah)* among the Israelites" as "no Israelite woman shall be married to a gentile slave, and no Israelite man shall marry a female slave *(ittita amah)*." He also mentions this in his Torah commentary on this same verse. However, this interpretation is not brought in either Talmud or the codes. It is, however, presupposed by the Hasmonean ban on non-marital sexual relations in private with gentile women, viz., every gentile woman is considered as if she were a gentile slave with whom sexual relations are already prohibited (B. *Abodah Zarah* 36b). That there is no valid marriage with a gentile slave woman is based by the Talmud (B. *Kiddushin* 68a/bot.) on Gen. 22:5 (see above, note 46). Maimonides, as usual (see *Sefer Ha-Mitzvot*, intro. sec. 2), ignores this indirect exegesis *(asmakhta)* and simply states the law *(Hilkhot Ishut*, 4.15—see, also, *Tur; Eben Ha'Ezer*, 44). See *Ran* on *Alfasi, Kiddushin*, chap. 3, end re Rabbenu Tam on B. *Gittin* 41a, *Tos.*, s.v. "lisa."

[50]Cf. B. *Hagigah* 16a and parallels.

[51]*Hilkhot Isuray Bi'ah*, 15.4. See *ibid.*, 12.11-14 where he simply includes the prohibition of marriage with a gentile slave woman in the general prohibition of intermarriage, although he mentions (12.1) that the Torah does exempt a Jewish bondsman *(ebed ibri)* from this prohibition if his master gives him a gentile slave woman for breeding purposes (Ex. 21:4—see, also, *Hilkhot Abadim*, 3.4, 12).

[52]B. *Kiddushin* 69a.

[53]See *supra*, note 41.

[54]For the difficulty in proving *mamzerut*, see, e.g., B. *Kiddushin* 76b/top. Even parents have some difficulty in declaring their own children to be *mamzerim*. See M. *Kiddushin* 4.8 and Maim., *Hilkhot Isuray Bi'ah*, 15.16, 18-20 and 19.17. Calling someone a *mamzer* without definite proof is an act punishable by lashing (B. *Kiddushin* 28a and Isserles' note on *Shulhan Arukh: Hoshen Mishpat*, 420. 38/end and 41). For the general rule that the burden of proof is on the accuser, see B. *Baba Kamma* 35b.

[55]*Bah* on *Tur: Eben Ha'Ezer*, 2/beg. Re *hilkhata de-meshiha*, see *Encyclopedia Talmudit*, 9:388-390. See S. M. Passamaneck, "Some Medieval Problems in *Mamzeruth*," *Hebrew Union College Annual* 37 (1966), 145.

[56]B. *Kiddushin* 68a and parallels. See M. *Yebamot* 4.13; also, B. *Ketubot* 29b, Rashi, s.v. "bo'u."

[57]*Ibid.*, 67b-68a and B. *Yebamot* 49a-49b.

[58]*Ibid.* and P. *Yebamot* 4.15/6b/bot.

[59]M. *Kiddushin* 4.2-3.

[60]B. *Kiddushin* 73a and parallels.

[61]M. *Yebamot* 10.1.

[62]B. *Yebamot* 87b/top, Rashi, s.v. "m'ai." See R. Yaron, "Mistake-Occasioned Palingamy," JOURNAL OF JEWISH STUDIES (1974), 25:203-204.

[63]*Ibid.*, s.v. "ve-ha-velad." See Maim., *Hilkhot Isuray Bi'ah*, 15. 10 and R. Vidal of Tolosa, *Magid Mishneh* thereto.

[64]M. *Gittin* 4.2.

[65]B. *Gittin* 33a.

[66]P. *Gittin* 4.2/45c. See B. *Yebomot* 10a, *Tos.*, s.v. "lefikhakh;" B. *Baba Batra* 48b, *Tos.*, s.v. "taynah;" *infra.*, 40ff.

[67]B. *Gittin* 33a, *Tos.*, s.v. "ve'afqa'inhu." This reasoning, viz., to prevent an uncle from protecting his promiscuous niece-wife from legal punishment, was employed to explain why *gittin* are to be dated (B. *Gittin* 17a/bot. and *Tos.*, s.v. "mishum"), i.e., so that a *get* cannot be produced when the woman is charged with adultery so as to show that she was divorced before the promiscuous act. Apparently this kind of marriage was considered meritorious (see B. *Yebamot* 62b-63a and Rashi and *Tos.*, s.v. "ve-ha-nose;" P. *Gittin* 4.3/45c/bot.; Maim., *Hilkhot Isuray Bi'ah*, 2.14 and *Magid Mishneh* thereto a la B. *Sanhedrin* 76b/top and *Rashi*, s.v. "tiqra," and *Beresheet Rabbah* 18.4, ed. Theodor-Albeck, 164). For rabbinic disapproval, however, of "May-December" marriages, see B. *Yebamot* 44a/top and B. *Sanhedrin* 76b/top.

[68]B. *Yebamot* 78b re M. *Yebamot* 8.3.

[69]*Ibid.*, s.v. "de-yadi'a."

[70]P. *Yebamot* 8.3/9c/bot. There it is stated in the name of R. Hanina that every 60 or 70 years God destroys all *mamzerim* and *kasherim* along with them so that their status will never be known.

[71]T. *Sanhedrin* 11.6; B. *Sanhedrin* 71a. See M. *Makkot* 1.10 and B. *Makkot* 7a; M. *Zabim* 2.2.

[72]P. *Yebamot* 8.3/9d/top.

[73]B. *Yebamot* 78b and P. *Yebamot* 8.3/9c-d.

[74]Cf. B. *Yebamot* 80a/bot. See D. Novak, *Law and Theology in Judaism*, 2:61-62.

[75]*Bekhorot* 45a.

[76]M. *Bekhorot* 7.6.

[77]*Bekhorot* 46b re Is. 3:9 and Rashi, s.v. "hakarat panim." Cf. B. *Baba Metzia* 87a re Gen. 25:1 and *Beresheet Rabbah* 53.6 re Gen. 21:2; *Tanhuma: Toledot* (printed ed.) re Gen. 25:1; L. Ginzberg, *The Legends of the Jews* (Philadelphia, 1925), 5:245, n. 204.

[78]See M. *Yebamot* 16.3.

[79]See *infra.*, 82ff.

[80]M. *Horayot* 1.3. See *infra.*, 40ff.

[81]See D. Novak, *Law and Theology in Judaism* (New York, 1974), 1:32.

[82]B. *Sotah* 37b. See M. *Gittin* 4.5 for the rejection of a situation leaving a person in permanently hopeless sexual and familial limbo.

[83]*Ibid.*, s.v. "ela."

[84]See M. *Kiddushin* 4.5.

[85]See *infra.*, 36ff.

[86]See B. *Gittin* 79b, Rashi, s.v. "gita" and B. *Kiddushin* 3b, Rashi, s.v. "d'aboha;" Rabbenu Asher *(Rosh)*, *Gittin*, 8.8 and R. David Ha-Levi *(Taz)* on *Shulhan Arukh: Yoreh De'ah*, 195, n. 7.

[87]See "Bitul Ha-Hoq Le-ma'an Qiyumo," PANIM EL PANIM, no. 705 (Jan. 12, 1973), 14ff.

[88]M. *Berakhot* 9, end. See *Rashi* thereon (B. *Berakhot* 54a) and B. *Berakhot* 63a and *Rashi*, s.v. "ume-reshayh." Cf. Maimonides' comment on this *Mishnah*, however.

Chapter Three

[1]See Ruth 1:13; B. *Gittin* 26b and A. Kohut, *Aruch Completum* (Jerusalem, 1969), 6:167-168.

[2]See. B. *Gittin* 2b-3a and Maim., *Hilkhot Gerushin*, end; M. *Yebamot* 15.4 and 16.5-7. For the *Mishnah's* standard of witness, see M. *Sanhedrin* 3.3-5 and *Babli* and *Yerushalmi* thereto.

[3]Thus, e.g., the Talmudic rule (B. *Yebamot* 121a) that if a man fell into a body of water whose end is in sight *(she-yesh lahem sof)*, he is presumed dead and his wife may remarry, has been interpreted to mean that since we now know where even great oceans end, we can thus assume that anyone lost at sea did not survive if not heard from within a short period of time. See, e.g., I. H. Herzog, *Hekhal Yitzhaq: Eben Ha'Ezer* (Jerusalem, 1960), 1, no. 29. (I thank my learned friend and colleague, Dr. Salamon Faber, for this important reference.) Also, see I. Klein, *A Guide to Jewish Religious Practice* (New York, 1979), 454.

[4]See M. *Gittin* 9.8; B. *Kiddushin* 50a re M. Arakhin 5.6; Maim., *Hilkhot Gerushin*, 2.20.

[5]See M. *Gittin* 9.8 and B. *Gittin* 88b.

[6]It is noteworthy that Baruch Spinoza, who might well be considered the first secular Jew, was the first (to my knowledge) to argue that "unusquisque igitur, ubicunque sit, Deum potest vera Religione colere, sibique porspicere, quod viri privati officium est." *Tractatus Politicus* 3.10, ed. S. Zac (Paris, 1968), 66.

[7]*Netibim Be-Mishpat Ha'Ibri* (New York, 1978), 246-247.

[8]B. *Kiddushin* 65b.

[9]Esp., Rabbenu Nissim *(Ran)* thereto (ed. Vilna, p. 28a/bot.) contra *Rashi* thereto, s.v. "hakha."

[10]See B. *Makkot* 24a/top; Maim., *Moreh Nebukhim*, 2.33.

[11]T. *Baba Kama* 7.5 re Lev. 25:55. Cf. P. *Baba Kama* 1.2/79d re Ex. 20:3 and Lev. 25:55; B. *Kiddushin* 22b.

[12]See B. *Berakhot* 47b re Lev. 25:46 and D. Novak, *Law and Theology in Judaism*, 2:89ff.

[13]M. *Sotah* 1.2.

[14]B. *Sotah* 24a/top.

[15]M. *Sotah* 9.9 re Hos. 4:14 and B. *Sotah* 47b re Num. 5:31.

[16]See M. *Sanhedrin* 8.1-5 and *Babli* and *Yerushalmi* thereto.

[17]See M. *Gittin* 9.10 and Meiri, *Bet Ha-Behirah* thereto, ed. Schulsinger, 374.

[18]See M. *Ketubot* 7.10; also, Isserles' note on *Shulhan Arukh: Eben Ha'Ezer*, 154.1.

[19]B. *Yebamot* 89a.

[20]See, e.g., *Sifre: Debarim*, no. 291, ed. Finkelstein, 310 re Deut. 25:9; M. *Yebamot* 12.3; P. *Yebamot* 12.6/13a re Deut. 25:10. Cf. P. *Kiddushin* 1.5/60c.

[21]See B. *Gittin* 90b re Mal. 2:13-14 and D. Novak, *Law and Theology in Judaism* (New York, 1974), 1:10-14.

[22]For marriage as male completion, see, e.g., B. *Yebamot* 62b. For marriage as female completion, see, e.g., B. *Gittin* 49b; B. *Kiddushin* 41a and, esp., B. *Sanhedrin* 22b re Is. 54:5.

[23]Thus R. David Aronson in his learned presidential address to the Rabbinical Assembly (Conservative) stated, "The husband's right to initiate the divorce proceedings constitutes a privilege not a *Mitzvah*, not a sacred obligation. . . . To obey the order of the court is a *Mitzvah*. Personal privilege must yield to a *Mitzvah*, and the rabbis did not hesitate to enforce this moral position." *Proceedings of the Rabbinical Assembly* (1951), 15:126.

[24]See M. *Hallah* 2.7.

[25] B. *Ketubot* 3a.

[26]See P. *Horayot* 3.5/48c; Novak, *Law and Theology in Judaism*, 1:2-4 and 2:xiii-xvi.

[27]B. *Ketubot* 74a. See, also, P. *Kiddushin* 3.1/63c.

[28]See B. *Nedarim* 29a.

[29]For the nonbinding character of such unions, not requiring annulment formally, see M. *Kiddushin* 3.12.

[30]B. *Yebamot* 110a and B. *Baba Batra* 48b.

[31]See B. *Sanhedrin* 90a. For the acceptance of rabbinic hyperbole, see *Hullin* 90b.

[32]See Rashbam's commentary on B. *Baba Batra*, s.v. "taynah" re B. *Yebamot* 89b commenting on Ezek. 10:8.

[33]B. *Kiddushin* 12b.

[34]B. *Yebamot* 122b.

[35]See B. *Kiddushin* 2b/top and *Tos.*, s.v. "u-khtib;" also, P. *Kiddushin* 3.3/64a. Prof. Atlas argues that the Hillelite view (M. *Kiddushin*, beg.), that marriage can be initiated with a trifling amount of money *(perutah)*, is to emphasize its symbolic rather than its real function in initiating the marital union. See *Netibim Be-Mishpat Ha'Ibri*, 250. Here he is arguing against the well-known theory of the late Prof. Louis Ginzberg in his "The Significance of the Halakhah for Jewish History," trans. A. Hertzberg *On Jewish Law and Lore* (Philadelphia, 1955), 78ff. The same point was developed by Prof. Ginzberg's student, Prof. Louis Finkelstein in *The Pharisees* (Philadelphia, 1938), 1:45.

[36]*Teshubot Ha-Rashba*, no. 551.

[37]*Ibid.*, no. 1206. Interestingly enough the term is *danti ba-dabar*, which perhaps means to theorize, not issue a practical ruling. See, e.g., M. *Nazir* 7.4. Cf., however, no. 1249.

[38]*Ibid.*, no. 1185. See L. M. Epstein, "Marriage Annulment," *Proceedings of the Rabbinical Assembly* (1928), 2:71-83.

[39]*Teshubot Ha-Ribash*, no. 399. For the quite liberal use of annulment by a widely followed Orthodox authority, see R. Mosheh Feinstein, *Igrot Mosheh: Eben Ha'Ezer* (New York, 1961), nos. 74-76.

[40]*Mahariq*, shoresh 84. See *Otzar Ha-Posqim: Eben Ha'Ezer* (Jerusalem, 1968), 11:47a.

[41]*Mordecai: Kiddushin*, no. 522.

[42]*Bet Yosef* on *Tur: Eben Ha'Ezer*, 28/end; Isserles' note on *Shulhan Arukh: Eben Ha'Ezer*, 28.21 and *Gera* thereto.

[43]*Shiltay Ha-Gibborim* on *Alfasi, Baba Batra* 48b (ed. Vilna, p. 45a).

[44]See A. Freimann, *Seder Kiddushin Ve-Nisu'in* (Jerusalem, 1945), 345; also, *Otzar Ha-Posqim: Eben Ha'Ezer*, 11:56a-56b; E. Berkovits, *Tenay Be-Nisu'in Ube-Get* (Jerusalem, 1966), 154ff.

[45]B. *Gittin* 33a.

[46]See Maim., *Hilkhot Gerushin*, 6.16. Re the subsequent use of minority opinion, see M. *Eduyot* 1.5 and *Rabad* thereto; also, B. *Berakhot* 9a/top and parallels.

[47]B. *Gittin* 33a, *Tos.*, s.v. "kol." Most authorities agree that this condition refers to contemporary courts. See R. Jehiel J. Weinberg, *Seriday Esh* (Jerusalem, 1966), 3:330, no. 114.

[48]Atlas, *op. cit.*, 209, n. 7. For the legally binding requirements of the betrothal statement, see T. *Kiddushin* 1.1 and B. *Kiddushin* 5b/top.

[49]See M. *Ketubot* 4.7; also, Isserles' note on *Shulhan Arukh: Eben Ha'Ezer*, 66.2.

[50]B. *Baba Batra* 48b, *Tos.*, s.v. "taynah."

[51]See n. 41; also, B. *Gittin* 33a, *Tos.*, s.v. "be'ilat zenut."

[52]See M. *Kiddushin* 2.2-5 and, esp., B. *Yebamot* 107a and *Tos.*, s.v. "Bet Shammai."

[53]Atlas, *op. cit.*, 214, n. 7. In general it is assumed that such intercourse is not fornication. See B. *Yebamot* 107a; M. *Kiddushin* 2.6; T. *Kiddushin* 4.4; P. *Kiddushin* 2.5/62d; B. *Ketubot* 73b and Maim., *Hilkhot Ishut*, 4.20; *Teshubot Hatam Sofer: Eben Ha'Ezer*, no. 108. Re retroactivity, see T. *Kiddushin* 2.4 and P. *Kiddushin* 3.1/63c.

[54]*Ibid.*, 215, 224ff.

[55]*Legal Fictions* (Palo Alto, CA, 1967).

[56]B. *Gittin* 33a, *Tos.*, s.v. "ve'afqa'inhu" re B. *Gittin* 17a.

[57]*Teshubot Maharsham*, 1, no. 9. Cf. S. Z. Auerbach's critique in MORIAH, 2.9-10 (1970), 6ff.; also, A. Rakeffet-Rothkopf, "Annulment of Marriage, etc.," TRADITION, 15.1-2 (Spring-Summer, 1975), 173-185.

[58]B. *Yebamot* 110a, *Tos.*, s.v. "le-fi-khakh;" B. *Baba Batra* 48b, *Tos.*, s.v. "taynah." For the radical character of *aqirah*, see B. *Ketubot* 74b.

[59] P. *Gittin* 4.2/45c.

[60] M. *Terumot* 1.4; P. *Terumot* 1.2/40d.

[61] M. *Yebamot* 10.1.   See *Ritba* and *Meiri* thereto.   See, also, R. Yaron, "Mistake-Occasioned Palingamy," JOURNAL OF JEWISH STUDIES (1974), 25:203-206 (Daube Festschrift). (I thank Prof. B. S. Jackson for this reference).

[62] B. *Yebamot* 89a, *Tos.*, s.v. "mai." The question of whether the *ketubah* is Scriptural or rabbinic in essence is a Tannaitic dispute. See B. *Ketubot* 10a; Maim., *Hilkhot Ishut*, 10.7; *Tur: Eben Ha'Ezer*, 66.

[63] *Ibid.*, 87b, *Rashi*, s.v. "ha'ishah."

[64] *Ibid.*, 89b.

[65] Cf. M. *Ketubot* 9.1 and M. *Baba Metzia* 7.11. Cf. T. *Kiddushin* 3.8 and B. *Kiddushin* 19b.

[66] See M. *Sanhedrin* 10.1.

[67] See B. *Gittin* 36a.   Cf. B. *Yebamot* 79a re I Sam.   21:10 and Maim., *Hilkhot Mamrim*, 2.4.

[68] See B. *Berakhot* 20a, *Rashi*, s.v. "sheb."   Note the criticism of R. Joseph Karo (*Kesef Mishneh* on Maim., *Hilkhot Berakhot*, 2.2) of B. *Berakhot* 16a, *Tos.*, s.v. "ve-hotem," for the needless invocation of this principle.

[69] See B. *Rosh Hashanah* 29b.   For the rejection of total abrogation of a Torah institution (*la'aqor kol guf* contra *la'aqor dabar*), see M. *Horayot* 1.3.

[70] Commentary on M. *Gittin* 4.2, nn. 38-39. See B. *Nazir* 43b, *Tos.*, "ve-hai."

[71] Auerbach, *op. cit.*, 11, n. 57.

[72] See n. 57.

[73] M. *Ketubot* 2.7.

[74] Maimonides' commentary thereto re B. *Yebamot* 33b and B., *Ketubot* 51b commenting on Num. 5:13; *Hilkhot Isuray Bi'ah*, 18.30 (see R. Vidal of Tolosa, *Maggid Mishneh* thereto). Cf. B. *Ketubot* 26b, *Tos.*, s.v. "ve'al;" 51b, *Tos.*, s.v. "asurah."

[75] *Eben Ha'Ezer*, 7.11.

[76] *Be'er Heteb* thereto.

[77] *Darkhay Mosheh* on *Tur: Eben Ha'Ezer*, 7, n. 13.

[78] See B. *Sanhedrin* 74b and *Tos.*, s.v. "ve-ha."

[79] Beginning in 1968 the *Bet Din* of the Rabbinical Assembly (Conservative) began granting such annulments.

[80] *Law and Theology in Judaism*, 1:41-42.

[81] See B. *Ketubot* 3a.   The only comparable situation in pre-modern times was the case of an apostate husband still legally married to his Jewish wife.   Frankly, the medieval halakhists did not solve this problem. See, esp., *Teshubot Ha-Rashba*, no. 1162 and Isserles' note on *Shulhan Arukh: Eben Ha'Ezer*, 154.1. (For the Karaite solution to this problem, see Abrabanel on Deut. 24:1, resp. to q. 14). However, this does not constitute an halakhic barrier today, but only a customary inhibition (see M. *Zebahim* 12.4). I also suspect that our *agunah* problem is more acute than theirs was.

Chapter 4

[1]From the introductory article, "Toward a Renascence of Judaism," JUDAISM, 1.1 (Winter, 1951) and printed at the beginning of every subsequent issue of JUDAISM.

[2]B. *Erubin* 13b.

[3]M. *Yebamot* 1.4. For the discussion of how this was halakhically possible, see B. *Yebamot* 14a-b.

[4]T. *Yebamot* 1.10 re Zech. 8:19.

[5]B. *Erubin* 13b. For the intolerance of the Shammaites at times, see B. *Shabbat* 17a.

[6]See *Beresheet Rabba* 1.15.

[7]See S. B. Hoenig, *The Great Sanhedrin* (Philadelphia, 1953), 44ff.

[8]B. *Horayot* 4a. See M. *Horayot* 1.3.

[9]For an interesting contemporary use of the Pharisee/Sadducee model, see D. J. Elazar, "The New Sadducees," MIDSTREAM, 24.7 (August/September, 1978), 20ff.

[10]"Plural Models Within the Halakhah," JUDAISM, 19.1 (Winter, 1970), 85-86. See D. Novak, *Law and Theology in Judaism*, 1:34-35.

[11]*Proceedings of the Rabbinical Assembly*, 30 (1966), 107-108.

[12]*Yoreh De'ah*, 198.48.

[13]Maim., *Hilkhot Mikva'ot*, 1.8. See *Hullin* 31a (cf. *Hidushay Ha-Rashba*) and M. *Hagigah* 2.6.

[14]Thus a child converted by others has the right to repudiate that conversion when reaching adulthood. See B. *Ketubot* 11a re M. *Erubin* 7.11; Maim., *Hilkhot Melakhim*, 10.3; B. *Sanhedrin* 68b, *Tos.*, s.v. "qatan."

[15]B. *Yebamot* 45b. See *Shulhan Arukh: Yoreh De'ah*, 268.3.

[16]P. *Kiddushin* 3.12/64d.

[17]*Hilkhot Isuray Bi'ah*, 13.9.

[18]Thus Nahmanides argues that if immersion is meant only as one indication of Jewish observance in general, Sabbath observance would have clearly been a more evident example since it is more public. For this reason Nahmanides (*Hidushay Ha-Ramban* on B. *Yebamot* 45b) is willing to accept the validity of such immersion for conversion *ex post facto* in these particular cases. For another example of an irregular conversion being accepted, see B. *Shabbat* 68a and *Tos.*, s.v. "ger" and R. Solomon ibn Adret, *Hidushay Ha-Rashba* thereto.

[19]See B. *Kiddushin* 68a.

[20]See B. *Berakhot* 22a; also, D. Novak, *Law and Theology in Judaism*, 2:136ff. My friend, Rabbi Benjamin Z. Kreitman, has argued that since the Talmud indicates that immersion for seminal emission (B. *Yebamot* 45b) suffices for a man's conversion, and since the Talmud ruled this need not be the same as immersion for a woman (B. *Berakhot* 22a), which requires a fully kosher *miqveh*, perhaps the standard for conversion for a man is not as stringent as that for a woman. (*Proceedings of the Rabbinical Assembly*, 33/1969, 219). Nonetheless, the Talmud only recognizes one type of immersion for both male and female converts which is "the place where the menstruant immerses herself" (B. *Yebamot* 47b). Indeed the *tebillah* described on B. *Yebamot* 45b can only be

understood as being the same for both men and women.

[21]See R. Shabbtai Ha-Kohen, *Shakh* on *Shulhan Arukh: Yoreh De'ah*, 268.3.

[22]T. *Demai* 2.5; *Bekhorot* 30b.

[23]Even though one could take upon oneself certain commandments as specific obligations (see Neh. 10:30ff.; M. *Shebu'ot* 3.6; B. *Hagigah* 10a re Ps. 119:106), this can never be taken as a limitation (see, e.g., P. *Berakhot* 1.5/3c).

[24]Acceptance of the Torah (especially by a convert) transcends his or her ability to perform all the commandments. See Nahmanides' comment on Deut. 27:26. What is required is an unconditional openness. Perhaps this is why the instruction for conversion prescribed in the Talmud (B. *Yebamot* 47b/top) is deliberately random.

[25]The Committee on Jewish Law and Standards of the Rabbinical Assembly however, by majority vote in 1983, accepted my responsum, "The Status of Non-Halakhic Conversions," a responsum which totally rejects the conclusion of Rabbi Bohnen's responsum.

[26]B. *Yebamot* 24b.

[27]Maim., *Isuray Bi'ah*, 13.17.

[28]*Melamed Le-Ho'il* (Frankfurt am-Main, 1962), 2, nos. 83, 85.

[29]*Mishpatay Uziel: Eben Ha'Ezer* (Jerusalem, 1964), sec. 18 re. B. *Kiddushin* 21a and Maim., Responsa *Pe'er Ha-Dor* (Amsterdam, 1764), no. 132.

[30]See B. *Yebamot* 24b, *Tos.*, s.v. "lo" re B. *Shabbat* 31a and *Menahot* 44a. Cf. B. *Pesahim* 50b.

[31]See *supra.*, 29ff.

[32]See Deut. 24:1; P. *Kiddushin* 1.1/58c; M. *Ketubot* 5.6; B. *Ketubot* 77a; M. *Gittin* 9.8; B. *Gittin* 88b; M. *Arakhin* 5.6.

[33]See, e.g., Responsa *Rashba* (B'nai B'rak, 1958), 1, no. 1162 and R. Moses Isserles' note to *Shulhan Arukh: Eben Ha'Ezer*, 154.1. Cf. R. Isaac Abranel's comment to Deut. 24:1, response to question 14; also, *supra.*, 29ff.

[34]See *Law and Theology in Judaism*, 1, chap. 4.

[35]*Supra.*, 35ff.

[36]B. *Gittin* 33a and parallels.

[37]R. Moses Isserles, *Darkhay Mosheh* on *Tur: Eben Ha'Ezer*, 7, n. 13.

[38]See M. *Hallah* 2.7; B. *Abodah Zarah* 26/bot. Cf. B. *Ketubot* 3a.

[39]See M. *Pe'ah* 4.1.

[40]Re this common good, see M. *Gittin* 4.2ff. Cf. Aristotle, *Nicomachean Ethics*, 1129b15, 1155a25; *Politics*, 1276a15.

[41]See, e.g., R. Jehiel J. Weinberg, *Seriday Esh* (Jerusalem, 1966), 3, no. 36. Cf. *Responsa Rema*, ed. A. Siev (Jerusalem, 1970), no. 56. All of this is based on B. *Kiddushin* 13a/bot.

[42]*Netibim Be-Mishpat Ha'Ibri* (New York, 1978), 246-247.

[43]The most pointed example of this is in cases where capital punishment is prescribed. Here the same two witnesses to the crime must *fore*warn *(hatra'ah)* the criminal and he must reject their forewarning before this act is legally considered a crime punishable by death. See *Encyclopedia Talmudit*, 9, s.v. "hatra'ah."

[44]See, e.g., B. *Shabbat* 130a and Rashi thereto; B. *Rosh Ha-Shanah* 22b; Maim., *Hilkhot Qiddush Ha-Hodesh*, 3.14. The classic example of a shift from initiatory to confirmational testimony is in the area of witnessing the new moon. The Rabbinites, as opposed to the Karaites, insisted that the witnesses required for the announcement of the new moon were only for publicity; the new moon would be declared by the court even without them by calculation. See Maimonides' comment to M. *Rosh Ha-Shanah* 2.6 and the commentary of Rabbenu Bahya to Ex. 12:2, ed. Chavel (Jerusalem, 1972), 86 and Dr. Chavel's note thereto.

[45]See B. *Makkot* 5b-6a re Deut. 19:15.

[46]M. *Niddah* 6.4.

[47]B. *Rosh Ha-Shanah* 22b.

[48]M. *Gittin* 1.1.

[49]B. *Gittin* 2b-3a.

[50]B. *Gittin* 2b, *Tos.*, s.v. "ed" (2).

[51]M. *Yebamot* 15.4; B. *Yebamot* 88a.

[52]*Hilkhot Gerushin*, end. See *Hilkhot Yibum Ve-Halitzah*, 4.31. Of course, this raises the question of the exclusion of women from initiatory testimony and its implications for such contemporary debates as to whether or not women may function as rabbis. See *infra.*, 61ff.

[53]M. *Gittin* 4.3.

[54]B. *Gittin* 36a and 86b.

[55]Alfasi on B. *Gittin* 36a, ed. Vilna, p. 18b. See Rabbenu Nissim *(Ran)* thereon.

[56]*Hilkhot Gerushin*, 1.15-16. See *Responsa Tashbatz*, 5, no. 1.

[57]Maim., *Hilkhot Isuray Bi'ah*, 13.17. See *Magid Mishneh* thereto quoting B. *Yebamot* 47b.

[58]See *Law and Theology in Judaism*, 2:129-130.

[59]Thus *edah* refers to the Sanhedrin wherein *edut* is possible. See M. *Sanhedrin* 1.6 re Num. 35:24-25 and re Num. 14:27; Malbim on Lev. 4:13, no. 241. And it is the *edut* of Israel that makes God either present or absent in the world of humans. See *Sifre: Ve-z'ot Ha-Berakhah*, ed. Finkelstein, 403-404 re Is. 43:10; B. *Sanhedrin* 74b re Num. 14:27.

[60]*Hilkhot Edut*, 12.1. Cf. Maim., *Hilkhot Mamrim*, 2.7.

[61]*Ibid.*, 11.6. See 10.3.

[62]B. *Sanhedrin* 26b. See B. *Rosh Ha-Shanah* 22a.

[63]See, e.g., B. *Ketubot* 5a/top.

[64]See, e.g., B. *Berakhot* 8a/bot. Cf. M. *Abot* 3.10.

[65]The *bet midrash* was called "the house of the rabbis" (see B. *Megillah* 28b; Maim., *Hilkhot Tefillah,* 11.6 and, esp., R. Joseph Karo, *Kesef Mishneh* thereto). Even though the rabbis disapproved of calling the synagogue "the house of the people" (see B. *Shabbat* 32a and Rashi thereto), the designation was, no doubt, true.

[66]*Hilkhot Edut,* 11.1 re M. *Kiddushin* 1.10 and B. *Kiddushin* 40b. Also, for various moral and religious criteria for testimony, see B. *Sanhedrin* 27a.

[67]*Ibid.,* 11.2.

[68]Just as the Talmud relates Hillelite ascendency to the fact that they were more cordial (B. *Erubin* 13a), so Josephus makes the same judgment about the Pharisees *(Bellum Judaicum,* 2.166). See, also, B. *Sanhedrin* 24a re Zech. 11:7.

[69]See M. *Shabbat* 1.3; B. *Gittin* 58a. The term we noted on B. *Horayot* 4a *(bay rab)* refers to the elementary school *(bet rabban).* See B. *Shabbat* 119b.

[70]B. *Yebamot* 65b re Prov. 9:8. See Rashi thereto.

[71]Surely this is a question of "profanation of the Divine Name" *(hillul Ha-Shem).* In such cases the law may be bent. See M. *Berakhot,* end re Ps. 119:126 and B. *Yebamot* 79a.

Chapter 5

[1]Since I am an old partisan in this controversy, the following writings of mine may be of interest: *Law and Theology in Judaism,* 1: chap. 2; 2: chap. 8; "Yes To Halakhah Means No To Women Rabbis," SH'MA 9/166 (Jan. 19, 1979), 45–47; response to Ruth Wisse's "Women As Conservative Rabbis?," COMMENTARY, 69.2 (Feb., 1980); response to Robert Gordis' "The Ordination of Women," MIDSTREAM, 27.4 (Apr., 1981), 60–61.

[2]On the indispensibility of authority in society, see T. *Rosh Hashanah* 1.18 and parallels.

[3]See Ernest Barker, intro., *The Politics of Aristotle* (Oxford, 1948), xvi.

[4]See *On Being A Jewish Feminist,* ed. S. Heschel (New York, 1983), esp., intro.

[5]M. *Kiddushin* 1.7; B. *Kiddushin* 33b–34a.

[6]See B. *Hagigah* 16b and *Tos.,* s.v. "la'asot" re Lev. 1:2, 4 and M. *Menahot* 9.8; Rashi on Ex. 33:8; B. *Erubin* 96a-b (cf. P. *Erubin* 10.1/26a) and *Tos.,* s.v. "dilma;" B. *Rosh Hashanah* 33a and *Tos.,* s.v. "ha;" B. *Kiddushin* 31a and *Tos.,* s.v. "dela;" *Rosh: Kiddushin,* 1.49; *Teshubot Rashi,* ed. Elfenbein (New York, 1943), 80–81; note of Isserles on *Shulhan Arukh: Orah Hayyim,* 38.3; *Shemot Rabbah* 4.2 (cf. *Mishnat Rabbi Eliezer,* no. 19, ed. Enelow/New York, 1933/, 342).

[7]See Meiri, *Bet Ha-Behirah: Kiddushin,* ed. Sofer (Jerusalem, 1963), 8; also, *Teshubot Ha-Rosh,* ed. Venice (1607), no. 42, sec. 1.

[8]See B. *Kiddushin* 7a and parallels; also, B. *Yebamot* 88a and B. *Gittin* 3a.

[9]See *supra.,* 29ff.

[10]See B. *Shebu'ot* 30a and *Tos.,* s.v. "kol;" B. *Yebamot* 77a re Gen. 18:9; also, *Teshubot Rashi,* 251–252; *Teshubot Ribash,* no. 235.

[11]See B. *Shabbat* 118b and Rashi, s.v. "ishti;" *Beresheet Rabbah* 17.7; also, B. *Baba Batra* 110a.

[12]B. *Sanhedrin* 74b; P. Berakhot 7.3/11c. The view of R. Simhah of Speyer that a woman may be included as the tenth participant in a minyan is upheld by no subsequent authority. See *Mordecai: Berakhot,* 7.158 and R. Joseph Karo, *Bet Yosef* on *Tur: Orah Hayyim,* 55; also, B. *Berakhot* 47b/bot. Even this is no precedent for women in the minyan.

[13]See Novak, *Law and Theology in Judaism,* 2:145-146.

[14]M. *Berakhot* 3.3.

[15]See B. *Kiddushin* 41b; B. *Berakhot* 20b, *Tos.,* s.v. "ba-tefillah." One can only be the agent of the congregation *(sheliah tzibbur)* if that person is under the same obligation as the congregation itself. See B. *Rosh Hashanah* 29a/top and Rashi, s.v. "af-al-pi." Re public Torah reading, see T. *Megillah* 3.11; S. Lieberman, *Tosefta Kifshuta: Moed* (New York, 1962), 1176-1177; B. *Megillah* 23a; Novak, *Law and Theology in Judaism,* 2:144-145; *Ran* on *Alfasi,* B. *Megillah* 23a and Meiri, *Bet Ha-Behirah: Megillah,* ed. Hirschler (Jerusalem, 1968), 73-74; R. Abraham Gumbiner, *Magen Abraham* on *Shulhan Arukh: Orah Hayyim,* 689.2.

[16]M. *Megillah* 4.3 and B. *Ketubot* 7a-b and Rashi, s.v., "be-makehelot" re B. *Berakhot* 21b and parallels.

[17]Whether or not this role is necessarily rabbinical, see B. *Kiddushin* 6a, Rashi, s.v. "lo" and *Hidushay Ha-Ritba* thereto; *ibid.,* 13a, Rashi, s.v. "hadar;" cf. *ibid.,* 6a, *Tos.,* s.v. "lo."

[18]M. *Niddah* 6.4.

[19]M. *Shebu'ot* 4.1. Cf. B. *Yebamot* 88a and B. *Gittin* 3a.

[20]See Maim., *Hilkhot Sanhedrin,* 3.8.

[21]B. *Shebu'ot* 30a re Deut. 19:15 and 17; P. *Sanhedrin* 3.9/21c; Maim., *Hilkhot Edut,* 9.2 and R. Joseph Karo, *Kesef Mishneh* thereto. See P. *Yoma* 6.1/43b.

[22]See B. *Kiddushin* 6a, Rashi, s.v. "lo" re Eccl. 1:15 on B. *Yebamot* 22b.

[23]Even though Maimonides' exclusion of women from all roles of public authority *(Hilkhot Melakhim,* 1.5 re Deut. 17:15 and *Sifre: Debarim,* no. 157, ed. Finkelstein, 208; see *Radbaz* thereon re B. *Niddah* 50a, *Tos.,* s.v. "kol") is not repeated in any of the other codes to my knowledge, it certainly reflects an opinion which would have been accepted by the overwhelming number of halakhists until this day.

[24]See *Bamidbar Rabbah* 18.1 ff. Even the egalitarian theology put in the mouths of the daughters of Zelophehad by the rabbis *(Sifre: Bamidbar,* no. 133, ed. Horovitz, 176 re Ps. 145:9) is only hypothetical and is subject to ultimate judgment by the categorical Divine decree to be brought by Moses.

[25]See B. *Shabbat* 88a-b re Ex. 19:17 and Est. 9:27; also, P. *Sotah* 7.5/22a re Josh. 3:16.

[26]Even converts are compared to native-born Jews, viz., they are "born again" *(ke-qatan she-nolad dami).* See B. *Yebamot* 22a and parallels. Furthermore, conversion is irrevocable. See *ibid.,* 47b.

[27]T. *Demai* 2.4 and B. *Sanhedrin* 44a/top re Josh. 7:11, *Rosh,* Baba Metzia, no. 52.

[28]See *Tur: Yoreh Deah,* 266 (end) and Karo, *Bet Yosef* thereon. Cf. Maim., *Ebel,* 1.10.

[29]See *Beresheet Rabbah* 3.7.

[30]See R. Zvi Hirsch Chajes, *Minhat Kina'ot* in *Kol Kitbay Maharatz Chajes* (Jerusalem, 1958), 2:982ff.

[31] *Contra Apionem*, 2.164-165.

[32]See B. *Berakhot* 55a re Ex. 35:30 and *Alfasi* thereon; B. *Sanhedrin* 16a/bot. re M. Sanhedrin 1.5; B. Abodah Zarah 36a and Maim., *Hilkhot Mamrim*, 2.7. The rule that popular usage determines the law (B. *Erubin* 14b/bot. and parallels) only applies to choosing between conflicting *traditions*. See I. H. Weiss, *Dor Dor ve-Dorshav* (Vienna, 1876), 2:62. Also, the oft quoted passage "My children have conquered Me!" (B. *Baba Metzia* 59a) simply refers to the right of the majority of the sages to choose between conflicting options already traditionally given, and that no new normative revelation is acknowledged.

[33]Thus Dr. Judith Hauptman, a Talmudist on the faculty of the Jewish Theological Seminary of America, attacked my assertion made at the April 1983 convention of the Rabbinical Assembly in Dallas, Texas that "Judaism is not an egalitarian tradition" *(New York Times,* Apr. 13, 1983, p. A23) as follows: "Rabbi Novak is right . . . However, the . . . Talmud . . . also delineates a number of mechanisms for legal change which are to be implemented when such change is shown to be ethically necessary." *(ibid.,* Apr. 23, 1983, p. 22) Nevertheless, Dr. Hauptman does not demonstrate the cogency of this "ethical necessity" on either philosophical or historical Jewish grounds.

[34]B. *Baba Kama* 93b.

[35]See Aristotle, *Nicomachean Ethics*, 1133a30; D. Novak, *Violence in Our Society: Some Jewish Insights* (New York: American Jewish Committee, 1983), 14ff.

[36]M. *Sanhedrin* 4.1.

[37]B. *Abodah Zarah* 64b; Maim., *Hilkhot Melakhim*, 8.10-11 and 10-11; *Encyclopedia Talmudit*, 5:337-338.

[38]"Die Naechstenliebe im Talmud," *Juedische Schriften* (Berlin, 1924), 1:159-160.

[39]Indeed, men and women are subject to virtually all the same prohibitions of the Torah. See M. *Kiddushin* 1.7.

[40]B. *Baba Kama* 15a. See Maim., *Hilkhot Sanhedrin*, 21.1.

[41]For the idea of punishment as atonement, see B. *Sanhedrin* 6b re II Sam. 8:15.

[42]See *Menahot* 43b/bot. and Rashi, s.v. "hynu ishah" re B. *Hagigah* 4a.

[43]See M. *Horayot* 3.7.

[44]See B. *Baba Kama* 15a, *Tos.*, s.v. "asher;" Maim., *Hilkhot Sanhedrin*, 2.1; *Shulhan Arukh: Hoshen Mishpat*, 7.4. Cf. *Hidushay Ha-Rashba* on B. *Baba Kama* 15a re Ex. 21:1 as regards allowing women to judge in civil cases; also, *Hidushay Ha-Ritba* on B. *Kiddushin* 35a. For the same logic, see B. *Sanhedrin* 18a re Zeph. 2:1.

[45]For the difference between proportional (indirect) and arithmetic (direct) equality, see Aristotle, *Nicomachean Ethics*, 1131a10ff.

[46]B. *Kiddushin* 68b re Deut. 7:4.

[47]M. *Kiddushin* 3.12.

[48]See, e.g., P. *Kiddushin* 3.14/64d; R. Aryeh Leib Yellin, *Yefeh Aynayim* on B. *Kiddushin* 68b.

[49]See *Bamidbar Rabbah* 19.4. The Yiddish phrase "avek mit der hant" expresses this notion even better.

[50]See B. *Shabbat* 23a. For the attempt to overcome the Deuteronomic prohibition of new legislation (Deut. 4:2), see *Sifre: Debarim*, no. 82, ed. Finkelstein, 148; also see, Philo, *De Specialus Legibus*, 3.143-144.

[51]M. *Nega'im* 12.5.

[52]See Louis Finkelstein, *The Pharisees* (Philadelphia, 1938), 1:264ff.

[53]M. *Yoma* 1.3. See B. *Yoma* 18a.

[54]See B. *Niddah* 14b; *Encyclopedia Talmudit*, 1:83.

[55]M. *Horayot*, end. See P. *Horayot*, end/48c re Prov. 3:15; also, B. *Abodah Zarah* 3a re Lev. 18:5 and parallels.

[56]Actually the verb *shft* in this context, especially, seems to mean administration not adjudication. See I Sam. 8:5-6.

[57]B. *Niddah* 50a, *Tos.*, s.v. "kol."

[58]See M. *Sotah* 3.4 and *Babli* and *Yerushalmi* thereon; Novak, *Law and Theology in Judaism*, 2:53ff. See, also, *Tosefta Kelim: Baba Metzia* 1.6 (cf. B. *Erubin* 53b/bot. re M. *Abot* 1.5); B. *Sanhedrin* 94b.

[59]B. *Hagigah* 3a.

[60]"Ha-Matmeed" in *Kol Kitbay Hayyim Nahman Bialik* (Tel Aviv, 1951), 75a/bot.

[61]See P. *Rosh Hashanah* 2.9/58b.

[62]See M. *Abot* 4.1 and Maim., *Shemonah Peraqim*, ed. Kappah (Jerusalem, 1965), 247.

[63]B. *Kiddushin* 40b and parallels.

Chapter 6

[1]See B. *Baba Kama* 91b; *Hullin* 10a; Maim., *Hilkhot De'ot*. 4.1 and *Hilkhot Rotzeah u-Shemirat Ha-Nefesh*, 11.5ff. In his *Introduction to the Mishnah: Sanhedrin*, chap. 10 (*Heleq*), Maimonides attempts to see such norms as the rational content of the Torah (ed. Kappah/Jerusalem, 1965), 2:136.

[2]Ed. L. Landman (New York, 1973).

[3]*Ibid.*, 30ff.

[4]See B. *Abodah Zarah* 35a and *Menahot* 29b; also, R. Ezekiel Landau, *Noda Bi-Yehudah: Hoshen Mishpat*, 2:no. 1.

[5]Similar reasons were used in rabbinic attempts to ban gambling. See B. *Sanhedrin* 24b; Maim., *Hilkhot Gezelah*, 6.10 and *Hilkhot Edut*, 10.4. For the sense of rabbinic impotence, however, in issuing such bans, see, e.g., R. Moses Isserles on *Shulhan Arukh: Orah Hayyim*, 338.5 re B. *Baba Batra* 60b/bot.

[6]See P. *Berakhot* 1.8/3c where the heart and the eyes are presented as the "two middlemen" (*sirsuray*) of sin. See Maim., *Hilkhot Teshubah*, 6.3 for the question of how habitual sin results in the loss of human freedom. Cf. Philo, *De Specialus Legibus*, 3.99.

[7]B. *Ketubot* 41b and parallels.

[8]Using similar reasons (with much better documentation), the late R. Nathan Drazin urged a ban on cigarette smoking. See *Judaism and Drugs*, 77ff., primarily based on M.

Aberbach, "Smoking and the Halakhah," TRADITION, 10.3 (Spring, 1969), 49ff.

[9]*Ibid.*, 205.

[10]*Ibid.*, 210-211.   Kraut, mostly basing himself on L. Grinspoon, *Marihuana Reconsidered* (Cambridge, MA, 1971), assumes that moderate marijuana use is neither physically nor mentally harmful. Most of this was disputed, however, by William Polin, M. D., Director of the National Institute of Drug Abuse, in his testimony before the Select Committee on Narcotics Abuse and Control, U. S. House of Representatives, on July 10, 1979.

[11]For an unsuccessful attempt in this direction, see B. *Baba Batra* 60b/bot.   Prof. Kraut's logic is that of the Talmudic *tokheah*, see, e.g., B. *Kiddushin* 4b.

[12]*Judaism and Drugs*, 193-194.   See B. *Megillah* 7b.   For attempts to soften this seeming invitation to a Jewish baccanalia, see Maim., *Hilkhot Megillah*, 2.15; Rabbenu Nissim *(Ran)* on *Alfasi (Rif)*, *Megillah*, ed. Vilna, 3b; R. Joseph Karo, *Bet Yosef* on *Tur: Orah Hayyim*, 695/end; R. Moses Isserles on *Shulhan Arukh: Orah Hayyim*, 695.2; R. Samuel Edels *(Maharsha)*, *Hidushay Aggadot* on B. *Megillah* 7b.

[13]See, e.g., *Sifra: Shemini*, ed. Weiss, 46b; T. *Keritut* 1.20; *Keritut* 13b; B. *Pesahim* 107a/top.   Many times Scripture or the rabbis were seen as using contemporary examples when enunciating a general principle, but the principle was by no means limited to these examples. See, e.g., M. *Baba Kama* 5.7; M. *Shabbat* 6.6.

[14]B. *Nedarim* 10a and parallels.   See Rashi and *Tos.*, s.v. "de-shnah;" *Ran* thereto; also, D. Halivni, *Meqorot u-Mesorot: Nashim* (Tel Aviv, 1968), 275.

[15]See B. *Ta'anit* 11a-11b; also, P. *Berakhot* 2.9/5d and P. *Nedarim* 9.1/4b. Re the attempt of R. Judah the Prince to limit the supply of wine in the Land of Israel to lessen "frivolity" *(ha-tiflah)*, see T. *Abodah Zarah* 4.2 and B. *Baba Batra* 90b. Re asceticism, see, also, B. *Yebamot* 20a and Nahmanides on Lev. 19:2. Re the teetotaling Essenes as objects of admiration for their abstention from alcohol, see Josephus, *Bellum Judaicum*, 2.133, 138 and Philo, *Vita Contemplativa*, 73-74. See *Responsa Radbaz*, 3, no. 861.

[16]Note R. Judah the Prince again: "Why is the section about the *Nazir* juxtaposed to the section about the wayward wife *(Sotah)*? —To teach us that whoever sees the *sotah* in her disgrace will vow as a *Nazir* to abstain from wine." (B. *Nazir* 2a and B. *Sotah* 2a).

[17]B. *Ketubot* 8b based on *Semahot* 14/end.   See Maim., *Hilkhot Ebel*, 13.8 and R. Joseph Karo, *Kesef Mishneh* thereto in the name of Nahmanides.

[18]B. *Baba Batra* 12b.

[19]B. *Sanhedrin* 43a re Prov. 31:6. See *ibid.*, 45a and parallels.

[20]B. *Pesahim* 106a.   For wine as a requirement for *habdalah* "over the cup," see M. *Berakhot* 8.5 and B. *Berakhot* 27b.   For wine as a wedding requirement, see B. *Ketubot* 7b.

[21]See *Teshubah Bi-Dbar Yaynot* (New York, 1922), esp., 7-12, 69-71.

[22]B. *Yoma* 76b.   For the possibility of vocalizing *teerosh* as *teerash*, see, e.g., Gen. 27:28.

[23]*Vayiqra Rabbah* 12.1 and 20.9, ed. Margaliot, 255, 426-463.

[24]*Zohar* 1:73b.

[25]1:73a.   In the text the answer precedes the question.   For the logical sequence of the passage, however, see the arrangement by R. Yudel Rosenberg in his *Sefer Zohar Be-Lashon Ha-Qodesh* (New York, 1955), 2:34.   The notion of experiencing sin in order to understand it was a major doctrine of the Sabbatean and Frankist heresies in the 17th and

18th centuries. See Gershom Scholem, "Redemption Through Sin," trans. H. Halkin in *The Messianic Idea in Judaism* (New York, 1971), 78ff. and *Sabbatai Sevi: The Mystical Messiah* (Princeton, 1973), 864-865 re B. *Nazir* 23b. Even though Scholem's thesis that the *Zohar* is a product of the 13th century *(Major Trends in Jewish Mysticism*/New York, 1946/, 156ff.) is accepted by most scholars now, no doubt the type of antinomian rationalization, used by the Sabbateans and the Frankists later, was used in earlier times as well. For the notion that too much experience with evil might well destroy the ability to overcome it, see Plato, *Republic*, 409A-C.

[26] 3:39a. Here the rabbinic proverb, "when wine enters, a secret *(sod)* comes out" (B. *Erubin* 65a/bot.) is paraphrased to refer to wine as antithetical *(megalay razin)* to mystical insight, which is to be esoteric.

[27] *Hilkhot Bi'at Ha-Miqdash*, 1.3. See *Sifra: Shemini*, 46d; B. *Erubin* 64a; B. *Sanhedrin* 42a; *Keritut* 13b. See, also, *Shulhan Arukh: Hoshen Mishpat*, 7.5; R. Jehiel M. Epstein, *Arukh Ha-Shulhan: Hoshen Mishpat*, 7.5.

[28] B. *Erubin* 65a. See T. *Terumot* 3.1; Maim., *Hilkhot Mekhirah*, 29.18 and *Hilkhot Nezirut*, 1.12; also, R. Simon ben Zemah Duran, *Responsa Tashbatz* (Amsterdam, 1739), 1:no. 23.

[29] M. *Baba Kama* 2.6.

[30] B. *Horayot* 10b re Hos. 14:10.

[31] B. *Erubin* 64b. Maim., *Hilkhot Tefillah*, 4.17 notes both the individual dysfunctional definition of drunkenness as well as the quantitative definition of how much alcohol will cause drunkenness in the average person. Cf. R. Moses Isserles on *Shulhan Arukh: Orah Hayyim*; 99.3 re R. Israel Isserlein, *Terumat Ha-Deshen*, no. 42.

[32] For the necessity of intention *(kavvanah)* in the *mitzvot*, see B. *Rosh Hashanah* 28b; *Shulhan Arukh: Orah Hayyim*, 60.4; R. Zvi Hirsch Chajes, *Mabo Ha-Talmud*, chap. 9 in *Kol Kitbay Maharatz Chajes* (Jerusalem, 1958), 1:315; A. J. Heschel, *God in Search of Man* (New York, 1955), 306ff., and esp., 317-319, n. 3.

[33] For the notion of *kenesset Yisrael* as the community related to God by *mitzvot*, see, e.g., B. *Berakhot* 53b re Ps. 68:14 and *Canticles Rabbah* 1.5 re Cant. 1:5. Thus, e.g., the definition of prohibited Sabbath labor was not based on an average level of exertion but, rather, on the 39 labors that were seen as being involved in the construction of the Sanctuary in the wilderness by the people of Israel (M. *Shabbat* 7.2; B. *Shabbat* 49b, 97b re Ex. 35:1; P. *Shabbat* 7.2/9b; *Mekhilta: Vayakehel*, ed. Horovitz-Rabin, 345). Just as the entire people participated in these labors as a community, so the entire people participated in refraining from them on the Sabbath as a community. Thus, as regards Sabbath observance, men and women are equal (B. *Berakhot* 20b re Ex. 20:8 and Deut. 5:12). For the idea of Sabbath as community-creating, see P. *Erubin* 3.2/20d and M. Buber, *Moses* (New York, 1958), 83-85.

[34] T. *Sanhedrin* 11.6 and B. *Sanhedrin* 71a. See D. Novak, *Law and Theology in Judaism*, 2:56-57.

[35] M. *Sanhedrin* 8.2.

[36] B. *Sanhedrin* 70b. The term *serikin*, which I have translated "drunkards," is interpreted by Rashi thereon to mean "empty ones who would habituate him in this." See A. Kohut, *Aruch Completum* 6:143.

[37] B. *Sanhedrin* 70b. See Maim., *Hilkhot Mamrim*, 7.2.

[38] See *Judaism and Drugs*, 69.

[39] There is an opinion, however, that grace after meals and other blessings may be recited when one is drunk (P. *Terumot* 1.6/40d re Deut. 8:10; *Mordecai: Erubin*, no. 512; Isserles on *Shulhan Arukh: Orah Hayyim*, 99.1). Nevertheless, a *haburat mitzvah* (i.e., an

occasion governed by the rules of the ancient Pharisaic fellowship, see *Encyclopedia Talmudit*, 12:509ff.) requires a level of attention *(kavvanah)* enabling the participant to comprehend the words of Torah said at it. Drunkenness, or any riotousness, would surely destroy the atmosphere which makes this possible (see M. *Demai* 2.3 and M. *Abot* 3.13; T. *Demai* 2.13). Such a level of attention is as high if not higher than that required for prayer, from which drunkenness is precluded (see B. *Erubin* 64a and B. *Berakhot* 31a/bot. re I Sam. 1:13). See, also, M. *Abot* 3.3 re Is. 28:8 and Maimonides' comment thereon (cf. comment of R. Obadiah Bertinoro, however).

[40]M. *Sanhedrin* 8.5.

[41]B. *Berakhot* 5a/top; B. *Yebamot* 103b; B. *Kiddushin* 30b re Deut. 11:18.

[42]B. *Sanhedrin* 70a.

[43]*Ibid.* See Louis Ginzberg, *The Legends of the Jews* (Philadelphia, 1925), 5:190, n. 58.

[44]See Maim., *Moreh Nebukhim*, 1.2.

[45]B. *Sanhedrin* 70a.

[46]*Tanhuma: Noah*, 13 (printed ed.).

[47]Thus the cry of the *metzora* (wrongly translated since LXX as "leper") in Lev. 13:45 is interpreted as a cry for our compassion and prayer (B. *Mo'ed Qatan* 5a). Moreover, the condition of the *metzora* is seen as the result of his or her "evil tongue" *(lashon ha-ra)*, i.e., estrangement from other persons (T. *Nega'im* 6.7; *Arakhin* 15b re Lev. 14:2).

[48]B. *Baba Batra* 54b and parallels.

[49]M. *Berakhot* 6.6.

[50]B. *Berakhot* 43b re Ps. 150:6. See, also, *infra.*, 100.

[51]M. *Berakhot* 8.5.

[52]Maim., *Hilkhot Shabbat*, 29.1 and R. Vidal of Tolosa, *Maggid Mishneh* thereon. See B. *Berakhot* 51b: the view of Bet Hillel; also, Louis Ginzberg, "The Significance of the Halachah for Jewish History," trans. A. Hertzberg, *On Jewish Law and Lore*, 105.

[53]Maim., *Hilkhot Shabbat*, 29.27. See B. *Shabbat* 70a re Ex. 35:3.

[54]B. *Pesahim* 102b, *Tos.*, s.v. "Rav." See R. Abraham A. Sperling, *Ta'amay Ha-Minhagim u-Meqoray Ha-Dinim*, no. 409 (Jerusalem, 1972), 185.

[55]B. *Betzah* 16a re Ex. 31:18.

[56]See Maim., *Hilkhot Sanhedrin*, 2.4ff.; *Hilkhot Mamrim*, 2.9; Louis Finkelstein, *Jewish Self-Government in the Middle Ages* (New York, 1964), 60, 242.

[57]See D. Novak, "The Opposition to Circumcision," SH'MA, 12/227 (Feb. 5, 1982), 53-54.

[58]B. *Sanhedrin* 60b; B. *Gittin* 52b-53a; P. *Gittin* 5.4/47a; B. *Abodah Zarah* 29b and Maim., *Hilkhot Abodah Zarah*, 2.5 and *Hilkhot Ma'akhalot Asurot*, 11.4.

[59]B. *Abodah Zarah* 36b. See Novak, *Law and Theology in Judaism*, 2:174ff.

[60]See, e.g., B. *Shabbat* 133b re Ex. 15:2 and B. *Pesahim* 109a re Deut. 16:14; also, Solomon Schechter, *Some Aspects of Rabbinic Theology* (New York, 1936), 148ff. The 4th century Babylonian sage, Rava, in one place (B. *Rosh Hashanah* 28a and parallels)

indicates that "the *mitzvot* are not given for pleasure" *(l'av layhanot)*, but in another place (B. *Sotah* 17a and parallels) he seems to indicate that a *mitzvah* "does involve pleasure" *(eeka hana'ah)*. It would seem, however, that the *mitzvot* are not for the sake of extrinsic pleasure, but themselves involve intrinsic pleasure *(simhah shel mitzvah)*. See Plato, *Philebus*, 60B-E and Aristotle, *Nicomachean Ethics*, 1172a15ff.

[61]Even though R. Akibah stated that love of neighbor as oneself (Lev. 19:18) is "the great principle in the Torah" *(Sifra: Qedoshim*, 89b and P. *Nedarim* 9.3/41c), he also indicated that "your life takes precedence over that of another" *(Sifra: Behar*, 109c and B. *Baba Metzia* 62a/top re Lev. 25:36). On the other hand, as R. Akibah's own life eloquently testified (B. *Berakhot* 61b re Deut. 6:5), God takes precedence even over our own lives (B. *Sanhedrin* 74a). In fact, in later kabbalistic thought, even love of neighbor was interpreted as love of the *godliness* in him or her. See R. Shneur Zalman of Ladi, *Tanya*, 1.32.

[62]One could, of course, interpret this verse as referring to God as the *knower* of all my desires (e.g., Rashi thereon). However, one can also interpret it, as did R. Judah Ha-Levi (see *Selected Poems of Judah Ha-Levi*, trans. N. Salaman/Philadelphia, 1924/, 87), that God is the *object* of all my desire.

Chapter 7

[1]See Aristotle, *Nicomachean Ethics* 1095a1-1095b10.

[2]See D. Novak *Suicide and Morality* (New York, 1975), 1-3, 115-127.

[3]See *supra.*, 2-3.

[4]See John Dewey, *Human Nature and Conduct* (New York, 1957), 284.

[5]Cf., e.g., B. *Sanhedrin* 91b for a direct answer to a non-Jewish inquiry, and *Bamidbar Rabbah* 19.8 for a metaphorical answer. Hermann Cohen severely criticized the popular work of the Jewish social psychologist, Moritz Lazarus *(Die Ethik des Judenthums*, Frankfurt am-Main, 1898-1899), for being methodologically inadequate, i.e., philosophically naive about what Jewish ethical teaching really is. Although one could disagree with Cohen's characterization of Jewish ethics, he was most insightful in distinguishing between dogmatic and apologetic presentations of Jewish ethics, on the one hand, and the philosophical one on the other hand. See "Das Problem der juedischen Sittenlehre" in *Juedische Schriften* (Berlin, 1924), 3:1ff.

[6]Maim., *Hilkhot Melakhim*, 8.10.

[7]*Teshubot Pe'er Ha-Dor* (Amsterdam, 1764), no. 50.

[8]B. *Sanhedrin* 59a re Deut. 33:4; cf. B. *Sukkah* 49b re Cant. 7:2.

[9]See, e.g., Leo Baeck, *The Essence of Judaism*, trans. V. Grubenwiser and L. Pearl (New York, 1948), 77ff.

[10]This was best illustrated by the law concerning Jewish use of non-Jewish wine. Any involvement with it was prohibited, even commercially, when it was assumed that every gentile was *eo ipso* an idolator. The ban began to be liberalized, however, when gentile monotheism was recognized. See D. Novak, *Law and Theology in Judaism*, 2:174-183.

[11]Thus certain distinctions between Jews and gentiles were either emphasized or de-emphasized depending on the political climate. See, e.g., Deut. 23:4-8; B. *Abodah Zarah* 26a-26b and *Tos.*, s.v. "ve-lo."

[12]B. *Sanhedrin* 59a; see B. *Yebamot* 22a. This whole topic is the subject of D. Novak, *The Image of the Non-Jew in Judaism: An Historical and Constructive Study of the Noahide Laws.*

[13]See Nahmanides' commentary on Gen. 34:13.

[14]See B. *Sanhedrin* 57a-58a; P. *Kiddushin* 1.1/58c; Maim., *Hilkhot Melakhim*, 9.8.

[15]See, e.g., M. Fox, "Maimonides and Aquinas on Natural Law," DINE ISRAEL (1972), 3:xivff.

[16]Herman Cohen, *Religion of Reason Out of the Sources of Judaism*, trans. S. Kaplan (New York, 1972), 123.

[17]M. *Ohalot* 7.6; cf. M. *Shabbat* 23.5.

[18]*Hilkhot Yesoday Ha-Torah*, 5.7. For the inclusion of this question in the context of Noahide law, see B. *Sanhedrin* 59a and *Tos.*, s.v. "leyka."

[19]There is discrepancy in the early rabbinic sources as to the exact point in time when the fetus is considered to be an independent body. In the text from the *Mishnah* just quoted independence is designated when the majority of the body or torso is out of the birth canal. In T. *Yebamot* 9.5 and M. *Niddah* 5.3 independence is designated when the forehead is out of the birth canal. In M. *Arakhin* 1.4 (see *Arakhin* 7a-7b) the fetus is designated independent when labor begins. In T. *Arakhin* 1.4 the fetus is designated independent when its hand extends out of the birth canal. These differences clearly indicate how talmudic law is essentially case law.

[20]B. *Sanhedrin* 80b; but cf. *Tos.*, s.v. "ubar."

[21]*Ibid.*, 72b.

[22]M. *Sanhedrin* 8.7.

[23]See B. *Sanhedrin* 73a re Deut. 22:26.

[24]B. *Pesahim* 25b.

[25]*Teshubot Noda Bi-Yehudah: Hoshen Mishpat* (Vilna, 1904), no. 59 re *Hilkhot Rotzeah*, 1.9. See R. Yom Tob Lippmann Heller, *Tosfot Yom Tob* on M. *Niddah* 5.3.

[26]B. *Sanhedrin* 91b.

[27]*Ibid.*, 57b; see LXX on Ex. 21:22.

[28]Thus, once the infant is mostly out of the birth canal, it can no longer be sacrificed for the mother's life because "we do not know who is pursuing whom" (P. *Shabbat* 14.4/14b).

[29]For the degree of proximity as a criterion in other moral questions, see Maim., *Hilkhot Mattnot Aniyyim*, 7.13 re Deut. 15:11.

[30]*Sifra: Behar*, ed. Weiss, 109c re Lev. 25:35 and B. *Baba Metzia* 62a/top.

[31]See *supra.*, 2-3,

[32]*Hilkhot Bikkurim*, 4.3 re P. *Bikkurim* 1.4/64a. See D. Novak, *Law and Theology in Judaism*, 1:164, n. 7.

[33]Thus, Gen. 2:16, "And the Lord God commanded the man" is interpreted on B. *Sanhedrin* 56b as "concerning man" (*al ha'adam*). Man is, then, taken to be both the subject and the object of God's first commandment.

[34]See A. J. Heschel, *God in Search of Man*, 321, 332-333.

[35]*Hilkhot Melakhim*, 9.1.

[36] *Moreh Nebukhim*, 3.26.

[37] For the antimetaphysical theory that insists that a specific norm can only be grounded in a more general norm, see Hans Kelsen, *The Pure Theory of Law*, trans. M. Knight (Berkeley, CA, 1970), 193-195.

[38] Thus it is mentioned on B. *Baba Kama* 38a and B. *Abodah Zarah* 2b and 64b that the sons of Noah "accepted *(qibblu)* for themselves the seven commandments". Cf. B. *Sotah* 35b.

[39] Such acceptance is at best reconfirmation, because in the *locus classicus* of Noahide law (T. *Abodah Zarah* 8.4) they are presented as Divine commandments to Adam, based on Gen. 2:16 where no convenant is mentioned at all. Thus, e.g., Cain's complaint, "Am I my brother's keeper?" (Gen. 4:9) implies that moral responsibility is contingent on personal acceptance of that responsibility beforehand. In Scriptural law one cannot become a "keeper" *(shomer)* without his prior consent. See Ex. 22:6 and *Mekhilta: Mishpatim*, ed. Horovitz-Rabin, 298. Hence, God's refusal to accept Cain's excuse means that moral responsibility does not presuppose an act of prior personal commitment, i.e., a convenant. In terms of Jewish responsibility, however, convenantal acceptance is crucial. See B. *Shabbat* 88a re Est. 9:27; *infra.*, 117ff.

[40] See J. Faur, "Understanding the Covenant", TRADITION, 9.4 (Spring, 1968), 40-41.

[41] *De Opficio Mundi* 69. See B. *Berakhot* 10a and Maim., *Moreh Nebukhim*, 1.1.

[42] Plato, *Phaedrus* 248A, *Theaetetus* 176A-B, *Laws* 899D; Aristotle, *Nicomachean Ethics* 1177b25-1178a1; Epictetus, *Discourses*, 1.9.

[43] *Moreh Nebukhim*, 1.71.

[44] See R. Obadiah Sforno's commentary on Gen. 1:26.

[45] This is based on *Shemot Rabbah* 3.6.

[46] See *Hilkhot Teshubah*, 5.4.

[47] Kant called freedom the *ratio essendi* of moral law. See *Critique of Practical Reason*, trans. L. W. Beck (Indianapolis, 1956), 4, n. 1.

[48] Thus Hermann Cohen wrote, "Jewish ethical teaching constitutes the inner source, strictly the substantive principle, of Jewish religious teaching. Jewish ethics is the principle and not the consequence . . . the principle of Divinity . . . cannot be otherwise defined except through the ethical teaching." "Das Problem des juedischen Sittenlehre," 5-6; cf. Kant, *op. cit.*, 130. Although Cohen in his later theology emphasized the God-idea to a greater extent than Kant did, he never accepted a relationship between God and man not grounded in the relationship between man and man. See, e.g., *Religion of Reason etc.*, 114 and J. Guttmann, *Philosophies of Judaism*, trans. D. W. Silverman (New York, 1964), 357-366.

[49] Aristotle, *Politics* 1253a10. See *De Anima* 414b18.

[50] See Novak, *Law and Theology in Judaism*, 2:110ff.

[51] Aristotle, *Nicomachean Ethics* 1097b10; *Politics* 1253a1. See *De Generatione Animalium* 488b24.

[52] Aristotle, *Nicomachean Ethics* 1113b21ff., 1134a25ff.; Maim., *Hilkhot Teshubah*, 5.4.

[53] Justinian, *Institutes*, 1.2, 1.2.1, 1.2.11; see 1.3, 1.3.2. See Novak, *op. cit.*, 91ff.

[54] See Novak, *Suicide and Morality*, 105-107.

[55]See *Philosophers Speak of God*, ed. C. Hartshorne and W. L. Reese (Chicago, 1953), 448-459, 471-478.

[56]M. Abot 3.14. Nevertheless, R. Akibah was criticized by a contemporary sage, Ben Azzai, for confusing a derivative ethical principle with a metaphysical ground. According to Ben Azzai this metaphysical ground is ". . . in the likeness of God He made him." (Gen. 5:1) *Sifra: Qedoshim*, 89b.

[57]See Reinhold Niebuhr, *The Nature and Destiny of Man* (New York, 1941), 1:125; A. J. Heschel, *Man Is Not Alone* (Philadelphia, 1951), 48; Jacques Maritain, *Existence and the Existent*, trans. L. Galantierre and G. B. Phelan (Garden City, NY, 1957), 84.

[58]B. *Berakhot* 54a re Deut. 6:5; cf. B. *Hagigah* 2a, *Tos.*, s.v. "yera'eh" and A. J. Heschel, *Man's Quest for God* (New York, 1954), 124-126.

[59]*Tzemah Tzedeq* on Gen. 1:26, quoted in *Sefer Ha-Hasidut*, ed. I. Werfel (Tel Aviv, 1947), 93a. See, also, Franz Rosezweig, *The Star of Redemption*, trans. W. W. Hallo (New York, 1970), 154-155, 186; Paul Ramsey, *Basic Christian Ethics* (New York, 1950), 254-255.

[60]See B. Yoma 85a. *Targum Onkelos* on Gen. 2:7 emphasizes the human ability to speak.

[61]B. *Shabbat* 129a and parallels.

[62]*Vayiqra Rabbah* 4.5.

[63]See the commentary of R. Abraham ibn Ezra on Deut. 27:1.

[64]T. *Sotah* 8.6.

Chapter 8

[1]For a critical discussion of these views, see Reinhold Niebuhr, *The Structure of Nations and Empires* (New York, 1959), 267ff.

[2]B. *Yoma* 67b.

[3]T. *Ta'aniyot* 2.13; *Mekhilta: Yitro*, beg., ed. Horovitz Rabin, 188; *Zebahim* 116a (cf. B. *Shebu'ot* 36a); Philo, *De Vita Mosis*, 2.53ff. Also, see L. Ginzberg, *The Legends of the Jews* (Philadelphia, 1925), 5:149, n. 53; S. Lieberman, *Tosefta Kifshuta: Moed* (New York, 1962), 1097.

[4]*Nicomachean Ethics*, 1112b12ff. See Plato, *Protagoras*, 357D-358D; Thomas Aquinas, *Summa Theologiae*, 1-2, q. 94, a. 2 and Germain G. Grisez, "The First Principle of Practical Reason," *Natural Law Forum*, 10 (1965), 168ff.

[5]Plato, *Apology*, 40C, trans. H. N. Fowler (Cambridge, MA, 1914), 40-41. See D. Novak, *Suicide and Morality* (New York, 1975), 7ff.

[6]*Beyond the Pleasure Principle*, trans. J. Strachey (New York, 1959), 71.

[7]See D. Novak, *Law and Theology in Judaism*, 2:108ff.; *supra.*, 99ff.

[8]For the Jewish concept of "just war," see, e.g., *Sotah* 8.7; B. *Sotah* 44b; *Sotah* 8/23a; Maimonides, *Hilkhot Melakhim*, 6.1-7.15.

[9]Thus the great 2nd century C.E. sage, R. Akibah, who was famous for his great exegetical acumen, was, nevertheless, criticized more than once by colleagues for interpretations which, although quite clever, were, however, contrary to accepted Jewish ruling and opinion. See B. *Sanhedrin* 51b; *Menahot* 89a; cf. P. *Pesahim* 6.1/33a.

[10]See B. *Sanhedrin* 108a-108b; *Beresheet Rabbah* 30.7.

[11]Thus in ancient Jewish law a criminal had to be forewarned (*hatra'ah*) of his act as a crime and its punishment before being prosecutable. See B. *Sanhedrin* 40b-41a.

[12]Song of Songs is called "holy of holies." See M. *Yadayim* 3.5.

[13]B. Nedarim 10a and parallels. See *supra.*, 73-74.

[14]The great exceptions, of course, were the Essenes. See Josephus, *Bellum Judaicum,* 2.133, 138; Philo, *Vita Contemplativa,* 73-74; also, B. *Yebamot* 20a and Nahmanides on Lev. 19:2.

[15]B. *Ta'anit* 11a.

[16]"Death in the Nuclear Age," quoted in *Jewish Reflections on Death,* ed. J. Riemer (New York, 1974), 44. For a philosophical analysis of how one's view of death affects his being in the present, see M. Heidegger, *Sein und Zeit,* 8th ed. (Tuebingen, 1957), 251ff.

[17]One rabbinic source interprets the incest of Lot's daughters with him, after the destruction of Sodom by fire and sulphur, as having been motivated by their fear that the whole world was once again to be destroyed. See *Beresheet Rabbah* 51.8. Cf. Josephus, *Antiquities,* 1.205.

[18]*Collected Poems: 1909-1935* (New York, 1936), 105.

[19]See B. *Sanhedrin* 109a.

[20]B. *Berakhot* 4a. See, also, B. *Sotah* 11a re Is. 54:9.

[21]Thus the Talmud views *halakhah* never practiced and never to be practiced as it does *aggadah.* See B. *Sanhedrin* 71a.

[22]B. *Yebamot* 16a. Rabbinic legislation on behalf of the poor applied to the gentile poor as well as to the Jewish poor. See *Gittin* 5.8-9 and B. *Gittin* 61a.

[23]*Bellum Judaicum,* 7.334-336, trans. H. St. John Thackeray, *Josephus* (Cambridge, MA, 1928), 3:598-599.

[24]B. *Gittin* 56b.

[25]See D. Novak, *Law and Theology in Judaism,* 1:80ff.

[26]The Talmud (B. *Ta'anit* 21a) reports that the sage, Nahum of Gimzo, was punished by God because he hesitated too long in attending to the needs of a poor man.

[27]In the Talmud the rabbis debated whether Samuel's warning was just a warning or the actual right of kings (B. *Sanhedrin* 20b).

[28]The term is Marshall McLuhan's. See *War and Peace in the Global Village* (New York, 1968).

[29]B. *Berakhot* 61b. See B. *Sanhedrin* 72a.

[30]See Ginzberg, *The Legends of the Jews* 1:179 and 5:201ff., n. 88.

[31]*Tanhuma: Mattot,* sec. 7.

[32]See B. *Makkot* 9b-10a re Hos. 6:8.

[33]M. *Abot* 2.16.

[34]*Beresheet Rabbah* 22.7.

[35]Quoted in *Seven Centuries of Verse: English and American*, 2nd rev. ed., A. J. M. Smith (New York, 1957), 687. See Ginzberg, *op. cit.*, 5:138-139, n. 17.

[36]This is the view of Nahmanides in his commentary thereon. Maimonides, on the other hand, seems to have regarded this love as more natural. See *Sefer Ha-Mitzvot*, pos. no. 206 (Cf. *Targum Pseudo-Jonathan* on Lev. 19:18). This contrast is made by Dr. C. B. Chavel in his edition of Nahmanides' commentary (Jerusalem, 1963), 119.

[37]See *Leviathan*, chap. 13.

Chapter 9

[1]T. *Sanhedrin* 11.6 and B. *Sanhedrin* 71a.

[2]*Major Trends in Jewish Mysticism*, 3rd rev. ed. (New York, 1961), 23. The body of my essay, however, disputes Scholem's continuation of this thought viz., " . . . that naivté which speaks to us from the classical documents of Rabbinical literature. Classical Judaism expressed itself; it did not reflect upon itself." *(ibid.)*

[3]See Schechter, *Some Aspects of Rabbinic Theology* (New York, 1936); Moore, *Judaism*, 3 vols. (Cambridge, MA, 1927-1930); Heinemann, *Darkhay Ha'Aggadah* (Jerusalem, 1954); Finkelstein, *The Pharisees*, 2 vols. (Philadelphia, 1938); Kadushin, *The Rabbinic Mind* (New York, 1952); Urbach, *Hazal* (Jerusalem, 1971).

[4]See *Torah min Ha-Shamayim*, 2 vols. (London, 1962-1965). In his proposed vol. 3 Prof. Heschel was to have developed the themes outlined and documented in the first two vols. However, the Ms. which he left at the time of his death in Dec., 1972, which I have examined, is too fragmentary to be published.

[5]See I. Heinemann, *Ta'amay Ha-Mitzvot Be-Sifrut Yisrael* (Jerusalem, 1959), 1:11ff.

[6]See, e.g., M. *Nedarim* 3.11; M. *Abot* 3.11; B. *Berakhot* 48a-49a. Cf. M. *Baba Kama* 1.2 where Jews are designated *benay berit*.

[7]B. *Shabbat* 88a. See P. *Sotah* 7.5/22a re Josh. 3:16; B. *Sanhedrin* 43b re Deut. 29:28; M. *Sanhedrin* 10.3; T. *Sanhedrin* 13.10-11; P. *Sanhedrin* 10.4/29c; B. *Sanhedrin* 110b re Ps. 50:5.

[8]*Bamidbar Rabbah* 19.1.

[9]*Sifre: Shemini*, ed. Weiss, 93b.

[10]B. *Sukkah* 28a. Re all tradition as Sinaitic in origin, see M. *Eduyot* 8.7 and P. *Megillah* 4.1/74d and parallels.

[11]B. *Berakhot* 33b. See Maim., *Moreh Nebukhim*, 3.48 who indicates that this statement is typical of only one kind of rabbinic theology, one to which he himself does not subscribe. See, also, D. Novak, *Law and Theology in Judaism*, 2:127-128 re the background of M. *Berakhot* 5.3 and M. *Megillah* 4.9, the text Maimonides interprets above.

[12]See B. *Baba Batra* 39b-40a and *Rashbam* s.v. "ve-khen" and *Tos.*, s.v. "meha ah." Also, see B. *Yebamot* 48a, *Tos.*, s.v. "ela" (end).

[13]See B. *Baba Kama* 28a re Deut. 22:26. Cf. *Mekhilta: Yitro*, ed. Horovitz-Rabin, 219 and 222; M. *Berakhot* 2.2.

[14]B. *Shabbat* 88a-88a.

[15]*Ibid.*, 88a.

[16]See, e.g., B. *Berakhot* 23b; B. *Sanhedrin* 27a re Ex. 23:1; B. *Makkot* 22b re Deut. 25:3.

[17]See B. *Megillah* 7a; P. *Megillah* 1.5/70d.

[18]See B. *Shabbat* 23a re Deut. 17:11; also, *supra.*, 150, n. 50.

[19]B. *Megillah* 7a.

[20]See Neh. 10:1-34.

[21]See Maim., *Hilkhot Mamrim*, 1.1ff; *supra.*, 5.

[22]Re the qualification of absolute heteronomy, see Eliezer Berkovits, *Not in Heaven: The Nature and Function of Halakha* (New York, 1983), 83-84. Cf. Paul Tillich, *Systematic Theology* (Chicago, 1951), 1:83ff.

[23]See B. *Shabbat* 88a, *Rashi*, s.v. "biymay" and *ibid.*, 88a, *Rashi*, s.v. "desaginan."

[24]*Debarim Rabbah* 7.10. See *Bamidbar Rabbah* 14.10.

[25]*Menahot* 43b re T. *Berakhot* 6.24 Cf. P. *Berakhot* 9, end/14d.

[26]B. *Berakhot* 45a.

[27]See *Tos.*, s.v. "ba-qolo" re *Alfasi*; also, R. Jacob ibn Habib, *Iyun Ya`aqob* in *Ayn Ya`aqob* thereon—all who argue that God is the reader and Moses the *meturgaman*. Cf. Maharsha, *Hiddushay Aggadot* thereon.

[28]*Bamidbar Rabbah* 14.10. See *Midrash Tehillim* 18.29 and Heschel, *Torah min Ha-Shamayim*, 2:264ff.

[29]See Heschel, *op. cit.*, 1:3ff.

[30]See Maim., *Hilkhot Tefillah*, 12.22.

[31]B. *Kiddushin* 54a and parallels.

[32]*Shemot Rabbah* 15.5. The ostensive meaning of *ve-khipper* is that the *sanctuary* is to be purged (see Ibn Ezra thereon). The point of this *midrash* is that God Himself is purged. For the notion of God's need for atonement, see, e.g., *Pesiqta Rabbati: Nahamu*, ed. Friedmann, 141b-142a; *Anokhi*, 149b.

[33]B. *Yoma* 56b-57a.

[34]*Tanhuma: Be-ha`alotekha*, printed ed., no. 6.

[35]*Bamidbar Rabbah* 15.4. See 12.3.

[36]See B. *Berakhot* 33b re Deut. 10:12.

[37]*Vayiqra Rabbah* 35.5.

[38]P. *Rosh Hashanah* 1.3/57b. See P. *Bikkurim* 3.3/65c; *Pesiqta Rabbati: Ba-Yom Ha-Shemini*, 7b; *Tanhuma: Ki Tisa*, printed ed., no, 33.

[39]B. *Berakhot* 6a. See *Zohar: Qedoshim*, 3:81a; also, A. Marmorstein, *The Old Rabbinic Doctrine of God* (New York, 1968), 2:65-67 re M. Joel, *Blicke in der Religionsgeschichte* (Breslau, 1880), 2:172; M. Silberg, *Talmudic Law and the Modern State*, trans. B. Z. Bokser (New York, 1973), 156, n. 16.

[40]B. *Shabbat* 133b. Rashi interprets *ve'anvehu* as "I and He *(ani ve-hu)* will make myself like Him to cleave to His ways." See *Sifre: Debarim*, no. 49, ed. Finkelstein, 114.

[41]B. *Berakhot* 7a/bot. Rashi makes the conceptual link between this *aggadah* and the *aggadah* on 6a which we just examined. Re Divine prayer as auto-suggestion to be merciful with Israel, see *ibid.*; also, B. M. Lewin, *Otzar Ha-Geonom* (Haifa, 1928), 1:12 re B. *Rosh Hashanah* 17b.

[42]*Vayiqra Rabbah* 35.6. However, contra Moritz Lazarus in *The Ethics of Judaism*, trans. H. Szold (Philadelphia, 1900), 1:163, this is not a proto-Kantian statement of the "autonomy of morality." Man "makes himslf" only in intimate relationship with God, whose Torah is already given (heteronomy). For a modern exposition of this concept, see Emil L. Fackenheim, *Quest for Past and Future* (Bloomington, IN, 1968), 204ff; *Encounters Between Judaism and Philosophy* (New York, 1973), 37ff.

[43]B. *Nedarim* 7b–8a.

[44]B. *Baba Metzia* 59b. Re majority rule, see B. *Berakhot* 9a and parallels; *Hullin* 11a.

[45]See *Makkot* 23b–24a re Deut. 33:4.

[46]B. *Baba Metzia* 59b.

[47]See *Canticles Rabbah* 8.13 re Hab. 3:3.

[48]B. *Pesahim* 119a. See *Rashbam* thereon.

[49]For the rabbinic use of *tzimtzum* see *Shemot Rabbah* 34.1; *Pesiqta Rabbati: Qorbani Lahmi*, 84b and *Aharay Mot*, 190a; *Pesiqta De-Rab Kahana: Rosh Hashanah*, ed. Mandelbaum, 2:337. For the kabbalistic development of this concept, see R. Mosheh Cordovero, *Pardes Ha-Rimonim*, 1:3.4 and Gershom Scholem, "Schoepferung aus Nichts and Selbstverschraenkung Gottes", *Eranos-Jahrbuch* 25 (1956), 90ff.

[50]B. *Berakhot* 32a.

[51]This reading follows Ms. Munich and *Masoret Ha-Shas*. See R. N. Rabonoviez, *Diqduqay Sofrim* thereon, n. 3.

[52]See Louis Ginzberg, *The Legends of the Jews* (Philadelphia, 1928), 6:54, n. 276. Re insistence that God keep His promises, see, e.g., B. *Ta'anit* 23a; *Pesiqta De-Rab Kahana*, 2:443–444.

[53]See B. *Erubin* 64b, *Rashi*, s.v. "ayn potehin" and *Tos.*, s.v. "potehin"; B. *Nedarim* 27b and *Ran* thereon; *Encyclopedia Talmudit*, 11:333ff.

[54]See B. *Nedarim* 77b and B. *Baba Batra* 120b and, esp. *Rashi*, s.v. "hakham mattir."

[55]See B. *Kiddushin* 2b.

[56]See *Canticles Rabbah* 1.4; 2.1.

[57]B. *Nedarim* 2b.

[58]M. *Nedarim* 2.2; B. *Nedarim* 16b; Maim., *Hilkhot Nedarim*, 3.6–8. See B. *Nedarim* 13b.

[59]B. *Baba Batra* 120b.

[60]P. *Ketubot* 7.7/31c; Maim., *Hilkhot Nedarim*, 13.2.

[61]M. *Nedarim* 9.9.

[62]Re Divine integrity in oathes, see Num. 23:19; B. *Abodah Zarah* 3a; *Canticles Rabbah* 2.6 re Ps. 77:16.

[63]*Canticles Rabbah* 8.13. Cf. B. *Shabbat* 88b-89a where Moses, with God's permission and protection, utters similar arguments against the angels, who are instruments of God's omnipotence.

[64]B. *Shebu'ot* 29a-29b. Note parallels.

[65]B. *Makkot* 23b-24a. See *Canticles Rabbah* 1.13.

[66]See B. *Shebu'ot* 29a, *Tos.*, s.v. "ki"; Nahmanides and *Rashba* thereon; also, *Ritba* (re *Alfasi*) and *Meiri* on B. *Nedarim* 25a.

[67]See the long comment of R. Nissim Gaon on B. *Berakhot* 32a, no doubt following the rationalist theology of R. Sa adyah Gaon contra philosophical and/or Karaite attacks on rabbinic anthropomorphism, who interprets this whole *aggadah* in a way that makes its concern be the power of God. For the philosophical basis of such theology and the problem in using it to interpret scriptural and rabbinic texts, see A. J. Heschel, *The Prophets* (Philadelphia, 1962), 247ff. Cf. Philo, *De Sac.*, 94-96.

[68]See *God in Search of Man*, 328ff.

[69]*Law and Theology in Judaism*, 1:11ff.

[70]See *Sifre: Debarim*, no. 49, p. 115.

INDEX